FOOTBALL, NATIONALITY AND THE STATE

Football, Nationality and the State

Vic Duke and Liz Crolley

LONGMAN

Addison Wesley Longman Limited,
Edinburgh Gate, Harlow,
Essex CM20 2JE, England
and Associated Companies throughout the world.

*Published in the United States of America
by Addison Wesley Longman Publishing Company, New York*

First published 1996

ISBN 0 582 29306 5 PPR

British Library Cataloguing-in-Publication Data

A catalogue record for this book is
available from the British Library

Library of Congress Cataloging-in-Publication Data
Duke, Vic.
    Football, nationality, and the state/Vic Duke and Liz Crolley.
    p. cm.
    Includes bibliographical references and index.
    ISBN 0-582-29306-5 (ppr)
    1. Soccer – Social aspects. 2. Soccer – Political aspects.
    3. Sports and state. 4. Nationalism and sports. I. Crolley, Liz,
    1966– . II. Title.
GV943.9.S64D85 1996   96-23692
796.336–dc20   CIP

*The cover photograph was taken by Vic Duke at the San Siro Stadium
before an Inter Milan match. The photographs in the text were taken
by Vic Duke with the exception of Figures 3.1 and 8.1, which were
taken by Liz Crolley.*

Set by 33 in 10 on 11pt Times Roman
Produced by Longman Singapore Publishers (Pte) Ltd
Printed in Singapore

Liz: *To my 'football family' at Anfield*

Vic: *To my uncle Jean Dekegel (1907–96), former player with RSC Anderlecht, who encouraged my youthful interest in international football, and my mother, Anna Duke (née Dekegel, 1915–96), neither of whom lived to see this book in print*

CONTENTS

List of figures and tables   ix
Preface   xi

1   **Introduction: the game of nations**   1
    The development of FIFA and the changing global politics
    of football   2
    Football, nationality and the state   3
    Football nations within the state   5
    Football as an extension of the state   6

PART ONE   Football Nations within the State   9
2   **UK 4 FIFA 0: the result of football's early development**   11
    FIFA and the UK associations: a history of separation and
    reconciliation   12
    The pervasive dominance of the UK associations   13
    Advantages and disadvantages in having four UK
    associations   15
    The future for separateness: Scotland and Ireland   17
    Making a case for separateness: the League of Wales   19
3   **Storming the Castile: footballing nations in Spain**   24
    Background to the state of autonomies   24
    Pre-Civil War period (1900–36)   25
    The Spanish Civil War (1936–39)   30
    Franco's regime (1939–75)   32
    Transition to democracy (1975–96)   40
4   **Playing in the right language: football in Belgium**   50
    Playing with a French ball: the early years of Belgian
    football   51
    The radical response: an alternative league structure
    1930–44   52
    The gradual response: *vervlaamsing* of leading clubs   53
    The where, the when and the why of *vervlaamsing*   54
    Case studies of *vervlaamsing*   56
    The paradox of Belgian football: a national structure in a
    federal state   60
5   **Playing across the border: football frontiers**   61
    Reasons for playing across the border   62
    Geographical proximity   62

Economic pragmatism   63
Status presence   65
Political pressure   66
Pushed across the border: Berwick Rangers into Scotland   67
Nowhere else to go: Derry City into the Republic of Ireland   70
Refugees on either side of the border: the case of Cyprus   76

PART TWO   Football as Extension of the State   **83**
6   **Red Star Dynamo Lokomotiv Torpedo FC: football in
    Eastern Europe**   85
    Football in Eastern Europe before socialism   86
    Political importance of football in Eastern Europe   88
    Socialist organization of sport   92
    Changes in the late 1980s in response to *perestroika* and
    glasnost   94
    Coping in the post-communist world   95
7   **Don't shoot me, I'm the *presidente*: football and politics
    in Argentina**   100
    Formation of early football clubs in Argentina   100
    Establishment of structures that integrate football and
    politics   101
    The role of fans in football and politics   106
    Politicization of the 1978 World Cup finals   111
8   ***Ultra*-political: football culture in Italy**
    By Rocco de Biasi, translated and edited by Liz Crolley   115
    Militant fans and political allegiances   117
    Are *ultras* right wing?   120
    The 'antagonistic left' and the fans of the *curva*   122
    The 'footballization' of politics?   123
9   **Women can't play, it's a male ball: her story in football**   128
    Reasons for women's exclusion from football   129
    Moral gender roles   130
    Physical gender roles   131
    Women as players   131
    Women's involvement as fans   139
    Women and the football media   141

References   145
Index   149

LIST OF FIGURES AND TABLES

Figure 1.1 The state and football are closely interlinked in
            Argentina. River Plate fans at the Estadio
            Provincial Malvinas Argentinas in Mendoza,
            Argentina, January 1994.   8
       2.1 Hampden Park, Glasgow. The design of the seats
            at the Scottish national football stadium
            incorporates the Scottish flag.   17
       3.1 The Campo Sarria ground, Barcelona.
            Non-Catalanists gather to the right of the terrace
            and Catalanists to the left while the scoreboard
            diplomatically spells the name of the club as both
            Castilian Español and Catalan Espanyol.   45
       4.1 The main stand of *FC Roeselare* with the club's
            main sponsor, the Rodenbach brewery, in the
            background.   58
       5.1 Scottish club Gretna welcome today's visitors.
            Visitors are always English as Gretna play in the
            English semi-professional Northern Premier
            League.   63
       6.1 As the communist regimes liberalized, so the
            English 'disease' of football hooliganism spread
            to Eastern Europe. Ferencvaros fans took a
            leading role in Hungary.   96
       7.1 The Boca end at La Bombonera, Boca Juniors
            Stadium. The match took place during an
            electoral campaign and the *barras bravas* were
            called to political duties elsewhere, hence the
            gaps in the centre of the middle tier.   111
       8.1 The Estadio delli Alpi, home to both Juventus
            and Torino, was temporarily abandoned by Juve
            in protest at the high charges demanded by its
            owners, the local authority.   127
       9.1 Arsenal Ladies about to kick off against
            Doncaster Belles in the match which decided the
            women's national division championship in April
            1995. The Stainforth Miners' welfare ground has
            no cover, seating or terracing.   138

Table 2.1 Key dates in the development of football in the UK 12

4.1 Name changes of Belgian football clubs: the progression to Flemish 55

5.1 Refugee clubs in the leading Cypriot divisions 77

PREFACE

Research work over several years has gone into the making of this book. We first worked together on a study of football spectator behaviour in Argentina in 1994, the findings of which are to be found in Duke and Crolley (1996). Following this we decided to combine our previous work on football in other parts of the world, most notably Liz on Spain, and Vic on Eastern Europe. All that remained was to research the additional countries and topics which comprise this book. Our colleague and friend Rocco De Biasi from the University of Milan agreed to contribute a chapter on Italian football, which Liz has translated and edited.

The introductory chapter sets out the framework for the book, and the following chapters form a series of case studies on the varied relationship between football, nationality and the state. It is intended that the case studies will serve as illuminating and innovative examples for students of the politics or sociology of sport. Moreover our aim has been to avoid specialist jargon and rely on everyday English in order to appeal to the general reader interested in the politics of football.

We are indebted to Richard Giulianotti for suggesting the eventual title, which is far more succinct and appropriate than our original broad title of 'the politics of football'. There are many others without whose assistance the book would not have been completed. Not least of these are the sponsors, who funded the research fieldwork required. For the trip to Argentina, Vic Duke was funded by the Nuffield Foundation, and Liz Crolley by Manchester Metropolitan University, who also funded her research visits to Spain. The British Council assisted in some of Vic Duke's visits to Eastern Europe, and his other research trips were subsidized by Salford University.

On Eastern Europe, Vic Duke has benefited over many years from the helpful advice and friendship of Pavel Slepicka, Vera Lapackova, Olda Uhlir and Rudolf Bata in the Czech Republic, and Gyongyi Szabo Foldesi and Zoltan Kovacs in Hungary. He is also grateful to Professor Roland Renson for arranging a visiting professorship to the Sport Museum of Flanders archive at the Catholic University of Leuven. Others providing assistance and conviviality while at Leuven were Jan Tolleneer, Richard Holt, Bart Van Heusel, Marijke Den Hollander, Marijke Taks and Erik De Vroede. M. De Wind of the Belgian Football Association was also courteous and helpful.

In Spain, Liz Crolley is indebted to the advice, assistance and generous hospitality of Juan Pedro and Isabel Ortega Gil and Fina and

Pepe Carceles Manzanares, to the *Real Federación Española de Fútbol*, in particular to Francisco Canigera, and to José del Olmo at the *Centro de Investigaciones de la Historia y la Estadística del Fútbol Español*, for providing information and data so promptly and efficiently on Spanish football past and present. She is also grateful to staff at various football clubs for collaborating in initial research projects, in particular to the staff of Espanyol, Real Madrid, Barcelona, and Athletic Bilbao.

Research in Argentina would not have been possible without the valuable assistance of the following people: Eduardo Archetti, Rafael Bayce, Miguel Cruzalegui, Julio Cesar Pasquato, Ariel Scher and Natalio Gorín, who kindly provided materials from the archives at *El Gráfico*.

Many individuals contributed to the research into women's involvement in football including Derek Marsden for information on girls' football at school level; Rachel O'Connor and Louise Aughty at the *Wharfedale and Airedale Observer* for their comments on women sportswriters; Marcela Mora at BBC World Service, especially for her help in interviewing fans; Helen Jevens at the FA Development Office; Pam Booth and Joy Calderbank; and to Sheila Andrew, Christine Wilkinson, Margaret Vaudrey and to Eileen Fraser, who is proof that Manchester United fans are not all that bad!

Other individuals helped in various ways on specific case studies: Dennis McCleary, Robin Murdie and the librarians at Berwick-upon-Tweed library on Berwick Rangers; Kevin Mahon, Arthur Duffy and Eddie Mahon on Derry City; Adonis Procopiou, Olgun Üstün, Memdah Asaf Sohak, Paris Menelaou, Haris Christoforou, Yiannikis Papatheodorou and Diofantos Chrysostomou in Cyprus; David Hand, Geraldine Muirhead, Mario Fazio and Billy Mitchell for constructive comments on earlier drafts of the manuscript. Flight distances for chapter 5 were promptly supplied by Air France, Air Portugal and Iberia; the missing distance from the airline which did not reply was provided by Gustav Dobrzynski, a cartographer at Salford University. At the proofreading stage we were ably assisted by Maddy Duke and John Cain. Finally, thanks to Liz's dad for coming out of retirement to contribute to one of the chapters, and to her mum for inspiring her interest in football in the first place.

CHAPTER 1

Introduction: the game of nations

Association football (often known as soccer) is the world's number one game. This statement applies whether one is referring to participation in the game, spectating at a match or viewing a match on television. The importance of football as a business as well as a sport is confirmed by the television audience for the final stages of the last two World Cups. Italy 1990 achieved a cumulative worldwide audience of over 25 billion, which was bettered by over 32 billion for USA 1994.

Football's popularity is in large part due to its simplicity and its low cost as a participation sport. The rules for casual play are basic requiring only a round ball and (if there are two teams) two improvised goals. No expensive equipment is needed and a match can take place anywhere there is an area of reasonably flat land. Children throughout the world seem to find kicking and running after a ball a natural and enjoyable activity.

Undoubtedly football has become the national sport in the vast majority of countries in the world. The term 'countries' is used quite deliberately as a catch-all at this juncture, because the *Chambers Dictionary* defines country as 'a region; a state; a nation; the land of one's birth or citizenship'. The terms region, state and nation will be clarified and distinguished later in this introduction, when the framework is outlined for the case studies, which constitute the rest of the book.

Exceptions to football's status as the national sport are few in number but comprise some populous and powerful countries. The USA is the most notable example with football as a spectator sport ranked well behind the big four of baseball, American football, basketball and ice hockey. Elsewhere in North America, ice hockey is the national sport for Canada. Mexico and the countries of Central America, however, are undisputed soccer territory.

Europe overwhelmingly adheres to football as the national sport, although there are a few exceptions. Finland and Slovenia prefer ice hockey as a spectator sport, and for Wales rugby union is regarded as the national sport. Football dominates in South America with the only deviation being Venezuela's preference for baseball. Africa is the football continent *par excellence* in terms of sporting dominance, particularly since the ending of apartheid in South Africa. The minority white elite preferred rugby union and cricket, but the black majority play and watch football in large numbers. Cricket has an area of dominance as the national sport in the Indian subcontinent and in the former British colonies in the Caribbean.

The development of FIFA and the changing global politics of football

The *Fédération Internationale de Football Association* (FIFA) was founded in 1904 by representatives from seven countries in mainland Europe. None of the first four football associations in the world (the four UK associations) was involved at this stage. Chapter 2 documents the unique position and turbulent history within FIFA of the four UK associations. Currently FIFA has more members than the United Nations, and the world population takes a greater interest in the activities of the former than of the latter. A prerequisite for FIFA entry in recent years is that the United Nations accept the political independence of the territory involved (not that this has been applied to the four UK associations – see chapter 2).

Eurocentrism was prevalent in FIFA until the wave of independence from European colonial powers in the 1950s and 1960s. On the eve of the First World War in 1914, FIFA's membership had risen to twenty-four. Of these, twenty were European, including the four UK associations; the other members comprised two South American representatives (Argentina and Chile) and two North American (Canada and the USA). By 1938 FIFA had fifty-six members, exactly half of them from Europe. Members from the rest of the world were distributed as follows: South America nine, North and Central America (including the Caribbean) eleven, Asia seven, and Africa one (Egypt).

In 1995 the membership composition and resultant balance of power look very different. Africa has moved from the lowest membership of one in 1938 to the highest of fifty-one out of a global total of a hundred and ninety-one. The second footballing continent is Europe, or more accurately the Union of European Football Associations (UEFA), which includes Israel as one of its forty-one members. Making up the rest are Asia forty-one, North and Central America thirty, South America ten and Oceania ten.

FIFA is an egalitarian institution in that each member has one vote irrespective of the size of the country. The Republic of China's vote (population over 1.1 billion) is of equal weight to those of San Marino (22,000) and the Cook Islands (17,000). However, any change to FIFA's rules requires a three-quarters majority to support it. Europe currently accounts for 25.7 per cent of the membership, so that a united Europe can prevent any change. Since the breakup of the Soviet Union, Yugoslavia and Czechoslovakia, Europe has increased its membership in FIFA. Moreover, the demise of Soviet-style communism has produced greater political uniformity, certainly in relation to the global politics of football.

Dominating the FIFA political agenda in the 1990s has been the issue of unequal distribution between the continents of places in the World Cup finals, which are held every four years. A growing African and Asian lobby is demanding greater representation at the expense of Europe and South America. At the 1994 finals in the USA, Europe's forty-nine members were represented by twelve finalists (including Germany as 1990 champions), which is exactly half the participants. Africa had only three finalists among its fifty-one members.

It is not a case of European countries beating African countries in the qualifying competition, because the qualifying stage is divided into continental groups. Europe was allocated eleven qualifying places (in addition, the holders of the trophy qualified automatically) and Africa only three. Asian countries are similarly aggrieved at receiving only two places in the finals for their forty-one members. South America, in contrast, was allocated four places to be competed for by the ten members. Admittedly, South American teams have won the World Cup eight times to Europe's seven in the fifteen finals thus far, but the other continents argue for a fairer share of the starting line-up for the finals.

Given that it has the highest number of members, Africa is particularly dissatisfied with the distribution of places in the World Cup finals. Egypt qualified for the 1934 finals in Italy by beating Palestine twice. The next African appearance in the finals was Morocco in 1970, when for the first time one place had been allocated to Africa. In between Africa felt harshly treated; in 1958 a joint African-Asian qualifying place was won by Wales! (this was caused by several withdrawals which left Israel as winners without playing a match, so being forced into a play-off against Wales); in 1962 Morocco beat Tunisia and Ghana before losing to Spain; in 1966 all the African entrants (and all the Asian entrants except North Korea) withdrew in protest at the allocation of only one place to Africa and Asia combined.

Since the breakthrough to an earmarked place in the 1970 finals, political pressure has intensified to increase the African quota. At the same time there was a steady increase in the number of African members of FIFA. The African quota in the finals was increased to two out of sixteen in 1982, and to three out of twenty-four in 1994. FIFA's solution has been to increase African participation as part of an overall enlargement of the scale of the World Cup finals. For the next World Cup finals in France in 1998, Africa will have five teams out of thirty-two finalists. Predictably, Europe's representation has been increased from twelve to fifteen, and South America's from four to five.

Football, nationality and the state

Returning to our earlier definition of a country as 'a region; a state; a nation', it is necessary to distinguish between the various components in order to establish the framework for the rest of the book. The extent of overlap between the state and nation in a given country is crucial to an understanding of the politics of football in that country. The specific definitions presented are adapted from Dearlove and Saunders (1984).

A *state* is a political unit, which claims the monopoly of legitimate force within a given territory: a state has its own army and police force as well as a foreign ministry for dealing with relations with other states. People know which state they live in because they pay taxes to the government of that state. States usually have a football team to represent them in international competitions. FIFA's members are the football associations of independent states, and the World Cup is competed for by teams representing individual states. (The exception to this rule is the UK: see chapter 2.)

A *region* is a geographical subdivision of a larger territorial unit such as a state. Regions may or may not be recognized and represented in the institutional structure of the state. They do not usually have football teams officially representing the region, although the best club in the region may be regarded as the region's football ambassador. Examples of historical regional rivalries in football are those between clubs in the north of England and London, and the enmity between northern and southern Italy.

A *nation* is a sociological entity with a defined territory, involving common sentiments and a common identity shared by its members: people feel themselves to be part of a nation. As an ideology nationalism became prevalent towards the end of the eighteenth century in Western Europe and North America (Hutchinson and Smith 1994). National movements are most often associated with the educated middle class, who have the most to gain from the replacement of colonial or monarchistic rule by a national republic.

Anderson (1983) has described nations as imagined communities. They combine both objective and subjective attributes. A finite territorial area is linked to a common bond based on a myth of common descent. Tomlinson (1994) suggests that nations attain their fullest expression in two ways – war and sport. The two were infamously combined in the war between El Salvador and Honduras in 1969 following on from riots at World Cup qualifying games between the two.

Football captures the notion of an imagined community perfectly. It is much easier to imagine the nation and confirm national identity, when eleven players are representing the nation in a match against another nation. If nationalism was a movement fostered by and favouring the educated middle class, its spread to the working class in the twentieth century was surely assisted by the development of international football. It has often been argued that only religious commitment can rival national loyalties in scope and fervour, but the passion of football supporters for their club is in the same league. When football support and nationalism are combined, the brew is particularly strong, as evidenced by the invading army of England supporters on numerous occasions throughout Europe in the 1980s and 1990s (Williams *et al.* 1984).

Another crucial feature stressed by Anderson is that nations should exhibit historical continuity in terms of an affinity with dead generations one has never met. The rise of football at the same time as the establishment of many nation-states has contributed to the development of this continuity. Tales of the legendary exploits of past international players, never seen but never forgotten, are passed on from generation to generation. In extreme cases of nations invaded or annexed by a neighbouring state, the legacy of previous international football matches becomes part of the very confirmation that the nation did exist, and indeed does exist.

A good example is the three Baltic republics, who have regained their independence from the former Soviet Union. Estonia, Latvia and Lithuania played international football from the early 1920s to the early 1940s, recommencing their international careers in 1991. Similarly, Croatia and Slovakia have reappeared in international football after disappearing in the 1940s.

Where the state overlaps to a large degree with the nation, the politics of football in relation to the state is straightforward. Nationalism becomes loyalty to the state, and support for the national team can be interpreted as support for the regime. Many political leaders have recognized the importance of football in this respect as the national and world sport. Equally however, opposition leaders or movements have been known to use the football stadium as an arena for resistance to the regime (for examples of both kinds see Kuper 1994).

In the cases where the state does not equal the nation, the existence of latent or submerged nations within a state provides the potential for political conflict. Politically unrecognized or unsatisfied ethnies (ethnic communities) are particularly prone to resistance to the centre. The 1960s witnessed an upsurge in nationalist movements demanding greater autonomy such as Scotland, Wales, Flanders and Catalonia. These movements may find expression in the football stadium. In authoritarian regimes football may be the only legal theatre for the expression of latent nationalism. Part one of the book presents case studies of the politics of football where there is more than one nation within the state. Part two provides examples, again via a series of case studies, of football as an extension of the state and closely linked to the political structures.

Football nations within the state

The first set of case studies relates to the existence of more than one football nation within the state. In the 1990s, the disintegration of the Soviet Union, Yugoslavia and Czechoslovakia into smaller independent states has diminished the extent of the phenomenon. However, several latent nations continue to exist within, and sometimes across, state boundaries. Football may provide an important means of expressing latent nationalism with the gathering of large crowds in the stadium.

Chapter 2 considers the unique position in world football of the UK, which has four football associations in the membership of FIFA, namely England, Scotland, Wales and Northern Ireland. This anomaly is due to the foundation of modern football in the UK in the second half of the nineteenth century. Some sections of the FIFA membership, particularly the African states, have recently questioned the UK's privileged position in world football. The Welsh football association responded to the threat by introducing a national League of Wales for the first time in 1992 in order to establish its separateness from England.

Chapter 3 analyses the role of football throughout different phases of twentieth-century Spanish political history. It focuses on the use of the football arena as a vehicle for expressing nationalism in the latent nations (or 'historic nationalities') of the Basque Country and Catalonia, and on the role of Real Madrid as promoting the notion of a single, centralized Spanish nation. The changing ways in which nationalist tendencies were expressed in football are documented from the start of the twentieth century when nationalist issues were becoming an important part of the political agenda; during and after the Spanish Civil War (1936–39) when Franco's regime proscribed any hint of nationalist sentiment; and more recently during Spain's transition to democracy when the 'historic nationalities' have gained a high degree of political autonomy and no longer rely on football as the sole exponent of nationalism.

Chapter 4 examines the case of Belgian football, where the language divide between the Flemish and French parts of the state has been manifested in distinctive ways. Belgian football was controlled in the early years of its development, as was the Belgian economy at this time, by the Francophone elite. The Belgian football association operated initially only in French. Most Flemish clubs in Flanders adopted the French name for the town in the club name prior to the First World War. A growing politicization of Flemish nationalism led to the formation of a short-lived alternative parallel Flemish football league structure in the 1930s. Of more lasting significance in football terms was the surge of support for Flemish nationalism in the 1960s, which led to a process of *vervlaamsing* (flemicizing) of club names from French to Flemish.

Chapter 5 contains several case studies of football clubs, which play across the border in a neighbouring state. Normally clubs are affiliated to the football association of the state in which the town is located, but FIFA does permit certain exceptions. Four reasons for playing across the frontier are outlined: geographical proximity, economic pragmatism, status presence and political pressure. The bulk of the chapter is taken up by three detailed case studies of playing across the border: Berwick Rangers, an English club, who play in the Scottish League; Derry City, a club from Northern Ireland, who play in the League of Ireland (the national league for the Republic of Ireland); and refugee clubs in Cyprus on both the Greek and Turkish sides of the partition.

Football as an extension of the state

The second set of case studies reveals a different kind of relationship between football and the state. The politics of football may come to reflect the structure of the political system. Football then appears as an extension of the state. In a totalitarian system the state's control and manipulation of sport is more likely to be deliberate and explicit. In other cases the importance of the national sport is such that the political and business elites forge links with football, leading to a convergence of both structure and values.

Chapter 6 documents the effects on football of the imposition of Soviet communism on the republics of Eastern Europe after the Second World War. Along with the new political system came a restructuring of sport along socialist lines. Football clubs were no longer independent private clubs, and instead became sponsored by a particular ministry, factory or trade union. The state attempted to alter the names of famous clubs, but predictably met with resistance from football supporters. National football teams were expected to play an important role in demonstrating the superiority of socialism over capitalism (especially in the Olympic Games football tournament). Post-communism in Europe since 1989 has created problems of a different kind for football clubs, as they face renewed professionalization and commercialization of football, plus the loss of key players to better pay and conditions in Western Europe.

Chapter 7 focuses on the relationship between football and politics in Argentina where the connections between the state and football structures are so closely interlinked that the two systems cannot easily be separated. Historically, as football predated the modern political system, there are grounds to claim that football provided the social model around which the political system was constructed. In times of military dictatorship, the state has deliberately controlled and manipulated football to serve its political ends and to promote a positive image of the country (as in the 1978 World Cup finals held in Argentina). The presence of an electoral system in football clubs ensures that club directors and entrepreneurs need the support of fans to succeed, just as politicians need the vote of their people. This gives the fans considerable power. Those who run football either at club level or in the Argentine FA are invariably involved in party politics in some way and the football club is used as a shop window and a stepping-stone to a political career (see Figure 1.1).

Chapter 8 provides an insight into the social phenomena which indicate the existence of interference between football and politics in Italy. Ritualistic behaviour, and particularly linguistic metaphors, used today in the political area had their origins in the footballing context and so many football chants have now taken on political connotations. The *'ultras'*, highly organized groups of football fans, play a key role in the development of the relationship between football and politics, and their political leanings/tendencies are examined in some detail. The *caso Berlusconi* (Berlusconi case) provides an example of how football and politics have merged and their cultural rituals transferred across social contexts.

Chapter 9 demonstrates how football reflects the political framework

Figure 1.1   The state and football are closely interlinked in Argentina. River Plate fans at the Estadio Provincial Malvinas Argentinas in Mendoza, Argentina, January 1994

of the state by examining how the structure and organization of women's football function within a patriarchal society in which sport, and in particular football, promotes certain 'male' values of power, strength and competitiveness. Distributional issues (the relative absence of women at all levels) and relational issues (how women's presence in football is seen in relation to men's) are examined at various levels of involvement in football – in the areas of playing, organization, supporting and the media. Women's involvement in football has been marginalized, even trivialized. Recent trends indicate an increased participation by women in football, although there remains strong evidence that women are restricted in terms of both distributional and relational issues.

PART ONE

Football Nations within the State

UK 4 FIFA 0: the result of football's early development

Numerous claims have been made regarding football's ancestry. Ancient civilizations possessing some version of a ball-kicking game include the Chinese (*Tsu Chu*), the Japanese (*Kemari*), the Greeks (*Episkyros*) and the Romans (*Harpastum*). In the Middle Ages more recent predecessors in Europe were *la soule* in Brittany, *calcio* in Italy and the annual folk football games in Britain. What is undisputed is that the modern game of association football (soccer) began in England with the formation of the (English) Football Association in 1863.

In the early nineteenth century, English public schools made the first modern attempts to regulate various games centred on the kicking of a ball. Such regulations referred to a set of binding rules including the notion of equal numbers on each team, and a clearly defined area of play. When pupils steeped in the pleasure of these public school contests wished to continue playing at university, the sheer variety of rules at different schools posed a problem. Hence the formulation in 1848 of the Cambridge (University) rules, which attempted to standardize play based on the dribbling game (to become soccer) rather than the handling game (to become rugby). It was the Cambridge rules which formed a partial basis for the Football Association rules in 1863.

Table 2.1 summarizes the key dates in the initial development of association football in the UK. The (English) Football Association was soon followed by the founding of the Scottish FA in 1873, the Welsh in 1876 and the Irish equivalent in 1880. Glasgow's West of Scotland cricket ground staged the first official international match between Scotland and England (a 0–0 draw) in 1872. Wales made its international debut in 1876 (a 0–4 defeat in Scotland) and Ireland in 1982 (a 0–13 defeat versus England in Belfast). A similar progression is evident in all four countries with respect to the setting up of a football association, a cup competition, international fixtures and a national league. The one anomaly is the failure of the Welsh FA to establish a national league (covering north and south Wales) until 1993. In the case study of Welsh football (pp. 19–23), the current repercussions are discussed in detail.

The four UK associations in Table 2.1 had a dominant position in the early years of the game. No other football association was formed until 1889, when both Denmark and the Netherlands started up. By the end of the century associations had been established in New Zealand 1891; South Africa and Singapore 1892; Argentina 1893; Belgium, Switzerland and Chile 1895; and Italy 1898.

*Table 2.1   **Key dates in the development of football in the UK***

Nation	Football association	National cup	First international	National league
England	1863	1871	1872	1888
Scotland	1873	1873	1872	1890
Wales	1876	1877	1876	1992
Ireland	1880	1880	1882	1890

Note: The Irish Football Association (IFA) originally covered the whole of Ireland but now administers only Northern Ireland. The Football Association of Ireland (FAI) formed in 1921 covers the Republic of Ireland.

International matches were played only between the four UK countries until the beginning of the twentieth century. A challenge match between teams representing the USA and Canada was played in November 1885, but this is not recognized as a full international. The first official international match in the world outside the UK took place in May 1901, when Argentina beat Uruguay 3–2 in Montevideo. Mainland Europe's first international was Austria's 5–0 demolition of Hungary in Vienna in October 1902.

This early development of association football in Britain left the UK with a legacy of four separate national stadiums for international matches. Moorhouse (1991) has described Scotland, Wales and Northern Ireland as submerged nations. Wales was formally absorbed into the English state in 1536, Scotland joined via the Act of Union in 1707, and Ireland followed in 1800.

FIFA and the UK associations: a history of separation and reconciliation

French initiative and vision were behind the moves to create an international football federation in 1904, and later in the founding of the World Cup for nations, and the European Champions Cup for clubs. A meeting in Paris established the *Fédération internationale de football association* (FIFA: International Federation of Football Associations). Founder members were France, Belgium, the Netherlands, Denmark, Sweden, Switzerland and Spain.

No representative of the UK associations attended the meeting. Aloofness with a hint of arrogance characterized the response of the English FA, which did not reply to the French proposal. Eventually an official reply stated that the FA could not see any advantages in such a federation, but that it was prepared to confer on matters of joint interest. Holt (1989) has suggested that the English felt that association football was their property, and they had no inclination to cooperate with foreigners. Despite this stance of splendid isolation, the Europeans retained a lingering admiration for the originators of the beautiful game.

FIFA began without any British involvement but the English FA soon joined in 1905, realizing that the new organization was here to stay; the other UK associations followed shortly after. Thereafter the four UK associations have acted in unison with respect to FIFA in a saga of separation and reconciliation. They all withdrew from 1920 to 1924, re-entered until 1928, then withdrew again until 1946, since when membership has been continuous if not always smooth.

Although the English were welcomed by FIFA in 1905, there was initial resistance to the separate membership of the other three UK associations. FIFA's rules stipulated that only one association was allowed from each state. Ultimately the founding influence and dominant role of the English FA, as well as the historical pedigree of the other three football nations, persuaded FIFA to admit Scotland and Wales in 1910, and Ireland in 1911. During this period there was a bizarre attempt to join FIFA by the (English) Amateur Football Association, which had split from the professional game administered by the (English) Football Association; the application was unsuccessful.

After the First World War there was a reluctance among certain countries, including the UK, to engage in sporting contests with the defeated enemies. A failed proposal that FIFA exclude Germany, Austria and Hungary led to the first withdrawal of the UK associations in 1920. The second exodus from FIFA in 1928 resulted from a disagreement over the issue of amateurism. A strict definition of amateurism was favoured by the UK associations to the effect that only necessary travel and hotel expenses should be paid for. By contrast, FIFA ruled that amateur players could in addition be paid compensation for any loss of earnings from their regular job (often designated as broken time payments).

One result of the tempestuous relationship between FIFA and the UK associations was that the latter missed out on another French initiative – the beginning of the World Cup competition for nations. The UK associations missed not only the first World Cup in Uruguay in 1930, but also the second finals in Italy 1934, and the third in France 1938. By the time England competed in the 1950 finals in Brazil, the two decades of isolation from top level competition had taken their toll. England lost two of its three games, including the infamous 0–1 defeat by the unrated USA team.

The pervasive dominance of the UK associations

Notwithstanding periodic disagreements with FIFA, the UK associations have retained a dominant position in the administration of world football. Three of FIFA's seven presidents have been English, the last being Sir Stanley Rous, who was not re-elected in 1974 when challenged by João Havelange of Brazil; since the early 1970s the pre-eminence of the UK associations has been strongly challenged.

It is surprising that separate representation of the four nations has been maintained. The one association per nation-state rule for new applications has not been retrospectively applied to the UK. If the 'British' rule had operated for other parts of the world, the fifteen Soviet republics could have been independent members of FIFA (as indeed they now are since the breakup of the Soviet Union). Moreover, why not give individual membership to the ten West German *Länder* or the fifty states of the USA?

There has been political opposition to the UK's privileged position in the early 1970s and in the early 1990s. In the former period, Havelange based his campaign partly on an anti-European ticket, beneath which lay a potential challenge to the position of the UK associations. He was able to build on South American resentment of European domination, particularly on the part of Argentina and Uruguay, who felt that officials (both on and off the pitch) were biased against them during the 1966 World Cup finals held in England. Argentina has still not forgotten or forgiven the sending off of its captain Antonio Rattin in the quarter-final match, which England subsequently won 1–0.

Havelange was able also to build on the aspirations of the newly independent African and Asian nations, who were recent additions to FIFA membership and demanded a greater presence in the World Cup finals at the expense of the European nations. Rous also alienated the Soviet Union (and its bloc vote of fellow communist countries) by insisting that a play-off between Chile and the Soviet Union take place in the National Stadium in Santiago, Chile. Earlier in the year, following a military coup in which the Marxist president was shot, the stadium was used for the torture and murder of political opponents; the Soviet Union refused to play there and was eliminated from the World Cup.

Rous (1978) in his memoirs expressed his fear that in 1974 the four UK associations might be required to unite, and pointed out that the balance of power in FIFA was tilting against Europe all the time. By the early 1990s there was a growing lobby in Africa for a UK team, which would reduce the number of European votes by three. In 1989 there were forty-eight African members of FIFA to Europe's thirty-four, and yet representation in the World Cup finals of both 1986 and 1990 was Africa two, Europe fourteen. Ironically the breakup of the Soviet Union, Yugoslavia and Czechoslovakia in the 1990s has seen European membership of FIFA rise to forty-nine, almost equal to Africa's fifty-one.

The four UK associations continue to control football's law-making body with respect to the rules of playing the game. The International Football Association Board was established in 1886 comprising eight members, two from each of the four FAs in existence. Two representatives elected by FIFA were added to the Board in 1913 alongside the original eight UK delegates. In 1928, when the four UK associations withdrew from FIFA, it retained their representation on the International Board. Currently FIFA has four members of the Board, but the four UK associations have sixteen. Given that a three-quarters majority is required in order to alter the playing regulations, clearly no change can occur without British approval.

Advantages and disadvantages in having four UK associations

Examined from the British point of view, the advantages in having four football nations in the UK have far outweighed the disadvantages. It is only in recent years that certain negative aspects of the arrangement have surfaced. An obvious but important factor favouring inertia in the historical set-up is the pure self-interest (conscious or not) of the administrators. Having a single UK association with a single UK national team and a UK Premier League would require only one set of administrators dealing with international relations and competitions. The career opportunities in international football administration in the UK would decrease by 75 per cent, not to mention the loss of travel opportunities to foreign meetings, conferences and away matches.

A further advantage is increased participation in international competitions between nations. All four football nations are allowed entry into the World Cup and the European Championship. Having a single UK team would reduce the possibilities for players, spectators, managers, referees and the media. The UK had at least one representative in each of the World Cup final stages between 1950 and 1990, reaching a peak in Sweden in 1958, when all four took part. Interestingly the two minnows of Northern Ireland and Wales were the most successful in reaching the quarter-final stage in this year. The only UK winner of the World Cup is England in 1966, when the team had the distinct advantage of hosting the final stages. For the 1994 World Cup finals in the USA none of the UK associations qualified; however, the Republic of Ireland did.

Similar benefits of enhanced participation in European competitions accrue to individual football clubs in the four UK associations. Each football nation is entitled to enter its league champions, cup winners, and in some cases other leading teams into the European Champions' Cup, the European Cup Winners' Cup and the UEFA Cup. English clubs have been the most successful, winning the Champions' Cup eight times (Liverpool four), the Cup Winners' Cup seven times and the UEFA Cup nine times. Scotland have had limited success with Glasgow Celtic winning the Champions' Cup in 1967 and Cup Winners' Cup victories for Glasgow Rangers in 1972 and Aberdeen in 1983.

Clubs in Wales and Northern Ireland have arguably benefited the most from the opportunity for European competition; these clubs are highly unlikely to be able to compete successfully in a UK national league and thereby qualify for European competition. The three leading Welsh professional clubs play in the (English) Football League Divisions 2 and 3 (actually levels three and four as the highest level is the Premier League). No Northern Irish club has progressed beyond the quarter-final stage of any of the European competitions.

In the case of Scotland it is likely that the leading clubs such as Glasgow Rangers and Glasgow Celtic could compete successfully in a UK Premier League, as evidenced by their European trophies. What all three submerged nations have in common is the tendency for their better players to be attracted to the higher salaries available in England. This migration of talent means that leading English clubs have often relied on Scottish, Welsh and Irish players. For example, when Liverpool reached the European Champions' Cup final in 1985 (the infamous Heysel confrontation with Juventus), only two of the starting eleven players were English (Phil Neal and Paul Walsh). The rest of the line-up comprised four Scots, three Irish and two Welsh.

As to the disadvantages of UK football having four national associations, these are less immediately obvious. The hypothetical argument suggests that a single UK national team in international competitions would have been considerably more successful than the one World Cup win achieved by England, and cites the spectacular success of English clubs in European competitions with teams comprising English, Scottish, Welsh and Irish players.

A more concrete and serious disadvantage to UK clubs emerged in the early 1990s, when UEFA began to impose restrictions on the number of non-nationals allowed in a team competing in the European competitions. Because the UK is regarded as four separate nations in football terms, English clubs had to classify Scottish, Welsh and Irish players as foreign (and vice versa). A century of migration of football talent from the submerged nations to England was under threat. In 1991–92 a quota of four foreigners was permitted in a squad of sixteen players. From the 1992–93 season the position was eased slightly to a maximum of three non-national players plus a further two assimilated non-nationals, who had played continuously in the country for five years.

However, the European Court's ruling in December 1995 on a case brought by a Belgian footballer (Mark Bosman) has declared the UEFA restrictions illegal. Article 48 of the Treaty of Rome guarantees free movement within the European Union for all workers, including footballers. It is illegal to restrict the number of European Union players who may play in a team; restrictions may still be applied to players from outside the European Union. The judgment has been welcomed by leading English and Scottish clubs because they can now continue their century-old practice of fielding as many UK players as they like.

A final disadvantage has emerged in the 1990s for the Welsh FA, which has been forced to justify its separateness with repercussions for Welsh semi-professional clubs as outlined in the case study below. The breakup of the Soviet Union and further splintering in Eastern Europe resulted in a flood of new applications to UEFA. Since 1989 UEFA has admitted Armenia, Azerbaijan, Belarus, Estonia, Georgia, Latvia, Lithuania, Moldova and Ukraine (from the former Soviet Union); Croatia, Macedonia and Slovenia (formerly part of Yugoslavia); the Czech Republic and Slovakia (former Czechoslovakia). One of UEFA's criteria for membership has been the existence of a national league. At this juncture the Welsh FA decided after over a century without one to establish a national league in order to confirm its separateness from England. Additional pressure arose via African demands for a greater say in world football and their questions regarding the validity of the four

UK associations. The problems arising out of the creation of the League of Wales are discussed on pp. 19–23.

The future for separateness: Scotland and Ireland

Scotland has had a long history as an independent kingdom, although it is not currently a political state. It is a territory with a clearly defined border with England. McCrone (1992) has pointed out that Scotland retained a separate civil society after the Act of Union with its own legal, religious and education systems. This institutional framework provides it with a solid basis for renewed independence if the political and economic will should arise.

Moorhouse (1991) has suggested that a characteristic of submerged nations such as Scotland is that football (the national sport) takes on an exaggerated importance (he terms this an overdetermined significance). The importance of FC Barcelona to Catalan nationalism is another example (see chapter 3). Moorhouse defines Scottishness as being anti-English, and football has provided a popular vehicle for expression of dislike of the English. This hostility was evidenced previously (until the fixture was banned in 1990) in the biannual invasion of Wembley by the Scottish hordes. The existence of a Scottish national team constantly reinforces the separateness of Scotland. At one end of the refurbished national stadium for football (Hampden Park in Glasgow) the pattern of the seating displays the Scottish flag (see Figure 2.1).

Figure 2.1   *Hampden Park, Glasgow. The design of the seats at the Scottish national football stadium incorporates the Scottish flag*

Scotland has established a presence in international football by qualifying for the World Cup finals on seven occasions and by the three European trophies won by Scottish clubs. One of the problems with the Scottish League is the overwhelming dominance of two clubs, Glasgow Rangers and Glasgow Celtic, who between them have won eighty-one of the first ninety-nine league championships. Throughout the world only Uruguay matches this degree of domination with Peñarol and Nacional winning seventy-eight of the first ninety-four titles. Rangers and Celtic might well prefer to play in a more competitive and more lucrative UK Premier League, or better still in some form of European League. Independence for Scotland would normalize the situation of a separate Scotland team and Scottish League, however, and this scenario remains a possibility. At the 1992 general election the Scottish National Party obtained 21.5 per cent of the Scottish vote, and support for independence in opinion polls has been around one-third since the mid-1980s.

The future of Northern Irish football is tied to the political future of the six counties of Ulster. Political opinion is divided with support for remaining part of the UK (Protestant majority), union with the Republic of Ireland (Catholic minority) and an independent Northern Ireland (supported by some). Historically, association football has been more popular in the predominantly Protestant North with closer ties to Scotland and England.

In the Catholic South there was originally greater hostility to cultural imports from England such as cricket and association football. The Gaelic Athletic Association was set up in 1884 to promote gaelic sports such as hurling and gaelic football. After the Civil War gave birth to the Republic of Ireland, a separate Football Association of Ireland (FAI) was formed in Dublin in 1921. Later that year, the League of Ireland began and in 1923 the FAI was affiliated to FIFA. The four UK associations recognized the FAI on condition that all clubs within Northern Ireland remained under the control of the (Northern) Irish Football Association. Nonetheless Northern Ireland continued to select players from the South for international matches until 1948.

Northern Ireland has a less distinguished pedigree in world football than Scotland, although the national team has qualified for the World Cup finals on three occasions (1958, 1982 and 1986). At the club level, however, there have been no successes for Northern Ireland. Undoubtedly an all-Ireland team would be a stronger force in world football, but the make-up of the team would then cross an international frontier between two states. An all-Ireland team has never ceased to exist in Rugby Union, which provides a successful sporting exemplar. An exception has been made in the case of Derry City, based in Northern Ireland but playing across the border in the League of Ireland (see chapter 5).

Making a case for separateness: the League of Wales

Wales has been the least successful of the four national football teams, having reached the World Cup finals only once in 1958 in Sweden. On this occasion Wales lost in the quarter-final to the eventual champions Brazil. Progress in the European Championship has been rare with only one quarter-final appearance in 1976. Welsh clubs have achieved little in the European club competitions, with only Cardiff City reaching the semi-final stage of the Cup Winners' Cup in 1968.

A possible explanation for the relative lack of success in Wales (its population is almost double that of Northern Ireland) may be the fact that in south Wales rugby union became the dominant football code. It is only in north Wales, closer to the football hotbed of Lancashire, that association football came to predominate. The first football clubs in Wales were in the north in Ruabon and Wrexham.

The independent status of Welsh football has been questioned by some in the early 1990s. Under pressure from African countries keen for more influence in FIFA, a motion was tabled in June 1990 demanding the amalgamation of the four associations into a single UK association, and a single UK national team. Although the attempt was unsuccessful, the Welsh FA (FAW) felt particularly threatened. The Welsh national team had a long history in international competition, but there was no national league in Wales. Mountains in the centre have always made transportation difficult between the north and south of the country.

With the breakup of the Soviet Union and Yugoslavia, FIFA and UEFA received several applications for membership in the early 1990s. Prospective football associations had to demonstrate control over the clubs within their territory: one indicator was the establishment of a national league. As a result the FAW came to see the setting up of the League of Wales as essential to asserting and maintaining its separate identity. This decision has led to a long-running and at times bitter dispute involving legal action between the FAW and several semi-professional clubs located in the territory of Wales.

When the FAW proposed the creation of the League of Wales to begin in season 1992–93, eleven clubs declined to join. All of these were Welsh clubs playing in the English league structure, including the only three full-time professional clubs in Wales – Swansea City, Wrexham and Cardiff City, all of whom play in the (English) Football League (Divisions 2 and 3 in 1995–96). As the rest of the members of the proposed League of Wales were at best semi-professional, these three clubs were allowed to continue playing in the Football League. UEFA's view is that these three should join when the League of Wales is established enough to cope with large professional clubs.

The other eight clubs declining to join the new national league were all semi-professional. In October 1991 the FAW insisted that these clubs must play in the League of Wales, and withdrew permission for the eight to play on Welsh territory in an English League. When the clubs appealed against the decision an independent committee (selected by the

FAW) was requested to adjudicate. In February 1992 the appeal committee confirmed the ruling for seven of the clubs, but gave a reprieve to Merthyr Tydfil.

Merthyr were the highest placed of the semi-professional clubs as they played in the Conference, which is at the top of the English semi-professional pyramid structure. The Conference champions are eligible (subject to ground and financial criteria) for promotion to the professional ranks of the Football League. Merthyr argued that they were in a position (i.e. only one promotion away) to join Swansea City, Wrexham and Cardiff City among the professional elite. The FAW gave Merthyr five years to attain Football League status or they must join the League of Wales.

Reactions to the appeal ruling among the other seven were varied. Bangor City and Newtown conceded defeat and (reluctantly according to press reports at the time) joined the League of Wales. Rhyl toyed with going into exile in England but ultimately judged this to be financially unviable. Having left an application to the League of Wales too late, Rhyl joined the Cymru Alliance (effectively the Welsh Division 2 north) just before the start of the 1992–93 season. By 1994–95 Rhyl had been promoted to the League of Wales.

The remaining four clubs chose to resist the FAW and continue playing in the English regional, semi-professional leagues. In order to do this, the clubs had to go into exile in England. They were barred from playing on Welsh territory by the FAW and each club had to seek a groundshare agreement with an English club and also join the English County FA in which the ground was located. For the 1992–93 season Colwyn Bay travelled 60 miles to Northwich Victoria for all their home matches, Caernarfon Town 105 miles to Curzon Ashton (in Greater Manchester), Newport AFC 50 miles to Gloucester City, and Barry Town AFC (under the Welsh name of Barri) 98 miles to Worcester City.

On 15 August 1992 the first set of matches were played in the new League of Wales. An article in the October 1992 issue of the magazine *When Saturday Comes* suggested that the league was more notable for who was not in it than for who was. Nonetheless an incentive for winning the league was provided by UEFA in May 1992, when a place was allocated to the winners in the European Champions' Cup for 1993–94 (Cwmbran Town were the eventual first champions). Playing in Europe is a profitable exercise for Welsh clubs. The three clubs in European competition in 1995–96 – Bangor City and Afan Lido in the UEFA Cup and Wrexham (from the English Football League) in the European Cup Winners' Cup – made £200,000 between them, despite elimination for all three in the preliminary round. This amount is four times the annual sponsorship from Konica for the whole league.

Why did the four rebel clubs take the drastic course of playing in exile in England? The original eight clubs which resisted the FAW gave four main reasons to the appeal committee as to why they did not want to enter the League of Wales. First, travel between north and south Wales is too difficult. For example Colwyn Bay can travel to Whitley Bay (the club's longest trip in the Northern Premier League) quicker by coach than to Cardiff, due to the superior standard of the English motorway system in comparison to roads connecting north and south Wales.

Second, the eight clubs considered that playing standards would be lower in the League of Wales than in the English semi-professional leagues. The manager of the first Welsh champions, Cwmbran Town, later admitted that the playing level was slightly below the Southern League Midland Division (roughly the English Division 7 Midlands). Third, the clubs argued that they would lose money because of lower attendances in the League of Wales. The combined attendance at all League of Wales matches on a given Saturday rarely matches a single attendance at one of the three professional Welsh clubs in the Football League.

Fourth, unlike the English pyramid structure, the League of Wales does not provide an opportunity for further promotion into the professional ranks (although it does provide access into European competition). The Caernarfon Town match programme of 29 March 1993 (versus Ashton United) stated that 'we wish to preserve our position within the English pyramid system at all cost'. All Colwyn Bay match programmes for 1993–94 (by which time the club was groundsharing at Ellesmere Port) contained 'a message to our visitors'. This began 'I am sure that it cannot have escaped your notice that you are in Ellesmere Port for today's game', and was followed by a polemic on the right to play on one's own ground in a league of one's choosing.

Football supporters have on the whole taken the side of the rebel clubs rather than the FAW. A newspaper poll in *Wales On Sunday* towards the end of 1991 indicated that 77 per cent of readers supported the rebel clubs. Over a four-year period from April 1992 to March 1996, twelve letters have been published in support of the rebels in the monthly semi-professional football magazine *Team Talk*. During this period only one letter was published in support of the FAW. The two most common arguments made in the letters were the unfairness of treating the three professional clubs (and Merthyr) differently from the rest, and support for the principle of free choice as to which league a club competes in.

After one season in exile in 1992–93, Barry Town gave in to the FAW, largely because of the heavy financial costs of playing in exile at Worcester City. Barry joined the Abacus League (Welsh Division 2 south) for 1993–94, and by 1994–95 had gained promotion to the League of Wales. Barry Town have since become the first full-time professional club in the League of Wales, and became Welsh champions in 1995–96.

The remaining three clubs continued in exile in 1993–94 with Colwyn Bay moving to Ellesmere Port, a mere 40 miles to travel for home matches. In May 1994 the dispute escalated with the three clubs taking joint legal action against the FAW alleging unreasonable restraint of trade by preventing them playing at home in Wales. To take legal action is to break FIFA statute 57, which states that football disputes should go to arbitration rather than civil law. Caernarfon Town, Colwyn Bay and Newport AFC now had the threat of suspension from world football hanging over them.

In July 1994 the court granted a temporary injunction preventing the FAW from restricting the trade of the three clubs pending a full High Court hearing in 1995. The clubs had won a battle if not the war, and were able to return to their home grounds in Wales for the start of the 1994–95 season, while still competing in English leagues. The judge commented that the clubs had a long history of playing in English football, and the English FA confirmed that the original transfer of clubs had taken place with the agreement of the FAW. On 20 August 1994 Caernarfon Town played the first match at The Oval for 849 days against Goole Town in front of a crowd of 721.

The High Court ruled in favour of the three exiled clubs in April 1995 by deciding that the FAW preventing the clubs from playing in Wales was an illegal restraint of trade. Although the clubs had won the war, FIFA issued a directive that all the clubs involved must play inside national borders (in football terms) by 1997. This exposed the existence of other anomalies, including the four football associations in one UK state.

Notwithstanding the case of the three Welsh professional clubs and Merthyr Tydfil, there are other examples of clubs playing outside the national border: English club Oswestry Town play in the Welsh Division 2 north; Scottish club Gretna play in the English Northern Premier League; English club Berwick Rangers play in the Scottish League Division 2; Northern Irish club Derry City play in the Republic of Ireland League (see chapter 5).

It has been estimated that the High Court ruling cost the FAW about £0.5 million; the three rebel clubs also suffered financially during the period of exile. Despite the provision of subsidized coach transport from the home towns to the home games in exile, attendances were markedly lower. Caernarfon Town averaged 98 in each of the two seasons of exile at Curzon Ashton in comparison to average crowds at The Oval of 236 in 1991–92 and 250 in 1994–95. Colwyn Bay averaged 186 at Northwich Victoria in 1992–93 and 160 at Ellesmere Port in 1993–94. Before and after the exile in England, the home crowds at Llanelian Road averaged 485 in 1991–92 and 468 in 1994–95. After averaging 323 at Gloucester City in 1993–94, Newport AFC returned home to Newport and achieved an average crowd of 1,191.

Two developments in the summer of 1995 further stirred the plot. First, Merthyr Tydfil was relegated from the Conference to the Southern League Premier Division (effectively English Division 6 south) for 1995–96, where the club is at the same level as Newport AFC. It is highly unlikely that Merthyr will now meet the reprieve condition of reaching the Football League by 1997.

Second, despite the High Court victory, one of the exiles, Caernarfon Town, resigned late from the (English) Northern Premier League and joined the League of Wales for the 1995–96 season. The club was welcomed as a political coup for the FAW, UEFA and FIFA. The decision to move to Welsh football split both the board of directors and the supporters. Caernarfon is a Welsh-speaking area and some felt that the club should play in the Welsh national league. Also local businesses sponsoring the club expressed a preference for the League of Wales. During 1995–96 average attendances at The Oval were just over 300, which is up slightly on the previous season in the English league. Caernarfon Town's aim is to qualify for European competition via the League of Wales.

Only two rebels remain of the original eight (although Merthyr may rejoin them when the time is up on its conditional reprieve). The unresolved issue is the FIFA directive that the clubs should play in a Welsh league by 1997. The clubs have the weight of English law on their side and FIFA may be reluctant to risk infringing English or even European Union law. A change of leadership at the FAW has led to more amicable relations with the two clubs, and the FAW have proposed a compromise to FIFA that no date be put on the return of the clubs to Welsh jurisdiction. Colwyn Bay would consider joining the League of Wales if it became stronger, which means the three professional clubs from the Football League transferring, along with Merthyr.

The hidden danger is that this minor border skirmish involving semi-professional clubs has revealed again the idiosyncrasies of UK football resulting from the historical legacy of four football nations in the one state. FIFA can either accept the FAW compromise proposal and back down or adopt a stance of confrontation, which may in turn lead to renewed calls (particularly from African countries) for a UK national team and a UK league in the UK state. What price the League of Wales then?

CHAPTER 3

Storming the Castile: footballing nations in Spain

The historical and contemporary links between football and the socio-political fabric of Spain are complex. Some themes in the game today predate Spain's major twentieth-century political upheavals of the Civil War (1936–39) and subsequent period of Franco's dictatorship (1939–75). The balance swings from football being used to promote an image of a single national identity (in the 1940s, during the early Franco years) to becoming a vehicle for nationalist/regionalist expression (particularly during the late Franco period and early phase of the transition to democracy).

The relationships between football, nation and the state will be examined throughout four phases:

- Pre-Civil War period (1900–36)
- The Spanish Civil War (1936–39)
- Franco's regime (1939–75)
- Transition to democracy (1975–96)

Some aspects of these relationships run throughout the century although they manifest themselves in different ways according to the period. In each period we shall explore the changing structures and organization of football institutions and how they reflect the political and social system at any given time, the notion of a single Spanish identity and the promotion of its image, other 'nationalisms' in Spain, with particular reference to Catalonia and the Basque Country, and how they are expressed in the footballing context. The links between football and politics are implicit or explicit throughout the investigation.

Background to the state of autonomies

Before Isabel of Castile married Fernando of Aragón in 1469, Spain had never been a single, unified kingdom. The allegiance between Castile and Aragón was a powerful one and gradually *los reyes católicos* (the Catholic Monarchs) conquered the rest of Spain. By the end of the fifteenth century Spain emerged territorially more or less as it is today. Although Castile played a dominant role, part of the reason for such rapid success in the unification of Spain lay in the high degree of autonomy granted to former kingdoms. As a consequence, the concept of a Spanish nation did not exist and neither did the notion of a Spanish nationality. Each former kingdom retained its own sense of identity and community which never gave way to any strong feeling of Spanishness. The regions of Catalonia, the Basque Country and Galicia, known today as the *nacionalidades históricas* (historic nationalities), maintained a high sense of collective identity and their people possessed characteristics and traditions in common that distinguished them from other Spaniards. Throughout the seventeenth century, Spain tried to become a modern state and unification policy became more defined. Philip IV refused to act upon the counsel of his adviser, the Conde-Duque de Olivares, who advocated the promotion of a political, administrative and legislative unification which, consequently, Philip IV failed to achieve. In Catalonia the local institutions remained intact, even continuing to use their own language officially. The Basques fought hard and maintained their unique legal and fiscal system known as the *fueros*.

It is the legacy of this autonomy of the different regions within Spain (known as *Comunidades Autónomas* or autonomous communities) that pervades Spanish society today. Following a thirty-six-year dictatorship in which General Franco centralized power and prohibited the regions from any signs of autonomy, the 1978 Spanish Constitution represented a turnabout in policy. It granted differing degrees of autonomy to the regions of Spain and the extent of regional autonomy reflects fairly accurately the degree of enthusiasm for home-rule as well as historical, cultural and linguistic singularity. The historic nationalities hold most power internally. The Basques and Catalans enjoy, therefore, a high degree of autonomy (including their own police forces), followed closely by the Galicians and also the Andalusians. They all control their own health services, dictate to a large extent their own education systems and have their own TV channels. The Basques in addition, saw the reinstatement of their system of *fueros* which had been taken away from them during the Franco dictatorship.

On closer examination of the history of the relationship between football, nationality and the state, we discover that this strong sense of identity and autonomy that the regions promote has at times been threatened and at other times strengthened.

Pre-Civil War period (1900–36)

Interest in the regional/nationalist issue in Spain grew at the end of the nineteenth century. Carlism (support of Carlos, second son of Charles IV, and his sons as legitimate heirs to the Spanish throne, to the exclusion of Ferdinand VII's daughter and her heirs) dominated the political history of nineteenth-century Spain and was strong in regions which had their own political institutions and in particular their own language, that is, in Catalonia, the Basque Country, Valencia, Navarre and Galicia. By the early twentieth century, domestic antagonisms were sharpened by the emergence of political and social movements based on regional and class exclusiveness. 'Regional' or 'local' nationalism developed in Catalonia and the Basque Country, expressing the pride and ambition of the only areas in Spain that were beginning to develop a modern industrial society. The *Renaixença* movement in Catalonia, which was originally a literary movement that began in the late nineteenth century, had by now taken on a political form and affected many aspects of Catalan life and society, emphasizing the distinct historical and cultural identity of the Catalans who began to press for regional autonomy in order to continue their own development unhampered by 'backward' Spaniards. Most importantly, the movement enjoyed the support of the Catalan bourgeoisie who attempted to promote Catalanism, making demands for home-rule for Catalonia and often enjoying the support of a wide-based popular movement. The Catalanist movement took on great dimensions and the Lliga, the first great Catalanist political party, was established.

Socioeconomic factors were relevant too in the rise of the nationalist movements. Catalonia was by this time transforming into a heavily industrialized region within a predominantly agricultural state. The implications of this meant that policies that would have favoured industrial areas were rejected by the centralist government. These social and political factors which distinguished the north-eastern regions from many other parts of Spain, bound up with strong notions of a distinctive Catalan character and work ethic, enhanced differences of situation and mentality between regions, and particularly between Madrid and Barcelona.

It is easy for the Catalans, and the Basques, to consider themselves more hard-working and progressive than the population of the rest of Spain. Even immigrants from the south often adopt a critical attitude towards what they see as a corrupt, inefficient Madrid that exploits the periphery. If Catalan rumours are to be believed, this attitude is one that is reflected in the world of football where central authorities do everything in their power to ensure the supremacy of Real Madrid rather than FC Barcelona, or *el Barça*.

As far as FC Barcelona is concerned, many of the characteristics of the club today date back to the beginning of the century, shortly after its foundation in 1899. In a recent publication which traces the history of the role of FC Barcelona, it is stated that

This is true whether we refer to the Catalan, European and international dimensions of *Barça*, its rivalry with Español and Real Madrid, or the unjust way the club has been treated by a centralist football association and by centrally appointed referees ... and the fact that Barcelona, the symbol of Catalonia, is more than a club.

(Sobrequés 1991)

Here, the main characteristics of FC Barcelona today can be found – its Catalan, European and international dimensions, its distrust of centralist powers and its rivalries with local team Español and with Real Madrid. Elements of all these characteristics that exist today were already present at the start of the century.

The first aspect of this statement, the identification between the club and the city, has existed since the establishment of the club. The first club emblem was the same as that of the city, the cross of St George on the left and the four bands of the Catalan flag (*senyera*) on the right. Today, the initials of the club, FCB, unite the top part of the emblem which represents that city and the bottom part which represents football. This desire to link the city and the club remains today and FC Barcelona is marketed as being *més que un club* (Catalan for 'more than a club').

Barcelona, however, prides itself not only on representing the city and Catalonia, but also on having a strong European and international outlook. Paradoxically, although FC Barcelona presents an image of being the club which represents the Catalans, its early teams depended largely on players from outside Spain. Partly for this reason perhaps, Barcelona has always been in favour of welcoming and encouraging foreign players (from outside Spain) in its ranks. Indeed, this was the root of one of the earliest disputes between Barcelona and its fiercest rivals in Catalonia, Español. When Español was established in 1900, as the *Sociedad Española de Football*, it supported a no-foreigner policy. This gave Barcelona an excuse to insult its rivals and label them as xenophobic. An early stance was taken by FC Barcelona in 1902 when it refused to play in a tournament in which foreign players were not eligible to participate. Barcelona supporters will claim that this was one of the earliest signs of support by the club for foreign players, but perhaps the fact that in the 1901 Barcelona squad no fewer than nineteen out of its twenty-two players were foreign imports might help to explain this stance. Even in recent times, however, Barcelona is keen to welcome foreign players (e.g. Stoichkov, Popescu, Lineker, Koeman, etc.) and managers (Terry Venables 1984–87, Johann Cruyff 1988–96).

The statement also refers to the treatment of FC Barcelona by officials and authorities. It has long been the belief of the club that it is persecuted and punished for what it represents. This passionate belief, at times approaching paranoia, dates back to the early twentieth century. As early as 1911, FC Barcelona felt harshly treated by the authorities when, in a tournament in which Athletic de Bilbao had been given special permission to field three ineligible players, Barcelona had a 4–0 win reversed to a defeat for unwittingly playing a goalkeeper illegally. In 1916, Barcelona stormed off the pitch during the semi-final of the Spanish FA Cup against Real Madrid because it thought that the referee was biased against them.

Serious complaints from Barcelona and its fans throughout the century involve their perceived persecution by an authority whose only objective is to benefit the team that represents the capital. They feel that it is precisely because it is seen as the team that represents Catalonia and anti-centralist Spain that they are treated unfavourably; talk about 'political refereeing' is common. Indeed, until a few years ago, it was not unheard of in Spain (where a referee's neutrality is never assumed, believed or claimed), for a referee to admit to supporting a particular team – frequently Real Madrid.

Associated with these attitudes is one of the greatest traditional rivalries in Spanish football, that between Barcelona and Real Madrid. The hostility between the clubs was, and still is, mutual. Real Madrid see Barcelona as anti-Spanish, anti-centralist and representing Catalonia, while Barcelona see Real Madrid (established in 1902) as the force that represents the centralist Spain that has deliberately persecuted them for so long. This tense relationship was not a product of post-Civil War resentment but existed even before then. During the dictatorship of General Primo de Rivera (1923–30) when nationalist feelings in Spain were repressed, football was the only way people could express their pent-up nationalism. Significantly, at this time, FC Barcelona saw a huge rise in the number of *socios* (club members who are season-ticket holders). One demonstration of such anti-centralist feelings took place before a testimonial match when the fans jeered the playing of the Royal March. This led to the club being banned indefinitely from participating in any sporting activity. (The ban lasted just three months because of a change of *presidente*.) It is also significant that at the end of the dictatorship in 1930, when once again freedom returned to express nationalist feelings outside the footballing arena, the number of *socios* at Barcelona dropped as there was no longer the need to use the football club as a vehicle to promote the 'nationalist' cause.

Within the city of Barcelona, the rivalry between FC Barcelona and Español is almost as intense as that between Real Madrid and Barcelona. If *Barça* fans see Real Madrid as representing centralist government from Madrid, then provocatively named Español (or Espanyol as it is spelt by Catalanists) represents centralist Spanish government within Catalonia. Again, this rivalry predates the Spanish Civil War. Reports of violence between Español and Barcelona both on the pitch and on the terraces date as far back as May 1911 during the Copa de Riva (Sobrequés 1991), and in 1912 matches between the sides had to be banned for two years following further violent incidents (Shaw 1987). In 1916 FC Barcelona suffered the reversal of another result when its 3–0 win over Español on 21 December was altered to a defeat after complaints by Español that Barcelona had fielded an Argentine in a competition from which foreigners were excluded. Barcelona felt particularly bitter about the decision as it had signed the player believing he was Spanish and had, moreover, agreed to let Español play two illegal players in the same match. This incident served to exacerbate the tense relationship between the clubs. In the 1919 Cup Final when Barcelona played Arenas de Guatro there are reports that Español fans distributed leaflets insulting *Barça*. On 23 November 1924, violence again broke out on the pitch and on the terraces in a match between the two clubs. This led to the match being abandoned at half-time and being played at a later date behind closed doors.

The tense relationship between Barcelona and Español that existed before the Civil War was to worsen afterwards. Barcelona, who always deny any links with political parties, was nevertheless identified with Catalan nationalism while Español represented the right-wing military of Franco's Spain. Barcelona was seen as separatist while Español was favoured by the new political situation after the Civil War.

In many ways, although less documented, the Basques were as ardent as the Catalans in the promotion of regionist/nationalist feelings via football. A similar process of industrialization took place in the Basque Country as that in Catalonia. Like the Catalans, the Basques considered themselves more hard-working, modern and progressive than the rest of Spain and as early as the end of the eighteenth century, nationalist political projects sprang up in the Basque Country. Despite the centralist regime of the Bourbons, the Basques' system of *fueros* (the traditional laws) survived into the twentieth century. This was important for their economy, but just as important as a symbol of Basque autonomy, thus the defence of the *fueros* became linked to Basque nationalism.

In the footballing context, Athletic de Bilbao (founded in 1898) decided to adopt a strict Basque-only policy in 1919 and from then on recruited only players who were born in the Basque Country. This enhanced the strong feeling of identity between the city and the club, who also openly supported the movement for Basque autonomy at that time. The link between football and politics was explicit. The leader of the Basque government in the 1930s, José Antonio Aguirre, was a midfielder for Athletic de Bilbao in the 1920s. Just as Barcelona was seen as a political symbol in Catalonia, Athletic de Bilbao was a symbol of Basque nationalism in the Basque Country. But the two clubs were radically different. Where Barcelona welcomed players imported from abroad, because of the Basque-only policy, Athletic de Bilbao players were home-grown, mainly from the province of Vizcaya, and came up through the ranks of the club. There was also a difference in the patterns of support. The support for Athletic de Bilbao was drawn largely from the working class whereas Barcelona had a large bourgeois, middle-class following.

Athletic de Bilbao was not the only team that represented the Basque Country. Real Sociedad of San Sebastian (established in 1909) represented the Basques, yet the two clubs had different perspectives. Real Sociedad also had a Basque-only policy, but there was more flexibility in defining what it was to be Basque. In order to play for Athletic de Bilbao, not only did a player have to be born in the Basque Country, preferably in Vizcaya, but also his parents and grandparents had to be Basque thus ensuring he was a 'pure' Basque. At Real Sociedad, this 'purity' was not so important and anyone born in the Basque Country, even children of immigrants, were eligible to play for the club.

Before the Spanish Civil War in the 1930s, Basque football teams enjoyed a high degree of success. Half of the national trophies won during this period were won by Basques. Their style of play was aggressive and direct, typically long balls played to a tall centre-forward. This successful style was widely respected and adopted by the national team, the *Selección*, in the 1920 Olympic Games and led to the belief in the *furia española* (Spanish fury).

At this time football was run democratically. All *socios* had the right to attend club annual general meetings and took part in the decision-making processes, including choosing their *presidente* (chairman) and boardroom directors, but this democratic process was not to survive the Civil War.

The Spanish Civil War (1936–39)

During the Civil War, the country was divided into Republicans versus Nationalists. The defeat of the Republicans in 1939 led to the establishment of a dictatorship led by General Franco. Spain remained divided territorially. The Civil War is one of the more revealing periods in the relationship between football and politics in Spain. A detailed account of football during the Civil War exists (Fernández Santander 1990) and the Centre for Historical and Statistical Research into Football in Spain (CIHEFE) holds a database of all the football played during this three-year period. Many players left Spain during the Civil War, especially those who lived in Republican areas. Many took part in the Civil War and inevitably many were killed.

The political divisions that existed between the regions during the Civil War were represented in football. As far as the football clubs are concerned, Barcelona and Athletic de Bilbao were synonymous with separatism, representing the nationalist aspirations of Catalonia and the Basque Country respectively. Osasuna (in Pamplona, Navarre) and Español represented Franco's Spain. Atlético de Madrid experienced semi-militarization and became known as Atlético Aviación (Aviation Athletic). The advantages for the club lay in the fact that it had first refusal on any players who had been in the forces, it enjoyed access to free transport and received various other subsidies. It is not surprising that Aviación won the first two championships after the Civil War, a time when most clubs were struggling to put a team together. This militarization was also reflected in the organization of football. Its main institutions were run by military figures. The Spanish Football Association (*Federación Española de Fútbol*) was run by a colonel, Troncoso, and the Minister for Sport was a general, Moscardó. The political motivation to continue playing football during the war was highlighted by Troncoso when he said, 'We all need to get used to the idea that in the immediate future, sport is not a pleasant leisure activity, but a necessary way in which the country can improve its men and have them prepared for action whenever they might be needed' (*Marca* 5 July 1939). Football was to be exploited in this way in order to keep men fit for military action.

The way football and politics were seen as two sides of the same coin was expressed explicitly by Moscardó when he took up his position as Minister for Sport at the end of 1938. In his inaugural speech he explained how he had accepted the post as part of his military duties because, 'I am a soldier and I obey my orders' (Fernández Santander 1990: 54).

Although there were no national competitions during the Civil War, football was organized on a regional basis (e.g. competitions took place in Catalonia, Levante, Galicia in 1936 and the *Liga Mediterránea* involving Catalan-speaking areas took place in 1937). Most significant for the purpose of this study are the tours abroad made by the Basque and Catalan 'national' teams. In June–July 1937 Barcelona was invited to go on an international tour. It was supposed to play six matches against first division opposition in Mexico, but stayed on and played another three, two of them against the Mexico national side. It also played in New York. In total, fourteen matches were played of which the Catalans won ten and lost four. Few players returned to Spain. Some stayed in Mexico, others went to play in France.

Similarly, in 1937, after the nationalists defeated the city of Bilbao in June 1937, the Basques formed a team of Basque players they called 'the *Euskadi* Republic' (*Euskadi* means 'Basque' in the Basque language) which went on tour in Eastern Europe and South America to raise money and prestige for the Basque cause until they were banned by FIFA. Back in Spain they were labelled as traitors by the Francoist press. By supporting the campaign for Basque autonomy and encouraging its players to form part of this *Euskadi* national team, Athletic de Bilbao lost the respect of the rest of Spain which its footballing conquests had previously commanded. Few of the players ever returned to Spain; most remained in Argentina or Mexico.

Marca's article entitled '*Euskadi* Republic's Football Embassy' (29 March 1939) referred to the team as 'That group of traitors captained by the separatist Vallana', and criticized them, saying, 'They couldn't accept that their duty was to become part of Nationalist Spain, who forgave and accepted those who had gone astray'. Then, recognizing the political motives that lay behind the tour, 'The aim of the tour was to make propaganda and it contributed, albeit unsuccessfully, to the Republican cause'.

The political motivations that lay behind both tours were no secret. The members of the *Euskadi* team themselves much later confessed their political motivations for the tour, among them the desire to promote Basque nationalism and a positive image of the Basque Country. When asked about the reasons for the establishment of a 'national' Basque team, Melchor Alegría admitted:

It is important to understand why the 1937 Basque team was formed. I suggested that the international campaign against the Basque government could be counteracted by the footballers' words and actions. Therefore, under the pretext of playing football, we talked in France, Poland and Argentina and managed to unveil the truth about what was really happening in the Basque Country. Some countries stopped us from playing, but we did our best to let the world know what was going on.

(*El Correo Español* 17 October 1987)

Similarly Luis Regueiro admitted that the motivation for the tour was to tell the world what was really happening in the Basque Country. What was important was not the results on the pitch but making friends and gaining sympathizers.

Soon after the Catalan and Basque tours, a Spanish national side was created, according to Fernández Santander (1990) to counter the propaganda of the *Euskadi* and Catalan tours. By this time, there were few Basque and Catalan players left in Spain: they had fled the country into exile, they never returned from the football tours or they were dead.

In December 1937, the Spanish national team, the *Selección*, changed its kit from the red shirts (the colour that was seen to symbolize the Republicans) and blue shorts to blue shirt (in keeping with the Nationalist colours) and white shorts. After the Civil War, footballers and officials who participated on Franco's victorious nationalist side were honoured and officially recognized (e.g. Jacinto Quincoces and Raimundo Blanco). Osasuna also benefited as it was given special permission to play in Division 1 even though it should have been relegated to Division 2. This decision was contested, however, by rivals Atlético de Madrid who were relegated in its place. Eventually a play-off took place which was won 3–1 by Atlético de Madrid.

Franco's regime (1939–75)

The victory of General Franco's forces in the Civil War led to a dictatorship that was to last thirty-six years until the death of the *Caudillo* on 20 November 1975. In Franco's Spain, particularly during the early years, football, just like other public institutions, was characterized by a high level of intervention by the authorities in its administration, organization, ownership and control, so the political regime of the country was reflected in the structures of the sport (see Part two).

Military figures were prominent in positions of power in the football authorities and also in most clubs. Football became a political intermediary between the state and society (*ABC*, 2 February 1941). The football authorities remained in the hands of the military (Troncoso and Moscardó) and the democratic electoral process that existed in football clubs before the Civil War gave way to one in which club *presidentes* were appointed by the regime.

Most football clubs, even Barcelona, the club which is today usually considered to have been that which demonstrated most *antifranquista* feelings, had a directorate which consisted almost exclusively of Franco followers, and were indeed appointed by Franco. This policy dated from 1938 when Moscardó, chairman of the Olympic Committee and of the Ministry for Sport (*Consejo Nacional de Deportes* or CND, later DND), outlined his programme for the future: 'Everything will be run by the State. We will appoint the chairmen of the football authorities who will make decisions in the interests of the country' (*Marca* 6 November 1938). It was for this reason, that is, because all football clubs were run by Francoist officials in the early period of the Franco regime, that there was little room for anyone to be disloyal to the *Caudillo* and a tight grip of control on the organization and structures within football was maintained.

The organization of football did not remain unchanged throughout the thirty-six years of Franco dictatorship. The changes that took place again reflected those changes that were occurring in the rest of the social and political system. The authoritarianism that characterized the early years gave way to a *democracia orgánica* (organic democracy) in which the personal power of individuals became more important. The organization of football clubs became more democratic too. In contrast to the early 1940s when the club *presidentes* were appointed by the Ministry for Sport (DND) in 1946 it was decided by the DND to make a recommendation to clubs that the board could elect their own *presidente*, provided of course, that the choice met with the approval of the DND. Some 200 *socios*, chosen at random (at least in theory) were to be allowed to attend annual general meetings. In 1948, Barcelona, frequently the pioneer of any moves towards democracy, allowed *all* its supporters to vote for the *presidente*; this provoked a rapid response by the DND who immediately made its recommendation which allowed 200 *socios* to vote legally binding. The only other real example of democracy in action during this period was again provided by Barcelona when, in 1962, Barcelona *socios* were all encouraged by the club to participate in choosing a name for the new ground.

There were no further moves towards democracy in football until the 1970s. One minor change in legislation was made in 1970 when it was decided that 5 per cent of *socios* rather than 200 were allowed to participate in elections, but the system was still not democratic and rumours were widespread that the *socios* who voted were carefully chosen. The Spanish FA (*la Federación Española de Fútbol*) was widely criticized for not being representative of clubs, but nothing was done to change the situation until after Franco's death, following which football rapidly became a democratically run institution.

Despite pledges to look at sport as the means to keep the nation of soldiers fit and ready for military action, sport was not very successful under Franco. Little money was invested in sport and the people who ran the DND have since been regarded as being largely incompetent (Shaw 1987). They were chosen for political reasons and their military success rather than their interest in and understanding of football. Not only did Franco's dictatorship affect the relationship between football and the state, but also attempts were made to change the notions of national identity. Much was done to promote a feeling of Spanish national identity throughout the country. Before each game, the players lined up on the field, held their arms aloft in a salute and sang the *Cara al Sol*, the fascist anthem, and chanted '*Arriba España! Viva Franco!*' (Long live Spain! Long live Franco!). The fact that football was used in this way as a vehicle for fascist propaganda has been recognized by historians. 'Football had a dimension that was not simply to do with sport. It was the best catalyst for promoting Spanish nationalism. The footballing victories against England in 1950 and Russia in 1964 were immensely important historical landmarks for official propaganda' (Fusi and Carr 1979).

There are two important issues that concern football and nationalism in Franco's Spain. The first concerns the role of football in promoting Spain's national image, especially abroad. The second involves the role of football either in support of or as opposition to the nationalist movements within Spain.

The role of football in promoting Spain's national image

The role of the national team, the *Selección*, was relatively insignificant in promoting Spain's image abroad. Spain was largely ostracized politically and many countries refused to play it. However, the few matches that did take place are of interest in the way they were presented within Spain. The role of the media was particularly significant. All Spain's victories were presented as a victory for Franco and contributed to his glory. They were attributed to the Spanish national character, to the *furia española*, and invariably achieved for patriotic reasons. They were achieved with the help of the Virgin and numerous Saints. Following a particularly impressive 4–1 Spanish victory in Dublin in 1949, Rienzi claimed, 'We can all be proud of Spain's performance, because not only were our racial virtues of energy, vehemence and resolution so overwhelming, but the outstanding natural talent of the Spaniards shone through' (quoted in Fernández Santander 1990: 98). Any losses were attributed to poor refereeing decisions or jealousy from outside Spain.

The media have been accused of exploiting football as a social drug (Fusi and Carr 1979; Shaw 1987). Matches were televised at politically sensitive times. If no matches were due to be played around that time, and the regime wanted to distract public attention from political issues, one would be arranged, compilations of the best goals of the *Selección* were shown or matches with no Spanish involvement at all were transmitted so that the attention would be distracted from more potentially dangerous thoughts. In chapter 7 similar tactics adopted by the dictatorships in Argentina will be examined. The press allocated a disproportionate amount of their coverage to sport, and especially to football. It was not unusual for a newspaper to dedicate six times more space to football alone than to politics (Essinague 1971), so accusations that the press kept the population depoliticized or politically passive might carry some weight.

The football press formed part of a wider culture of escapism along with the cinema, magazines and popular theatre. *Marca*, previously a weekly sports newspaper, became a daily in 1942 and rapidly became Spain's best-selling newspaper. It is difficult to say whether football's rise in popularity following the Civil War was owing to Franco's policies or whether it would have happened anyway. It is certainly unlikely that people flocked to the football grounds because of the quality of the football: there were so few experienced footballers left in the country that the standard of football was low. Football was, nevertheless, a useful political tool.

It has been claimed by many commentators that Real Madrid fulfilled the role of a national team in many respects during the Franco period. The team became known as the *'el equipo del régimen'* (the team of the regime). The club were exploited by politicians as being ambassadors for Spain at a time when Spain's image abroad needed a lift. Indeed, it is easy to find evidence that supports this claim, especially in the late 1950s. In a speech following one of Real Madrid's great victories during this period, Fernando María Castiella, then Defence Minister, claimed that Real Madrid was 'one of Spain's best ambassadors' (quoted in Fernández Santander 1990).

Minister José Solís in 1959 similarly recognized the role of football as a powerful tool of diplomacy when, at a time when Spain was largely ostracized from the rest of Europe, he gave a speech praising the Real Madrid players after a match saying:

You have done much more than a handful of ambassadors could do. People who hated us now understand us, thanks to you, because you broke down the barriers. Your victories are a real pride to all Spaniards everywhere. When you return to your changing-room at the end of a match you know that all Spaniards are behind you, proud of your triumphs.

(Boletín del Real Madrid 1959)

Solís said in 1961: 'Real Madrid is a style of playing. Its players are authentic ambassadors for sport. It is the best ambassador we have sent abroad' *(Boletín Real Madrid* 1961). There were many more such comments. Much has also been made of the fact that most of the directors of the club, in particular its chairman Santiago Bernabéu, were linked to the Franco regime in some way, and of the fact that Franco himself, along with many other government officials, went regularly to see the team play. From these comments stating how Real Madrid represented the nation and were ambassadors for Spain abroad, and from the apparent close links between the club and government, it can be seen how easily the step can be made to label Real Madrid as *'the team of the regime'*. At a time when Spain was still largely ostracized from the rest of Europe, apart from being the greatest club side in Europe in the 1950s, Real Madrid was not far from being Spain's sole ambassador abroad. So it should not come as any surprise to find that the regime basked in the glory brought to the country by the football team. 'There is no doubt that the regime benefited from Real Madrid and its prestige abroad which often led to an identification between the excellence of the team and the state of the political system which it indirectly represented' (Fernández Santander 1990: 155).

This image of Real Madrid being 'the team of the regime' existed within Spain as well as abroad. There is some debate over whether or not Real Madrid enjoyed this role or whether it was a victim of exploitation. There have been many suggestions, for example, that Real Madrid enjoyed the favours of referees' decisions. Did referees really award them dubious penalties or were Real Madrid forwards simply so good that they were frequently brought down in the penalty area?

There appears to be little evidence to suggest that Real Madrid ever encouraged associations between the club and the regime or welcomed its status as a national symbol. Given the quality of football guaranteed, it is hardly surprising if Franco and other government officials went to see Real Madrid, and indeed many also went to see Atlético de Madrid. Nevertheless, even though it is debatable whether or not the club itself encouraged such an image, the fact that the club did much for Spain's national self-image is not. Real Madrid represented the state. Within Spain it represented the capital and centralist policies.

The role of football in opposition or nationalist movements within Spain

If Real Madrid represented Franco's Spain, then there were clubs in other parts of Spain that represented the opposition. Franco tried to destroy all institutions that held traces of regionalism or separatism. Languages other than Castilian were proscribed and flags of the Basque Country and Catalonia (the *ikurriña* and *senyera* respectively) were burnt. In 1941 the names of clubs were hispanicized following a directive from the Home Office Department for Press and Propaganda (*Delegación Nacional de Prensa y Propaganda*). Football Club Barcelona became Club de Fútbol de Barcelona, Athletic de Bilbao became Atlético Bilbao and Sporting Gijón became Deportivo Gijón. Political leaders were exiled and even minor manifestations of regionalism, nationalism or opposition to the centralist regime were suppressed, sometimes brutally, by the police and the military who acted as occupying forces in Catalonia and the Basque Country during the 1940s. By the 1960s and 1970s, this opposition began to strengthen. This importance of sport as a catalyst for regionalist/nationalist sentiment and opposition to the centralist regime was recognized by Luis María Cazorla Prieto (1979): 'Sport is sometimes used as a political protest. . . . A close link between sports and politics is always present in nationalist and regionalist issues and was frequently exploited as such during the Franco period.'

There are a number of examples where the clubs, the players or the supporters have displayed nationalistic feelings. These clubs were consistently portrayed in a negative light by the Madrid-based press. The relationship between Barcelona and Catalanism has been related many times; the club is often portrayed as being the club with greatest *antifranquista* feeling during the dictatorship. Nevertheless, Atlético de Bilbao and also Real Sociedad in the Basque Country made just as many political gestures and were arguably more nationalistic in nature than the Catalan club, reflecting the attitudes of the Basque Country towards the Franco regime and their nationalistic tendencies. In both Catalonia and the Basque Country they refused to give the fascist salute which was normally performed at the start of each match. They sang their own anthems and waved their *senyeras* and *ikurriñas* respectively.

In the 1960s and 1970s, as the opposition movement increased its activities in both the Basque Country and Catalonia, football again became a catalyst for nationalism. In the Basque Country, the colours of Atlético Bilbao and Real Sociedad were substituted by the red, green and white of the *ikurriña* flag and their stadiums, the San Mamés and the Atocha, became centres where Basque nationalist feelings were tolerated and Euskera, the language of the Basques, could be spoken freely without fear of punishment. Real Sociedad *presidente*, José Luis Orbegozo, wrote club publications in both Castilian and Basque from 1972 onwards. Similarly, in Barcelona, the stadium was one of the few public places where Catalan could be spoken freely although still officially proscribed from all spheres of public life.

It seems that Franco did not see these political, nationalistic demonstrations that took place in the footballing context as being potentially dangerous. In fact, it has been suggested that football was actually promoted as a sort of 'escape valve' (Vázquez Montalbán 1975, quoted in Shaw 1987). This opinion is shared by many commentators including Carles Rexach, a former player, who said that 'Franco tried to erase all regional rivalries in Spain except in football. He promoted football as a healthy way for regions to get rid of their tension' (*National Geographic* 1984).

Rexach also suggests that this was a mistake on Franco's part and that Franco underestimated the strength of feeling that accompanied the songs in Catalan at football.

> He [Franco] tried to get rid of all regional rivalries in Spain, apart from in the footballing context. He promoted football as a healthy way for the regions to relieve their tensions. But with *Barça* the dictator made a mistake. As the Catalans had no political parties, or regional government, or any right to use their own language, they put all their cultural pride into *Barça*. At a *Barça* match, the people could shout in Catalan and sing traditional songs at a time when they couldn't do it anywhere else.
>
> (*National Geographic* 1984)

In the Basque Country, it was Real Sociedad and Atlético Bilbao who were the principal representatives of Basque nationalism. The social significance of the two clubs and the way they represented the nation was summarized in an interview by Francisco Cerecedo (1974): 'Athletic Bilbao and Real Sociedad represented the same thing in their respective areas of the Basque Country. Both teams do their bit to promote the race by not allowing players from outside the region into their squads.' This Basque-only policy which began at the start of the century was more strict in Bilbao than at Real Sociedad. In Bilbao they admitted players predominantly from Vizcaya and only a few from other parts of the Basque Country. At Real Sociedad, the aim was always to promote a more 'pan-Basque' image.

Both Basque clubs, like all other football clubs, were eventually taken over by Franco followers who were appointed to occupy the positions of power. Along with the weakened power structures, another factor contributed to the weakening of the power of football in the Basque Country. Real Sociedad and Atlético Bilbao did not perceive themselves for a long time as working together for the same cause and the Francoist directors were careful that this was not the case. It was not until the 1960s and 1970s, with the increasing surge of nationalism, that relationships between the two clubs improved and their common identity as Basques became important. It appears that the forces of Basque nationalism have played a part in suppressing internal conflict between the two Basque clubs in order to present 'us' as a unity. Indeed, suspicions were rife that ideas of the Basque National Party (*Partido Nacional Vasca*), demanding democracy and regional autonomy, were infiltrating the directorates of both Basque clubs at that time; it has even been rumoured that some members of the boards supported the Basque separatist terrorist group ETA (*Euzkadi ta Askatsuna*).

Players were also affected by the rise in regional sentiment. The Bilbao goalkeeper, José Angel Iríbar was a popular figure all over Spain, yet he was not afraid to voice his opinion of the Basque issue: 'I speak Basque, my wife, my children and my parents speak Basque. It is our language. Now it seems there is a renaissance and people are realizing what they should hold on to and every day more people speak Basque' (*Cuadernos para el diálogo* 1971). It was the same Iríbar who encouraged the Atlético Bilbao team to wear black armbands in respect for two members of ETA who were executed after a military hearing, which was rumoured to have been rigged, in September 1975. The black armbands symbolized the political, nationalistic stance displayed by the Basque clubs throughout the transition to democracy.

In Catalonia, although sharing features with the Basque Country, the situation was rather different. FC Barcelona stood as a symbol of Catalan identity, as it still does. Just as the Basques sent a 'national' team on tour abroad to further the Basque cause, so Barcelona went on tour. As with the Basque clubs, Barcelona had a Francoist directorate appointed in positions of power in the club. But unlike Basque clubs where opposition to the regime was demonstrated via promotion of a Basque identity, opposition to the regime by Barcelona was displayed most predominantly in its relationship with Real Madrid, the symbol of the centralist Franco regime.

Hostility during matches between Barcelona and Real Madrid heightened. There are many documented incidents of violent outbursts between rival supporters when games were played both in Barcelona and in Madrid. Suggestively, it was those played in Barcelona which were penalized most heavily, and by 1944 the situation was so tense that matches due to be played in Barcelona were held at a neutral venue. Barcelona was seen by the press as non-Spanish and anti-Spanish. Indeed, when Barcelona knocked Real Madrid out of the European Cup in the 1960–61 season, it was accused of knocking Spain out of Europe. Carreras, chairman of FC Barcelona in 1968, declared, 'We must fight against everything and everyone, because we are the best and we represent what we represent' (quoted by Vázquez Montalbán, *Triunfo* 1969) in an intelligent statement which alluded to the political and nationalist tendencies of the club while remaining ambiguous enough to avoid repercussions from the authorities. The political significance of FC Barcelona has already been documented in detail (most thoroughly and convincingly by Vázquez Montalbán, *Triunfo* 1969) and there can be no doubt as to its role of representing Catalonia. It is perhaps Vázquez Montalbán himself who best summarizes FC Barcelona's political role: 'It can definitely be said that FC Barcelona has served the purpose of the army that Catalonia has never had' (interview quoted in Shaw 1987).

It was during this period that Barcelona's suspicions of ill-treatment by the footballing authorities that existed before the Civil War almost became a persecution complex. Several incidents will serve as examples of how it felt harshly treated by the centralist authorities. In June 1943, the national cup semi-final took place over two legs between Real Madrid and Barcelona. During the first leg in Les Corts, Barcelona, the Catalan crowd jeered and whistled at the Real Madrid team. They were awarded the maximum fine and the fans were banned from travelling to Madrid for the second leg. During the second leg, Real Madrid fans jeered and whistled at the Barcelona team. They were fined the minimum amount and their actions condoned because they were said to have been provoked during the first leg.

In 1953 the famous *caso di Stéfano* took place. It concerned the transfer of Alfredo di Stefano who was at the time playing on loan for Colombian Millonarios de Bogotá but officially registered with Argentine club River Plate. Barcelona thought it had signed Di Stefano from River Plate but the Spanish FA stopped the transfer, according to Barcelona, claiming he was a Millonarios player (yet it had no legal rights over him). Real Madrid meanwhile nipped in and negotiated his transfer with Millonarios. The Spanish FA was called in to arbitrate over who had actually signed the player and made an unusual decision. Di Stefano was instructed to play alternate seasons for Real Madrid and Barcelona. An insulted Barcelona declined the offer and withdrew from the deal. Real Madrid subsequently built its team around Di Stefano and rose to glory winning five consecutive European Cups. Barcelona went through a lean period for which it never forgave the Spanish FA.

In June 1970 arguably the most controversial penalty decision in the history of Spanish football took place when referee Emilio Guruceta gave a penalty for a foul judged by most commentators to be between two and five metres outside the area (depending on the allegiances of the commentator). The *caso Guruceta* took place during the second leg of a cup quarter-final match between Barcelona and Real Madrid in the Nou Camp, Barcelona. It was perceived as yet another attack on Catalonia and since then all dubious refereeing decisions have been known as *Gurucetas*.

Even in recent times, the legacy of the accumulation of many years of dubious refereeing decisions going against it continues as Barcelona eyes with suspicion any poor refereeing decision and is frequently accused of sour grapes or paranoia by non-Catalans. The rivalry between *Barça* and Español was like a local version of Real Madrid and Barcelona. In contrast with FC Barcelona, Español was considered to be the anti-regionalist, Franco-supporting club in Catalonia who drew its support from right-wing aristocrats and civil servants who had been stationed in Barcelona. Its ground was moved into the wealthy area of Barcelona in the Franco period. This image of Español as being the non-Catalan club continues today although it is not entirely accurate.

Transition to democracy (1975–96)

The death of Franco in November 1975 led to huge transformations in the Spanish political system. It marked the official beginning of a transition to democracy, but this transition did not occur overnight. It has already been seen how Franco's dictatorship was loosening its grip during the 1960s and early 1970s as demonstrations of anti-Francoism became more open and more tolerated by the state. One of the first major changes to take place in the organization of football was the democratization of its structures. Football very quickly became a democratic institution and members of football clubs (*socios*) were able to vote for their *presidente*, as was the practice prior to the political upheavals of the 1930s.

The 1978 Constitution saw the creation of a 'state of autonomies' with seventeen *Comunidades Autónomas* which have varying degrees of autonomy in legislation and administration. A rise in the expression of regional/national identity has followed the creation of these *Comunidades*, perhaps exaggerated by a backlash of reaction against the repression of any anti-centralist tendencies which was suffered during the Franco years. This rise in regional/national interest is reflected in all aspects of culture – traditional folklore, dance, songs, promotion of regional languages – and also in football. Football grounds have played an important symbolic role in this explosion of regionalist sentiment. Catalan and Basque leaders who had been in exile under Franco reappeared and took their applause in football grounds (e.g. Jordi Pujol, Josep Tarradellas in Catalonia and Carles Garacoechea in the Basque Country).

Many regions now have a strong identity of their own (not only the historic nationalities, but also Andalusia, Asturias and Galicia) and it seems that people are often more concerned about how their local team fares than the success or failure of the national team. The local football club is increasingly perceived as representing the *Comunidad* rather than just the city in which it is located.

Local authorities are recognizing the potential of the football club in promoting the region. They now take the opportunity to use the success of a football team to promote regional pride. An example of this is the '*Zaragozamanía*' which invaded the *Comunidad* of Aragón following

Zaragoza's FA Cup win in 1994 and subsequent Cup Winners' Cup final win against Arsenal in 1995. Local government exploited the link between club and regional identity in a self-publicity campaign which bore the motto '*A Victory for Zaragoza is a victory for Aragón*'. The result was a rise in *socios* from 13,000 to 25,000. This is, of course, expected when a club enjoys an unprecedented period of success, but more significant in this case was the fact that the many new *socios* came from the surrounding towns and villages throughout the *Comunidad* of Aragón, rather than from the city of Zaragoza.

This phenomenon of the rise in regional issues reflects again what is happening in Spanish society in general. The sense of the region has become much stronger. It is not necessarily, in the case of many *Comunidades Autónomas*, that the people are indifferent to the country as a unit, but rather that the importance of regional autonomies is increasing all the time. Some degree of supposed indifference might apply, of course, in the case of the historic nationalities. As far as the Spanish national team is concerned, it is logical that not all Spaniards display the same degree of support for the *Selección*: some Basques and Catalans do not feel that the national side represents them as a nation. If they see themselves as different nations, why would they be interested in the success or failure of the Spanish national team? Thus, for example, support for the *Selección* in Catalonia and the Basque Country during the 1982 World Cup in Spain was low-key.

Indeed, it has reached the point when footballers might prefer to play for their club than in the *Selección*. This led to an article in a national newspaper entitled, 'The National Team Must Go' (*ABC*, 19 April 1991) where players, and to a lesser extent fans, were criticized for their lack of enthusiasm for the national team and it was suggested that the *Selección* would soon disappear through lack of interest.

Recently, these fears have been expressed as desirable by Italian politician and media tycoon Silvio Berlusconi as he presented his plans for football in the twenty-first century. He foresees the disappearance, or at least the decline in prestige, of the national teams and a rise in importance of local teams as a European League is established at club level. This aspect of the globalization of football is representative of what is happening in Spanish society. There is an apparent decline in the importance of the nation as a unit, even in areas where the illusion of a single nation was strongest, and conversely there now exists an increased awareness and importance of the regions.

This potential indifference or lack of identification with the *Selección* on the part of some regions in Spain has been recognized by the authorities, and in an attempt to encourage support and interest all over Spain, it has been the policy of the Spanish FA for some years now to hold international matches not only in the capital but all over the country (e.g. Seville, Bilbao and Barcelona).

The importance of club teams continues but indications are, however, not too pessimistic for the national team. Whereas in the late 1980s there were fears that there was no longer much interest in the *Selección*, in the mid-1990s a note of optimism can be detected. It appears that the national team has a rather fickle support. When the team does well, the public become interested, when the team is not doing well, the public are less vociferous and demonstrative in their support. The 1994 World Cup saw Spain surpass its own expectations as 'Forgotten patriotisms were dug up . . ., fanaticism returned with footballmania and false idols were once again at the altar' (*Tiempo* 18 July 1994). So it appears, then, that interest in the national team lies dormant for long periods of time when the *Selección* is not so successful.

Although many Spaniards do not feel that the *Selección* represents them, nationalist feelings are not expressed in the same terms as during the Franco period. There are two reasons for this. First, as people no longer need to take out their frustrated nationalist aspirations out on opposing football clubs and fans, football is no longer the sole vehicle for nationalist expression as it was under Franco: there are other outlets. Second, the situations of both *Comunidades Autónomas* have changed drastically since the Franco period. Catalonia and the Basque Country are now two of the most powerful nations without states in Europe. Not only do they enjoy a certain degree of autonomy, but also they are economically strong regions. There is evidence to suggest that attitudes in the football world are changing too.

It can no longer be assumed that all Catalans or all Barcelona fans are separatists seeking independence from Spain. Some Catalans and Basques feel that they have achieved what they wanted. Recognition as a different nation is sometimes all that is desired. According to a survey carried out by the CIS (Centre for Sociological Research) in Catalonia, only 15 per cent of Catalans say that they do not feel Spanish and just 35 per cent feel more Catalan than Spanish (*Tiempo* 25 September 1995). Nationalism, therefore, appears to be more moderate than is assumed by many outsiders. Political developments have perhaps been a factor contributing to the results of this survey. Whereas in Franco's Spain, historic nationalities such as Catalonia and the Basque Country felt that they were repressed, 75 per cent of Spaniards see Catalonia as the *Comunidad Autónoma* most favoured by the socialist government, PSOE (*Partido Socialista Obrero Español*), in power between 1982 and 1996. Even within Catalonia, the government is no longer perceived to favour Madrid. Significantly, the PSOE relied on the support of the Catalans to maintain their position of power in Spain for so long and it was in their interests to keep the Catalan government sweet. Thus Catalonia has enjoyed a considerable increase in its powers of self-government.

There are some in Catalonia who are content with the autonomy they now have. There is even support for the *Selección* in Catalonia. Javier Clemente, manager of the *Selección*, commented on the Spanish flags waved by Catalans in the Nou Camp when Spain played Malta there in 1994 (*Cambio 16* 20 June 1994) and during the 1992 Olympics the crowd was not anti-Spanish (Hargreaves 1995).

Claims that FC Barcelona is a huge political party with separatist aspirations, who uses Catalan folklore as nationalist propaganda against centralist powers, must now be modified to take into consideration these changes in the political climate. The importance of nationalist movements is declining as European political union involves the surrendering of power upwards to a new supra-national identity as well as downwards to the *Comunidades*. National boundaries have less and less importance in Spain.

Although Barcelona is still the main source of Catalan pride, owing partly to its recent successes in Europe, other events, such as the 1992 Olympics, have attracted considerable attention from outside and improved the confidence of the city. They have given a boost to the image of the Catalans outside Spain and an increased awareness of their cultural and national identity. When Barcelona wins a trophy, there are as many red and yellow *senyeras* of Catalonia on display in the streets as there are red and blue flags of FC Barcelona and the famous Barcelona Ramblas are invaded as are, significantly, the most important political buildings in the city – the *Generalitat*, home of the Catalan government, and the *Ayuntament*, the Town Hall.

Barcelona is still the club most closely associated with nationalistic feelings today. Shaw (1987: 62) claims that 'FC Barcelona is in effect the national team of Catalonia and as such can count on the support of most of its population of six million'. In a sense this is ironic because of all the clubs in Spain, Barcelona is probably the one with the fewest links on the pitch with its local people. While both Real Sociedad and (more strictly) Bilbao have maintained the policy of recruiting players largely from local talent (from players who were born within the Basque Country), the manager and most of the players at Barcelona are either foreign or from other parts of Spain. Paradoxically then, as FC Barcelona has spent massively on imports, it has become increasingly recognized as one of the most important Catalan institutions.

So how has this occurred? One factor was that the club adopted a linguistic policy. The club magazine, *Barça*, began to introduce Catalan as early as the 1950s. At that time the magazine was very popular and also useful for the many immigrants who came to Catalonia and needed an introduction to the language. The club changed its name back to its original Catalan version, *Fútbol Club Barcelona*, in the 1974–75 season. This linguistic policy is now prevalent throughout the club. All staff address the public in Catalan first. The club is also involved in promoting Catalan folklore and culture and helps fund such activities, particularly through its many *peñas* (social/supporters' clubs).

Another factor relevant in the promotion of Barcelona as being the symbol of Catalonia is that it is proving to be a successful marketing technique. Barcelona has been marketed for some time now as being *més que un club* (more than a club). The logo is to be found on club merchandise. This invites support from anyone who resents Madrid-based dominance to show their frustrations in the football context. Barcelona now represents for many Spaniards not only the symbol of Catalonia but also *anti-madridismo* (anti-Madrid feeling) and some support Barcelona simply because they dislike Real Madrid. In recent years the Real Madrid–Barcelona rivalry has continued. Both teams enjoy support all over the country and the past geographical divisions of nationalist versus republican areas are beginning to fade in the footballing context. The legacy of political divisions remains in the notion of 'second teams', a very important part of football support in Spain. Many football fans in Spain 'support' a second team, either Real Madrid or Barcelona, as well as their local team. Rivalry is still tense and hostile. Both clubs feel that they have something to prove which is still at least partly based on the historical events, hostilities and conflicts experienced outside football.

This rivalry exists still on the part of fans, players and even managers, but the club directors and *presidentes* are careful to play down signs of tension whenever possible. This has rarely, however, involved the fostering of friendly relationships between the clubs. Neither Real Madrid's longstanding chairman, Ramón Mendoza, ousted in the club's presidential election (1995) nor Barcelona's, Josep Luis Núñez (1978–present), will attend matches in the rival stadium. This trend was broken by Real Madrid's newly appointed chairman, Lorenzo Sanz, who travelled to Barcelona's Nou Camp to follow Real Madrid in February 1996.

Suspicions held by Catalans that referees and the football institutions are against their club still prevail. Barcelona manager and chairman, Cruyff and Núñez respectively, still talked about political refereeing in 1995. In November 1995, Cruyff was in trouble for comments and gestures made to the referee in a match against Valencia (*Don Balón* 20 November 1995). Núñez also accused the Spanish FA (now renamed the *Real Federación Española de Fútbol*) of conspiring against Barcelona by calling up nine players for international duty for the Spain–Lithuania match in February 1993, thereby forcing most of the Barcelona team to miss the club fixture on the weekend preceding the match (*El País* 23 February 1993).

Despite all the talk about Barcelona being the nationalist club and rumours about its political connections, the club is still careful to deny any links with politics. The Catalan Nationalist Party backed a candidate, Cambra, at the club's presidential elections in 1989, but his failure to achieve victory meant that football and politics were not linked directly (Kuper 1994). Official links between Barcelona football club and political parties are now frowned upon and Núñez was discouraged from taking on political responsibilities in October 1994 (*El País* 21 October 1994).

Again, the role of Español is worthy of note. There was an attempt made to change the image of the club from one of anti-Catalanism (inherent in its name) to 'Real Club Deportivo de Cataluña' and for a while the policy of recruiting players only from local talent was adopted. However, the reaction to these changes by fans who had no desire to be anything other than anti-Catalanists was so hostile that they were dropped. Español has traditionally attracted the support of those migrants to Catalonia who continued to feel Spanish rather than Catalan and never assimilated or integrated totally into Catalan society. The typical Español fan was a civil servant, sent to work in Catalonia during the Franco regime; Español fans still have a reputation for being fascist sympathizers.

However, it can no longer be stated that Español represents the centralist forces in Catalonia: this would be too simplistic. Español support is bitterly divided on this issue. While many other supporters are now keen to embrace Catalanism, one group of supporters in particular, the *ultra*-style *Brigadas Blanquiazules*, still chooses to be associated with its opposition. Feelings are such that supporters with these opposing ideologies segregate themselves in the ground and patterns of support differ widely. While the *Brigadas Blanquiazules* wave Spanish flags and sing '*Viva España*', the rest of the ground whistles and waves *senyeras* (see Figure 3.1).

The club itself, like Barcelona, refuses to be drawn into the political debate and plays down relationships between football and politics. Interviews with club officials render nothing more controversial than statements claiming that anyone is welcome to support Español, whatever their political leanings, and they deny that Catalanism is an issue of importance at the club. However, the same week as these interviews took place, the club newspaper, *Blanc i Blau* (December 1995) carried an article urging supporters to put aside their political biases and join forces together to support Español. Interviews with

Figure 3.1   The Campo Sarria ground, Barcelona. Non-Catalanists gather to the right of the terrace and Catalanists to the left while the scoreboard diplomatically spells the name of the club as both Castilian Español and Catalan Espanyol

supporters suggest that bitter, sometimes violent, rifts between groups of supporters are present and confirm that the club is doing its best to improve the image of its supporters. Liaison between club and *ultra* leaders (leaders of supporters' clubs) has led to a system of self-policing among the *Brigadas Blanquiazules*.

Español fans feel that they share something in common with Real Madrid and the two sets of supporters enjoy a friendly relationship. Indeed, many Español fans support Real Madrid as a second (or even first) team. When the clubs play each other there is no segregation. In December 1995, the two teams linked arms before the match in the centre circle as all the fans insulted Barcelona in unison.

Atlético de Madrid are also seen as representatives of central Spain, although to a lesser extent, partly because of their relative lack of success on the pitch in recent years. Nevertheless, they feel strongly enough to taunt Barcelona fans when they play in the Vicente Calderón with chants of '*Viva España!*' The same chant could be heard from Real Madrid fans when the club, which really takes pride in representing Spain, played in the Champions' Cup against Juventus on 6 March 1996.

As in Catalonia, the necessity to express nationalist aspirations through football is declining in the Basque Country. A legacy of anti-Franco associations, of opposition to the dictatorship, means that there remain many Athletic de Bilbao *peñas* all over Spain. Athlétic de Bilbao and Real Sociedad continue to defend the autonomy of their clubs and region. The policy of recruiting players only from within the Basque Country continues. Bilbao is at present reviewing its policy and considering two changes.

First, it is debating whether to relax the definition of a pure Basque and allow players who were born outside the Basque Country to play for the club, providing they have Basque ancestors (*El País* 11 October 1995). There have already been examples of players born outside the Basque Country but brought up there (De la Fuente, Ferreira, Luis Fernando). Second, Bilbao is considering permitting players from outside the Basque Country in Spain to join its ranks: the club is not suggesting extending its catchment area throughout Spain but it is expanding its definition of Basque nationality to include players who were born in the Basque Country in France, *Iparralde*.

The relationship between the Basque Country and the rest of Spain still comes to the fore in the footballing context. During the 1982 World Cup finals held in Spain, the linguistic barrier which proved insurmount-able between the English and the Spanish meant that contact between the Spanish locals in the Basque Country and England fans was limited to 'thumbs up' to England and, significantly, 'thumbs down' to Spain, and the aligning of the *ikurriñas* alongside the Union flags to symbolize Basque allegiance with England in preference to Spain. (Although the Cross of St George is the flag of England, England fans usually carry Union flags.)

It was noted several times during the British media coverage of the 1982 World Cup in Spain how low-key was the support for the national team by the press located in Bilbao to follow England. Williams and colleagues notice the contrast in attitude between the Basque Country and Madrid when commenting on the support for the Spanish national side in Madrid: 'It was the first time the English had experienced support of any substance for the Spanish side. In Bilbao, Spanish fans had remained noticeably reserved in their support for their team. Here in Madrid the situation was very different' (Williams *et al.* 1984: 101).

Other clubs outside the Basque Country and Catalonia have adopted regionalist (rather than nationalist) stances in recent years. Valencia has assumed an image as a regionalist club (while carefully avoiding being associated with anything Catalan); its supporters even show their allegiances when Barcelona play there by chanting 'Madrid'. Similarly, Deportivo La Coruña in Galicia threatened to withdraw from the Spanish League altogether in summer 1995 to play in the Portuguese League. Many club colours have been designed to represent the regional flags: Real Betis de Sevilla play in the green and white stripes of Andalusia, Las Palmas wear the yellow and blue of the Canary Isles and Celta de Vigo the sky blue and white of Galicia.

A phenomenon since the mid-1980s in the relationship between football and nationalism in Spain involves the rise of organized groups of supporters, akin to Italian-style *ultra* groups. Increasingly popular youth movements in Spain are frequently linked to football clubs. The first evidence of neo-fascist *cabezas rapadas* (skinheads) was in 1985 after a match between Barcelona and Español when a Barcelona fan was stabbed by a group known as the *Brigadas Blanquiazules* of Español. Many of the members of these groups hold extreme right-wing beliefs and have since joined forces in similar violent nationalist groups such as the *Boixos Nois* of Barcelona, the *Ultrasur* of Real Madrid and the *Frente Atlético* of Atlético de Madrid.

Football, it appears, is being used as a vehicle for extreme political groups, and the football grounds as the battlefields where the members of these extreme right-wing groups (*cabezas rapadas*) turn support into extreme nationalism, racism and xenophobia. This trend occurs not only in Spain but also in Germany and Italy (see chapter 8 for an analysis of complex relationships between fans and politics in Italy). It is ironic that the Europeanization of footballing culture is taking the form of a rise in nationalist, racist groups.

Some of the most violent groups in Spain are to be found among the *Celtarra* (Celta de Vigo), the *Riazor Blues* (Deportivo de la Coruña) and the *Ultra Boix* (Sporting de Gijón). According to the researchers from the government's Anti-violence Committee, there are now around 2,000 *cabezas rapadas*, most affiliated to club *peñas* (social/supporter clubs). It appears that the clubs themselves, in providing finance for *ultras* to travel to away games, are indirectly supporting these groups (see chapter 7 for more complex and structured links between clubs and fans in Argentina). *Juntas Españolas*, an extreme right-wing group, even claims to have contacted Jesús Gil y Gil, *presidente* of Atlético de Madrid, to discuss the creation of a new *frente patriótico nacional* (Patriotic

National Front). It is significant that the group turned to the president of a football club for support. As in Argentina, the system whereby the *socios* vote for a presidential candidate to run the football club ensured a dialogue and some relationship between club and fans. Chairmen need the support of fans if they wish to remain in control of a club; this might help to explain the reluctance on the part of some directors to speak out against recent outbreaks of violence in football. A crucial change in the Spanish system took place in 1992 when all clubs except four (Real Madrid, Barcelona, Valencia and Albacete) converted to *Sociedades Anónimas* (public limited companies), thus abandoning the former system of electoral campaigns.

Some *ultra* groups known for their independent convictions are *Ultras Mujica* (Real Sociedad), *Herri Norte* (Bilbao) and *Boixos Nois* (Barcelona). These groups are sometimes reputed to be associated with violent political movements and frequently participate in nationalist demonstrations in their respective *Comunidades Autónomas*.

One of the best known groups is Real Madrid's *Ultrasur*. While claiming to be apolitical, it extols extreme right-wing, nationalist ideology and displays 'evidence of a nationalism close to Francoism' (Broussard 1990). Occupying the section of the ground that used to be populated by Franco's admirers, the group is proud of Spain's fascist past and opposes any independence/separatist movements, holding particular contempt for Barcelona.

Although not all members of the *Ultrasur* are violent, the group admits responsibility for confrontations between certain sets of supporters, claiming that their politically motivated violence is justified against Catalans, Basques and Galicians who, in their opinion, do not love Spain as much as they should do. When they travel to clubs based in the historic nationalities, these *ultras* complain that they feel resented for representing the powerful capital.

The changing role of football since the Franco era has been of considerable significance in reflecting, or arguably shaping, the national/regional identities and nationalist feelings of the nations of Spain. The way in which football has been organized has provided an accurate reflection of the manner of government of the existing power structure in Spain.

The recent changes in the political structures in Spain allow greater freedom of expression for the regions today, an outlet for frustrated feelings of uniqueness, of distinctive identities within the Spanish state which were quashed by Franco's attempts to impose a single Spanish national identity. Differences between the regions are officially recognized and even encouraged. This appears to have been all that was desired by many in Catalonia and the Basque Country. Nationalist movements do not enjoy the support they once had in Catalonia when such freedom of expression was denied to the population. Even in the Basque Country, where ETA's violent campaign ensures that the issue of Basque separatism is always in the political foreground, there are channels other than football where nationalism can be expressed.

Football is now just one form of expression and its role in this sense has become diluted. Although football clubs remain an important symbol of identity in the *Comunidades*, they are not the sole representatives of nationalism they once were.

Old rivalries still exist and take on new forms. The motivation for the hostility has not been forgotten, but new trends push former nationalist feelings in two directions; downwards, reflecting the rise in importance of the *Comunidades*, and upwards, via extreme nationalist movements which choose football as their breeding ground. It will be interesting to monitor the patterns of support for the *Selección* in years to come and discover whether or not its support in the more independent *Comunidades Autónomas* rises or falls.

CHAPTER 4

Playing in the right language: football in Belgium

The language issue has been prominent in Belgium since its foundation as an independent state in 1830. From the beginning, the country was composed of two language communities. In the north the region of Flanders was predominantly Flemish-speaking, Flemish being a dialect of Dutch. Flanders shared the Dutch language with its neighbours the Netherlands to the north but was Catholic rather than Protestant. In the south, the region of Wallonia bordering on France was overwhelmingly French-speaking.

Following the French Revolution the francophone bourgeoisie came to power in Belgium. This group came to dominate both the Belgian economy and Belgian society even in Flanders. In the nineteenth century French was the single official language of the Belgian state. In the capital Brussels (*Brussel* in Flemish, *Bruxelles* in French), business was conducted mostly in French although the majority of the city's population were of Flemish origin. This higher prestige status afforded to things French led to growing Flemish discontent (to surface politically in the twentieth century) as the French language dominated most aspects of organized society, including football.

At the end of the nineteenth century the two language communities had approximately equal populations, but a higher birth rate among Flemish Catholics produced a marked demographic shift during the twentieth century. By 1973 the Flemish-speaking area accounted for 56.4 per cent of the population and the French-speaking area only 32.1 per cent. The remainder of the population comprised 0.6 per cent in the German-speaking area to the east and 10.9 per cent in Brussels, now officially bilingual.

The advance of the Flemish population in demographic terms was enhanced by a parallel shift in economic power. Prior to the Second World War, French-speaking Wallonia had been the centre of Belgian industry and material wealth. After the war Wallonia's core industries of coal and steel began to decline (as in the north of England) and the economic infrastructure of the region became increasingly outdated. New growth industries tended to locate in Flanders, which contributed to the gradual shift in economic power to the Flemish community.

Inevitably the demographic and economic trends were reflected in an increased prominence for the politics of language in Belgium. The Flemish movement grew in strength in the 1950s, which was to lead eventually to constitutional change in the direction of a federal state divided by language differences. From the 1960s onwards organizations and structures have increasingly split along language lines throughout economic and social life. It is during this period that the issue of Flemish football clubs playing in the right language reached its peak. We shall trace the history of Belgian football from its French-controlled origins through to the gradual *vervlaamsing* (flemicizing) of both the structure and the clubs. This chapter would not have been possible without access for a two-week period to the excellent archive at the Sport Museum of Flanders, in the Faculty of Physical Education, Catholic University of Leuven. The Belgian Football Association was also helpful in confirming the date of key changes of name by football clubs.

Playing with a French ball: the early years of Belgian football

In its official form, Belgian football was founded and played in French, and controlled by the French elite. *Union Belge des Sociétés de Sports Athlétiques* (UBSSA) was established in 1895. UBSSA was a multi-sport organization, although the majority of members were football clubs. As such the Belgian FA is one of the oldest on the European mainland. In 1912 the switch was made to a football-only association – *Union Belge des Sociétés de Football Association* (UBSFA). Throughout this time, the language of administration was French and the rules of the game were disseminated in French. Only in February 1913 did the association's notepaper add the Flemish translation of the Belgian Football Association (*Belgische Voetbalbond*).

At the club level *vervlaamsing* was markedly slow prior to the First World War. The official publication to celebrate the fiftieth anniversary of the Belgian FA (Boin 1949: 336–7; produced in both French and Flemish versions) lists all the member clubs of UBSSA in December 1906 after more than ten years of existence. Out of a total of fifty-three affiliated football clubs, only one had an unequivocal Flemish name – *Atheneum Voetbal Vereeniging* from Stokkel in Brussels (*Voetbal Vereeniging* is Flemish for football club). In contrast, most clubs adopted the French (or English) 'Football Club'. A further three clubs were entirely English in their nomenclature, most notably the oldest sports club in Belgium – *Antwerp Football Club*. Note the use of Antwerp (English) rather than *Antwerpen* (Flemish) or *Anvers* (French). Antwerp is in the north of Belgium and clearly part of Flanders.

Forty-nine of the fifty-three clubs were French by name in that either the club name or the town name (usually both) was in French. For example *Club Sportif Anversois* from Antwerp had both club and town names in French. *Union Sportive Roularienne* used the French name of *Roulers* rather than the Flemish *Roeselare* for the town in Flanders. Clubs from Wallonia and Brussels could reasonably be expected to have French names, but eighteen clubs with totally French names were from Flanders.

Boin (1949: 350) lists the one hundred and seven football clubs active in 1914 immediately prior to the First World War. Three clubs possess

English names including a new club in Brussels called *White Star Athletic Club* (long since part of a series of mergers which created the current first division club *Racing White Daring Molenbeek*). By 1914 eleven clubs had clearly Flemish names (just over 10 per cent of clubs). Distinctly Flemish club names were beginning to appear such as *Sport Vereeniging* (sports club), *Sportkring* (sports circle – a Catholic organization), *Voorwaarts* (forward), and *Vlug en Vrij* (fast and free) from Hasselt. The town of Lier figured prominently in this early *vervlaamsing* with two Flemish clubs prior to 1914 – *Liersche Sportkring* (currently in the first division) and *Turn en Sport Vereeniging Lyra*.

Flemish clubs were therefore on the increase but the eleven Flemish clubs were overshadowed by the other forty-two clubs from Flanders with French names at this time. Additions to this group since 1906 included *Association Sportive Ostendaise* (*Oostende* is the Flemish name for Ostend), *Football Club Roulers* (from the Flemish town of *Roeselare*) and *Sporting Club Tirlemontois* (*Tienen* is the Flemish name for the town called *Tirlemont* in French).

The radical response: an alternative league structure 1930–44

After the First World War, not only was universal male suffrage established in 1919 but also football underwent a process of democratization. Football ceased to be an elite sport with more working-class participation; it also expanded away from the cities into the rural areas, particularly into Flemish villages. This new hotbed of football was confronted by continuing French dominance of URBSFA (conversion to a royal society in 1920 added R for *Royale*), regulations written in French and the imposition of francophone referees even for matches between Flemish villages.

One response to this situation was a radical one, that of setting up an alternative football league structure for Flemish clubs. *Vlaamsche Voetbalbond* was founded in February 1930 (this section relies heavily on the pioneering work of Jan Tolleneer 1996). The Flemish Football Association grew rapidly from 89 clubs in 1930 to 420 clubs in 1937. This network of clubs consisted mostly of Flemish villages, and an alternative league competition was run in parallel to the official structure of the Belgian FA. *Vlaamsche Voetbalbond* operated as a renegade organization, outlawed by the Belgian FA and by FIFA. Member clubs were not allowed to play matches against official Belgian clubs or clubs in other countries affiliated to official football associations.

Although successfully organized in terms of football administration, *Vlaamsche Voetbalbond* developed political connections which ultimately led to its downfall. The organization's leadership became more politically militant during the 1930s, including links with *Vlaamsch National Verbond*, a political party whose aim was the secession of Flanders from Belgium to join the Netherlands. Fascist sympathies were also present among some party members; many actively collaborated with the Germans during the Second World War occupation of Belgium. Not surprisingly the immediate post-occupation period witnessed prosecution of, and retribution against, those who had collaborated with the Germans. *Vlaamsche Voetbalbond* was quickly dissolved in 1944 and its leadership fled, in one case to Argentina.

In retrospect *Vlaamsche Voetbalbond* was a marginal body, which brought small village teams together into a competitive football league. It was no real threat to the official structure. Most of the Flemish players and spectators were not politically conscious at the time, they just wanted to play and watch football respectively. It was the organization's leaders (eventually) who were political militants. However, the Flemish FA may be seen to have had some impact on official thinking and behaviour. In the postwar period, the Belgian FA made more efforts to use Flemish where appropriate.

The gradual response: *vervlaamsing* of leading clubs

Political and social change are not always the result of radical action. It may be more effective in the long run to set in motion a gradual process of change, which eventually develops a momentum of its own. The strategy of establishing a separate Flemish league structure came to an abrupt end. Even during the lifetime of the Flemish FA, the gradual process of *vervlaamsing* of football clubs was underway. By 1996 almost all football clubs in Flanders had a Flemish name.

In 1914 just over 10 per cent of clubs affiliated to the Belgian FA had Flemish names. By 1949 the Flemish proportion had increased significantly. The fiftieth anniversary publication of the Belgian FA provided a list of all the affiliated clubs active in the 1948–49 season (Boin 1949: 177–83). A complete categorization of all the 1,334 clubs listed would be time-consuming as well as difficult in a minority of specific cases. There is, however, an easier way of classifying the older clubs as either French or Flemish.

After a period of twenty-five years' continuous membership of the Belgian FA and in the absence of any scandals, a football club could become a royal society; the choice of royal designation reveals the French or Flemish nature of the club.

There are twenty-two *Koninklijke* (i.e. Flemish) football clubs in the 1949 list and sixty-six *Royal* (i.e. French) football clubs. Thus among the older clubs the proportion of Flemish clubs had risen to 25 per cent. Moreover, nineteen of the sixty-six French-designated clubs were from Flemish-speaking Flanders. Therefore a slight majority (22:19) of the older clubs in Flanders now had Flemish rather than French names. The list of exceptions retaining a French name in a Flemish town/city still contained some of the leading clubs in Belgian football, including the two main clubs from Bruges and the two main clubs from Ghent (these examples will be covered in more detail on pp. 58–9).

In the 1962–63 season, the Belgian national league had settled into a structure of eight divisions of sixteen clubs (a first division, a second, two regionalized third divisions and four regionalized fourth divisions), with fifty-six *Royal* clubs and forty-eight *Koninklijke* clubs. The gap was closing with only a narrow French advantage remaining. These figures reflect both the growing power of the Flemish movement and the shift in economic power to Flanders as more Flemish teams rise up to the national league.

By the 1985–86 season the position had been transformed even further. One hundred and thirty clubs were in the national league structure (the first division had been increased to eighteen clubs): only thirty-one were *Royal* and no fewer than sixty-five were *Koninklijke* football clubs. Flemish clubs were now dominant in the Belgian league, which more than reflected the demographic situation of Flemish advantage, emphasized the economic power of Flanders and indicated that the process of *vervlaamsing* was virtually complete.

The where, the when and the why of *vervlaamsing*

Table 4.1 describes the process of *vervlaamsing* for a set of leading football clubs from Flanders, all of whom have been in the first or second divisions at some point: Table 4.1 gives club names before and after *vervlaamsing* and the year in which the change was made. In most cases the clubs switched from the French *Royal* to the Flemish *Koninklijke*. In the case of *Berchem Sport* (a suburb of Antwerp) this was the only change made in 1967. Two exceptions who retained their French royal designation are the *Racing Clubs* of *Gent* (*Gand*) and *Tienen* (*Tirle-mont*). Not included is the oldest club in Belgium, which has retained its unique nomenclature of *Royal* (French) *Antwerp* (English) *Football Club*.

Some clubs in Table 4.1 have changed the football element in the club name. For instance, *Association Sportive* became *Athletische Sportver-eeniging*, and *Cercle Sportif* became *Sportvereeniging Cercle*. Most clubs in the list have altered the town name from the French version to the Flemish. Most prominent are the four towns with two leading clubs subject to *vervlaamsing*, namely *Mechelen* (*Malines*), *Brugge* (*Bruges*), *Gent* (*Gand*) and *Tongeren* (*Tongres*).

The earliest examples of *vervlaamsing* in Table 4.1 are from 1937 with the changes to *Racing Club Mechelen* and *Athletische Sportver-eeniging Oostende*. An earlier case of *vervlaamsing* took place in 1935 as *Football Club Roulers* became *Football Club Roeselare*. The latter club is currently in the third division and has never competed at a higher level. In the cases of *Oostende* and *Roeselare* the name changes brought the clubs into line with their main rivals in town, which both possessed Flemish names from their foundation (*Van Neste Genootschap Oostende* and *Sportkring Roeselare*).

Political developments account for the wave of *vervlaamsing* in the 1930s and early 1940s. During the 1930s the Catholic workers'

Table 4.1 **Name changes of Belgian football clubs: the progression to Flemish**

Old club name	Year	New club name
Racing Club de Malines SR	1937	Racing Club Mechelen KM
Association Sportive Ostendaise	1937	Athletische Sportvereeniging Oostende
R Cercle Sportif Tongrois	1939	K Tongerse Sportvereeniging Cercle
R Sporting Club Meninois	1941	K Sporting Club Meenen
Association Athlétique Termondoise	1942	K Athletische Vereeniging Dendermonde
Patria Football Club Tongres	1946	Patria Football Club Tongeren
R Courtrai Sports	1950	K Kortrijk Sport
R Vilvorde Football Club	1962	K Vilvoorde Football Club
R Stade Louvaniste	1963	K Stade Leuven
R Excelsior Football Club Hasselt	1964	K Sporting Club Hasselt*
R Berchem Sport	1967	K Berchem Sport
R Beerschot Athletic Club	1968	K Beerschot Voetbal en Atletiekveren.
R Cercle Sportif Brugeois	1968	K Sportvereniging Cercle Brugge
R Racing Club de Gand	1969	R Racing Club Gent
R Football Club Malinois	1970	K Voetbalklub Mechelen
R Football Club Brugeois	1972	Club Brugge K Voetbalvereniging
Association R Athlétique La Gantoise	1972	K Atletiek Associatie Gent
R Cercle Sportif Hallois	1972	K Cercle Halle
R Racing Club Tirlemont	1973	R Racing Club Tienen
R Association Sportive Renaisienne	1987	K Sportkring Ronse**
R Football Club Renaisien	1987	K Sportkring Ronse**

Notes:
R = Royal
K = Koninklijke
SR = Société Royale
KM = Koninklijke Maatschappij
* New club formed in merger between R Excelsior and K Hasseltse Vlug en Vrij.
** New club with the Flemish town name of Ronse results from a merger of two clubs
with the French town name of Renaix.

movement, which had militant Flemish sympathies, grew in strength (for a succinct history of the Flemish movement see Wils 1992). Catholicism was traditionally stronger among the small market towns of Flanders than in the more industrialized and more secular Wallonia. The Flemish movement was encouraged in 1932 by legislation which recognized Flanders as Flemish-speaking, Wallonia as French-speaking and Brussels as bilingual. Furthermore the various Flemish nationalist parties increased their share of the vote to 14 per cent in 1936 and 15 per cent in 1939.

During the Second World War period of German occupation of Belgium the occupiers adopted a policy of *Flamenpolitik*, which gave preferential treatment to the Flemish language (which is more like German than French is) at the expense of French. The policy held considerable appeal for some Flemish nationalists, who became involved in collaboration with the occupying regime. *Flamenpolitik* also sanctioned the process of *vervlaamsing*, which explains a spate of name changing among football clubs during this period.

The impact of the political surge forward of Flemish nationalism in the 1960s is clearly visible in Table 4.1. *Vervlaamsing* reached its peak in the period 1967–73 when nine leading clubs altered their names, including the two clubs from *Brugge* and the two from *Gent*. Pressure on football clubs to make the change came from club members demanding political change, and from local political authorities. Local councils often owned the football stadium in which the town team played, and moreover the political majority was frequently Flemish nationalist. The local authority was in a position to say *geen vlaams geen senten* (no Flemish no money).

At the 1961 election the Flemish nationalists made a political breakthrough in the form of the *Volksunie* (People's Union). In 1962 the language boundary was fixed, with Brussels decreed bilingual and the Ministry of Culture being split into Flemish and French sections. The elections of 1965 and 1968 produced substantial gains for the language parties in all three parts of Belgium. Pressure grew on the leading political parties such that they split into Flemish and French wings – the Christian Democrats in 1968, followed by the Liberals and finally the Socialists in 1978.

Since the burst of *vervlaamsing* in the late 1960s and early 1970s, the Belgian language divide has been further institutionalized. Constitutional reform in 1980 took a first step to full-scale federalism by decentralizing significant powers to the three regions. Further reform in 1988 increased the proportion of state expenditure under regional control from 7 per cent to 70 per cent. By the time the Belgian state was cemented into a federal system divided along language lines, the process of *vervlaamsing* of football clubs was completed.

Case studies of *vervlaamsing*

In the early history of Belgian football rival clubs were formed in the same town, often within months of each other, hence the important tradition of the local derby match in Belgium, which mirrors football histories in Britain and Argentina. The Flemish town of *Mechelen* (*Malines* in French) is a classic example. *Racing Club de Malines* was formed in August 1904 by a group of students, and *Football Club Malinois* in October 1904 by a different set of students. Both clubs in this predominantly Flemish town were founded with French names.

One of the founder players of *Racing Club* worked at the local prison, which resulted in the club playing its early matches inside the prison walls. The club's first account book was in French, although Flemish was used at club meetings. Govaerts and Vankesbeek (1929) comment that the first secretary probably found French more fashionable, which understates French elite control of Belgian football at the time.

From the very early days *Football Club Malinois* was associated with the *burgerij* (bourgeoisie) in the town, and the *arbeiders* (workers) were correspondingly linked to *Racing Club de Malines* (Jacobs *et al.* 1978). As a result *Football Club* was more likely to incorporate the French business elite. It is significant that the working-class *Racing Club* was the first to undergo *vervlaamsing* in June 1937 to *Koninklijke Racing Club Mechelen*. The more middle-class *Football Club Malinois* was not to follow suit until over thirty years later. The inaugural meeting of *Football Club Malinois* adopted the club name *sans discussion* (without discussion). To this day the letters FCM are visible above the entry gate to the stadium. An advantage of the *burgerij* connection is evident in the club's adoption of the town colours red and yellow. Only in July 1970 at the height of *vervlaamsing* was the switch made to *Koninklijke Voetbalclub Mechelen*. This represents the longest time period that two major clubs in a Flemish town have sported the town name in different languages.

An even closer example is in the Flemish town of *Roeselare* (*Roulers* in French), where two clubs emerged within ten days of each other out of the same original meeting, which broke into rival camps. Thus in the early history of Belgian football, if one of the dominant political creeds in town had a team, then the other one should form one as soon as possible.

Students were instrumental in forming the first local club, *Red Star Roeselare*, around 1900. By 1903 a club called *Union Sportive Roularienne* was affiliated with UBSSA but after only six years the club disbanded in 1909. A meeting was called on 9 June 1910 at a well-known Catholic café with a view to forming a new football club. At the suggestion of forming a Catholic club, those of a liberal disposition objected and were asked to leave the meeting.

The Catholic majority continued with the meeting to form *Sport Vereeniging Roeselare*. Both the club and town names were Flemish from the very beginning, which reflects the strong links between Catholicism and the Flemish language in Flanders. *Sport Vereeniging* displayed its Catholic origin by playing in green and white. After the First World War *Sport Vereeniging* was reformed as *Sportkring Roeselare*, at the same time adopting the town colours of black and white (Depestel 1960).

As for the liberals expelled from the original meeting, they reconvened on 18 June 1910 at another café to found *Football Club Roulers* – another connection between liberals, business and a French inclination. An early publication (Janart 1919) describes the results of the club's matches for the 1912–13 season as '*victoire, défaite* and drawn'. The team with the liberal/business connections adopted the town colours of black and white from the beginning. In the mid-1990s, *Roeselare* still provides the unique situation of both town clubs playing in the same black and white colours, in the same Belgian third division. In Belgian football tradition, the home team changes colours for the derby match. In 1929 *Football Club Roulers* moved to a new ground next to the Rodenbach brewery, where the club still play and are currently sponsored by Rodenbach (see Figure 4.1 for the proximity of main stand and brewery). The switch to the Flemish town name as *Football Club Roeselare* was made in June 1935, twenty-five years after the club's foundation and that of its instantly Flemish rival.

Figure 4.1   The main stand of **FC Roeselare** *with the club's main sponsor, the Rodenbach brewery, in the background*

The city of Bruges experienced an influx of British expatriates following the end of the Franco-Prussian War. From the 1870s cricket and football became regular features on the Assebroek fields. Football matches between the English 'red caps' (from the English college) and local schools began in 1885. A Flemish-named club, *Brugsche Football Club*, was the first Belgian club in the city in 1890. Discord between Flemish and French members led to a breakaway and the founding of *Football Club Brugeois* in November 1891. By December 1894 a third Bruges club, *Vlaamsche Voetbal Club*, appeared on the scene, its name reflecting the strength of Flemish players in the city.

In October 1897 the two original clubs, *Brugsche FC* and *FC Brugeois*, merged for financial reasons in the name of the latter. Ostensibly the reason for the choice of name was that *Football Club Brugeois* had a contract for renting a ground (the evocatively named *Rattenplein*, literally rat's field), which forbade letting other clubs play on it. The merger agreement stated that the French name would be retained until the club moved to *Brugsche FC*'s ground. However, this never happened. Marien (1973) suggests that adoption of the French name may be linked to the formation of the French UBSSA in 1995 as the national association.

The main rivals in Bruges were formed in April 1899 as *Cercle Sportif Brugeois*, a merger of existing clubs *Rapid Football Club* and *Vlaamsche Voetbal Club*. As was customary at the time the new club was given a French name (Marien 1973). Note that the two mergers of four clubs in Bruges, two of which had Flemish names, produced two clubs with French names. *Cercle Sportif* was founded by former pupils of the Catholic high school and still play in green and black. *Football Club Brugeois* comprised a combination of liberal and socialist members and have always played in blue and black. Despite the Flemish majority in Bruges, and the early tradition of Flemish clubs and players, there was no *vervlaamsing* until the late 1960s, when political pressure was at its peak. Bruges provides another example of the Catholic club changing name first (but only by four years). The name changes were to *Koninklijke Sportvereniging Cercle Brugge* in September 1968, and to *Club Brugge Koninklijke Voetbalvereniging* in July 1972. *Club* have been the more successful of the two, winning the championship nine times (eight since the name change), whereas *Cercle* have been champions three times (the last in 1930). Since 1975 the two clubs have shared the new municipally owned Olimpiastadion.

Ghent has a similar pattern of two rival football clubs, both originally with the French town name (*Gand*) and switching late to the Flemish name (*Gent*). The oldest football club (as opposed to sports club) in the city was *Racing Club Gantois* (later *Racing Club de Gand*) founded in April 1899. In 1864 this club's more famous neighbour originated as an athletics club, *Association Athlétique La Gantoise*; it entered UBSSA as one of the ten founder members in 1895. A football section was formed in 1900 and French was adopted as the official language even though most players were Flemish.

Name changes for both the Ghent clubs occurred during the peak of *vervlaamsing*, to *Racing Club Gent* in 1969 and *Atletiek Associatie Gent* in 1972. The process caused internal conflict at *AA La Gantoise* in September 1971 with the football and athletics sections in favour, and tennis and hockey against. In the end the local authority as sponsors of the football team proved decisive.

Antwerp Football and Cricket Club was founded in 1880, when the football referred to in its title was rugby. No association football team existed at the club until 1897 when the name registered was simply *Antwerp Football Club*. A century on, a French *Royal* is the only addition to the English town and club name: the oldest football club in Belgium has resisted *vervlaamsing*.

Other clubs in the city of Antwerp have changed with the times but not until the late 1960s under political pressure. The main rivals to *Antwerp Football Club* historically were *Beerschot Athletic Club* founded in 1899 (and becoming *Royal Beerschot AC* in 1925). *Beerschot* was a derivation of a medieval historical district called Bernescot. In November 1967 *Beerschot* sold its stadium to the local council for 43,625,000 Belgian francs. Within months of the ground becoming municipally owned, the club changed name to *Koninklijke Beerschot Voetbal en Atletiek Vereniging* in July 1968. In May 1967, in another suburb of Antwerp, *Royal Berchem Sport* became *Koninklijke Berchem Sport*.

The paradox of Belgian football: a national structure in a federal state

As the Belgian state has moved progressively towards a fully federal structure, so more and more aspects of economic, political, social and cultural life have been divided along language lines. Many sports are divided into Flemish and French authorities; some activists are even calling for separate Flemish and French Olympic Committees. This chapter has demonstrated the gradual *vervlaamsing* of football clubs, but in other ways Belgian football has remained relatively unscathed.

The paradox of Belgian football is that it has retained a national structure at a time when most aspects of Belgian life are bifurcating along the regional–language dimension. Examination of the clubs in the national football league in 1995–96 (first and second divisions with eighteen clubs in each, two third divisions with sixteen, and four fourth divisions with sixteen) reveals that they are *not* divided according to language. Even in the regionalized third division, where one might expect a replication of the language boundaries, this is not the case.

Division 3A is made up of clubs from the east and the south of the country: nine are Flemish, six are French and one is from Brussels (*Royal Union St Gilloise*). The two clubs from *Roeselare*, *SK* and *FC*, will play *Royal Olympic Club Charleroi*, *Royal Football Club Namur* and *Royal Albert Elisabeth Club Mons*. Division 3B comprises clubs from the north and west of Belgium: thirteen are Flemish, two are French and one is from the German-speaking enclave (*Alliance Sportive Eupen*).

Football is relatively well off as *the* national sport and is less dependent than other sports on funding from the public sector. The new community laws, which devolved most public expenditure to the regional–language level, cannot apply pressure on the Belgian FA in terms of *geen vlaams geen senten*. The Belgian national football team is one of the few symbols accepted and supported by all communities in Belgium. There has been no demand for a Flemish football team from the Flemish nationalists, who are happy to cheer for Belgium in the World Cup or European Championship.

Playing across the border: football frontiers

Chapters 2–4 were concerned with the existence of different football nations (actual or latent) within one state. Most professional football clubs aspire to play in their own national league; if successful, they can take part in one of the continental competitions. For leading British clubs 'getting into Europe' is a major objective. For a small number of clubs, however, playing abroad is for various reasons the norm; this chapter considers football clubs (not players) that play across the border. The increasing globalization of sport has precipitated a rapid growth in players exercising their trade abroad. Duke (1994) has documented the spread of Czechoslovak and Hungarian players across Europe in the early 1990s and there is a growing literature on the topic of sports migration (see Bale and Maguire 1994).

Playing across the border is not necessarily a question of travelling long distances to away matches; some of the longest football journeys are regularly made within national competitions. The three clubs from Funchal on the island of Madeira (Marítimo, Uniao and Nacional) travel 625 miles to reach Lisbon in the Portuguese league. Club Deportivo Tenerife face a 1,252 mile flight to Madrid for Spanish league matches.

Formerly the largest country in the world, one would expect the Soviet Union to provide an extreme case of long-distance travel in the national championship. Ironically it was not until the breakup of the Soviet Union into fifteen independent states that a team from Vladivostok reached the top division, i.e. national level rather than regional level. In 1993 Luch Vladivostok in the Russian first division had to make the flight of over 4,000 miles to Moscow six times to play Spartak, Dynamo, Lokomotiv, CSKA, Torpedo and Asmaral.

French colonial centralization has resulted in the native football associations not affiliating directly with FIFA. Instead they have operated as regional associations of the French FA and consequently were able to enter the French FA Cup. Those clubs emerging from the regionalized early rounds are then drawn to play against teams from mainland France thereby adding spice to the cup competition. For example, in 1978 Lille travelled to French Guiana (4,411 miles) to play Club Colonial de Cayenne; in 1979 Martigues played La Gauloise Basse Terre in Pointe à Pitre, Guadeloupe (4,206 miles); in 1982 Central Sport de Papeete from Tahiti in the Pacific Ocean travelled 9,763 miles to Montreuil to lose 1–2 against Club Sportif de Thonon; in 1990 Clermont Ferrand flew to Reunion Island in the Indian Ocean (5,822 miles) to play

Jeunesse Sportive Saint Pierroise (for these and other examples see Cazal *et al.* 1993). The French commitment to the development of world football clearly goes beyond establishing the World Cup and the European Champions' Cup.

Reasons for playing across the border

There are several reasons why clubs play across the border. For any one club a combination of reasons is often involved rather than a single explanation. We shall discuss in turn geographical proximity, economic pragmatism, status presence and political pressure as alternative explanations for playing across the border. We then consider three of the most interesting and distinctive cases – Berwick Rangers, Derry City and Cyprus.

Geographical proximity

Nearness to the political frontier and to other clubs in the neighbouring state is an encouragement to play at least occasional friendly matches across the border. Pressures for this arrangement to become more regular and institutionalized are most likely in two kinds of geographical situations. First, in the case of small states, to travel anywhere in any direction is to cross the frontier, for example, Liechtenstein and San Marino. Second, the shape of the frontier and the distribution of population renders foreign places/clubs nearer than domestic places/ clubs. The England–Scotland border provides two examples with Berwick Rangers (from Berwick-upon-Tweed, the northernmost town in England) playing in the Scottish League, and Gretna playing in the Northern Premier League for English semi-professional clubs.

Liechtenstein is a small country wedged between Switzerland and Austria, only 62 square miles in area with a population of 27,000 people. Mountainous terrain dictates an easier orientation towards Switzerland which has resulted in all seven registered clubs in Liechtenstein competing in the Swiss regional league structure. There is no national league in Liechtenstein but an annual cup competition was started in 1946 with the winners partaking in the European Cup Winners' Cup since 1992.

The independent Republic of San Marino covers only 24 square miles with a population of 22,000. It is totally surrounded by Italy and all San Marino football clubs played in the Italian regional leagues until 1986, when a San Marino national league championship was set up; it currently comprises sixteen clubs in two divisions. One club, Calcio (literally FC) San Marino, continues to play in the lower reaches of the Italian regional league structure, partly on the basis of a higher playing standard in Italy (thus involving status presence too). However, the prospect of entry into the European competitions has increased the attractiveness of the national league over the Italian regional leagues.

Gretna is the only Scottish football club to play in a league affiliated to the (English) Football Association. The town's location on the border with England contributed to its decision to move to an English league (see Figure 5.1 for the club welcome to English visitors). Formed in July 1946, the club spent only one season in the (Scottish) Dumfrieshire Junior League before joining the Carlisle and District League in 1947. The main justification for the move was to minimize travelling and costs (an element of economic pragmatism is also evident). Gretna has remained in English football ever since. Geographical proximity also played a part in the switch to Scottish football of Berwick Rangers (see pp. 67–70).

Economic pragmatism

For some clubs it simply makes economic sense to play across the border rather than in their own country. Lower travel costs are a key factor, which reinforce and overlap with geographical proximity. Economic

Figure 5.1   Scottish club Gretna welcome today's visitors. Visitors are always English as Gretna play in the English semi-professional Northern Premier League

pragmatism must also take into account relative income as well as relative costs. Playing across the border in a higher standard of competition should increase attendance and income at home matches, as well as providing a higher level of income from away matches (here economic pragmatism overlaps with status presence).

The three professional Welsh clubs (Cardiff City, Swansea City and Wrexham) who play in the (English) Football League do so out of a combination of economic pragmatism and status presence. Their average attendances for Football League matches against English professional clubs are much higher than would be the case if they played in the national League of Wales against Welsh semi-professional clubs. Chapter 2 considered in detail the case of the Welsh semi-professional clubs (Colwyn Bay and AFC Newport) who have resorted to litigation in order to defend their right (and preference) to continue playing in the English league structure for semi-professional clubs rather than the national League of Wales. In the opinion of these clubs the benefits of playing in England far outweigh the disadvantages. An element of economic pragmatism is also present in the cases of Berwick Rangers and Gretna on the England–Scotland border.

Arguably the most bizarre concentration of cases involving economic pragmatism occurred in Singapore in 1994. The Republic of Singapore has a population of 2.8 million and comprises 239 square miles. The main island is immediately to the south of and connected by bridge to the Malaysian peninsula. Historically Singapore and Malaysia were part of the same British colony. A Malaysia Cup competition between regions was begun in 1921. Singapore was the first winner of the trophy and in 1994 won it for the twenty-third time.

Singapore became self-governing in 1959 and joined the Federation of Malaysia in 1963. Political conflict rendered Singapore's participation in the federation short-lived and it seceded in 1965 to become an independent republic. However, the Singapore representative side continued to compete in the Malaysia Cup in the 1970s. An element of status presence was behind the decision but economic pragmatism was also involved. Although a national Singapore League was in existence from 1975, local supporters exhibited a greater interest and attendance for the Singapore representative side in the Malaysian competition.

In December 1994 Singapore completed a league and cup double by winning the Malaysian Cup final in Kuala Lumpur. The final attracted a capacity crowd of 81,000 of which it was estimated that 50,000 crossed the border from Singapore. However, after the end of the season, Singapore withdrew from the Malaysian League following a major match-fixing scandal. Singapore's withdrawal was explained officially as a protest against the Malaysian FA's allegation of a lack of cooperation on the part of Singapore in punishing the guilty parties. Significantly the Singapore association added that it was time to go it alone and concentrate on its own national league. In 1995 Singapore has declared its intention of forming a fully professional league akin to the J League in Japan.

As Singapore was winning (presumably) its last championship in the Malaysian League, a new Australian challenge emerged in the Singapore League. Two clubs, Darwin Cubs and Perth Kangaroos, joined the Singapore League in 1994. Both Darwin and Perth are almost 2,000 miles from Sydney, the epicentre of the Australian National League. Darwin in the extreme north and Perth in the extreme west of Australia have to travel inordinate distances to play anybody other than a rival local team. From Darwin, the flight to Singapore is shorter than that to Sydney. For the Darwin Cubs, playing in the Singapore League was considered far more viable financially than the Australian National League. Perth is closer to Sydney than Singapore but the air fare to Singapore is only slightly higher than flying to the east coast of Australia. Moreover, by 1994 Perth had lost patience with the repeated delays in admitting a Western Australian club into the Australian National League. For the east coast Australian clubs, economic pragmatism dictates resistance to a Western Australian presence in the national league.

The historic foray of Australian clubs into the Singapore League ended with Perth Kangaroos crowned as champions, just as Singapore was confirmed as double winners in Malaysia. The globalization of football is taking on a new dimension in Asia and Australasia.

Status presence

A desire to play at a higher level is another factor which may influence a football club to play across the border. Particularly for small states, the option of playing abroad may be the only way of achieving a higher status in football. It may well be politically and culturally important to establish a status presence in the neighbouring state. We have described the case of the Singapore representative side playing in the Malaysian League, which clearly has an element of status presence. Similarly Cardiff City, Swansea City and Wrexham play in the (English) Football League partly because of its higher status than the League of Wales.

Gretna's continued presence in the English league structure is related to finding an appropriate level at which to play. The club regards the pyramid structure of semi-professional football in England as providing greater incentives for ambitious clubs. Undoubtedly Gretna have had a successful career in England progressing from the Carlisle and District League in 1947 to the Cumberland League in 1951, the Northern League in 1982 and the Northern Premier League in 1992. In contrast, there is little opportunity to progress as a semi-professional club in Scotland.

Monaco is a tiny principality surrounded by France and the Mediterranean. A population of 29,000 is crammed into an area of 0.7 square miles. In football terms, Monaco has established its status presence by competing in the French League. This development has been assisted greatly by the patronage of Prince Rainier, a keen football fan. *Association Sportive de Monaco* was founded in 1924 and turned professional in 1948, encouraged by Prince Rainier to enter the French second division. AS Monaco soon made its mark in French football, attaining promotion to the first division in 1953, winning the French Cup in 1960 (and a further four times since) and the French League championship in 1961 (and four more times since).

Royal financial support remains the cornerstone of the club's success. A new stadium, Stade Louis II, was opened in 1985 with a capacity of 20,000, which can accommodate more than two-thirds of the total population. The club cannot exist at this level without financial sponsorship because attendances at Stade Louis II are too low. In 1990–91, AS Monaco won the French Cup and was runner-up in the league but the average attendance that season was only 4,313. Large crowds can be guaranteed only for the visit of Marseille and matches in the European competitions.

In order to stimulate increased attendances on a regular basis the club has considered playing abroad across two frontiers. Monaco is only a few miles from the Italian border at Ventimiglia, and in 1991–92 the club debated the possibility of joining the Italian League. However, there is no certainty that AS Monaco would be welcomed; it is unlikely that any club would be allowed to enter directly into the first division (*Serie A*). More likely would be a requirement to start at the third or fourth division level (*Serie C1* or *C2*). Monaco's desire to play the likes of AC Milan, Juventus and Sampdoria regularly would not be achieved quickly.

Political pressure

Football cannot escape the impact of international political conflicts. Political pressure may be such that a football club has to play across the border or not at all. The most extreme scenario is for a club's ground to be located on the frontline in a war zone. It was for this reason that Zeljeznicar Sarajevo was forced to withdraw from competitive football in 1991–92.

Military conquest inevitably changes the political map at least temporarily and football's boundaries are consequently altered. During the Second World War football clubs in those previously independent countries occupied by the German Third Reich were obliged to participate in the German national championship. The final stages of the championship were decided on a knockout basis and among the participants in the period were: Wiener Sport Club Admira, First Vienna FC and Sport Klub Rapid Wien from Austria; SS SG Strassburg (Strasbourg) and FC 1893 Mulhausen (Mulhouse) from France; FV Stadt Dudelingen (Dudelange) from Luxembourg; Nationalsozialistiche TG Prag (Prague) from Czechoslovakia; and SG Ordnungspolizei Warschau (Warsaw) from Poland. The political symbolism of some of the imposed club names is transparent.

Political pressure is central to an understanding of Derry City playing across the border. The club is from Northern Ireland's second city, the predominantly Catholic (London)Derry. Owing to the high level of political violence between Protestants and Catholics in Northern Ireland, City was unable to play in the (Northern) Irish League after 1972. Since 1985 the club has played across the border in the League of Ireland, the national league of the Republic of Ireland. The case of Derry City is documented later (pp. 70–6).

Different examples of playing across the border are to be found in Cyprus. Since the Turkish invasion of 1974 the island has been divided into the Greek south (roughly two-thirds) and the Turkish north (roughly one-third). On both sides there are refugee football clubs who cannot play in their home town on their own ground but continue to function in another location. Cyprus constitutes the third case study (pp. 76–81).

Pushed across the border: Berwick Rangers into Scotland

Berwick Rangers is the only football club in the Scottish League with its headquarters in England. Rangers began life as an English club, briefly played on both sides of the border, then opted for Scotland in 1905. Following a long period in the East of Scotland League, the club progressed into the Scottish League C Division (third) in 1951 and then the B Division (second) in 1955. Berwick Rangers has never been in the top division of the Scottish League and is currently (1995–96) located in the second division, the third tier below the premier and first divisions.

Both geographical proximity and economic pragmatism played a part in Berwick's historic decision to affiliate with Scotland. The England–Scotland border runs from south-west to north-east such that the northernmost part of England, which contains the town of Berwick-upon-Tweed, tapers into the eastern flank of Scotland. The nearest large settlement in England is Newcastle upon Tyne, 63 miles to the south, whereas the Scottish capital Edinburgh is only 57 miles to the north. Economic pragmatism on the part of other English clubs played a central role in the switch to Scotland in 1905.

A centenary history of Berwick Rangers was produced by a local journalist (Langmack 1981); for the club's early history it made use of an earlier book (King 1946), which in turn relied heavily upon an interview in the *Edinburgh Evening News* in October 1908 with Peter Cowe, one of the club's original players and organizers. It is in the nature of reminiscences that the rich detail provided does not always emerge in the right order nor with complete historical accuracy. As a result both books are prone to some chronological confusion and occasional inaccuracy over dates, particularly regarding the crucial period of Rangers' switch to Scotland.

Neither of the two histories therefore captures the vagaries and vicissitudes of 1905 for Berwick Rangers. Detailed research on the archives of the *Berwick Journal* has revealed the full story. What began as an attempt to become more firmly entrenched in English football became a permanent switch to Scottish football.

Berwick Rangers Football Club was founded in 1881. According to Langmack (1981) the inspiration was provided by an exhibition match at Berwick between North Eastern Railway (from Newcastle upon Tyne) and Tynefield (from West Barns, Dunbar). Note that the inspiration was part-English part-Scottish. In the first season there are reports of early Rangers matches with Alnwick and Tynefield, again reflecting contact with both sides of the border. Berwick Rangers is regarded as a pioneer of association football in the Scottish borders taking the game to Coldstream, Kelso and Eyemouth. In 1885 Rangers joined the North-umberland Football Association and began competing in the cup competition. However, King (1946) reports that many of the players in the early days were Scots and adds that the deliberate canny Scottish style was much in contrast to the dash of the English player.

By the mid-1890s Berwick Rangers demonstrated its orientation towards England by entering the (English) FA Amateur Cup. In November 1894 Rangers travelled to Goole in Yorkshire to lose 1–3 to Howden Rangers. The next year in October 1895 a home tie was lost 2–5 to Tow Law from County Durham. At the turn of the century, Rangers won the 1899–1900 North Northumberland League championship, a competition comprising only English teams.

A new initiative in 1901 led to the creation of the Border League. As this league was not affiliated to either the English or Scottish football associations, it was not restricted to clubs from only one side of the border. The Border League's founding members consisted of four Scottish clubs (Coldstream, Duns, Eyemouth and Kelso) and three English clubs (Berwick Rangers, Percy Rovers and Tweedside Albion). At the same time Rangers continued to enter the Northumberland cup competitions. Here is the beginning of a period with a foot in both camps.

That Berwick saw its future development in the English game is apparent from the club's annual general meeting in August 1903 where there was a proposal to enter the (English) FA Cup; the proposal was eventually withdrawn because of the expense involved. After winning the Border League championship in 1903–04 Rangers set its sights higher, again in an English direction, by applying to join the North-umberland League in September 1904. Upon its successful admission, club officials commented that Rangers had risen above the low dead-level of Border League mediocrity. Furthermore the new league would mean the visit of better-class teams and a wider recognition of Berwick in the realm of sport.

So Berwick Rangers entered the critical year of 1905 with its first team playing in the all-English Northumberland League and its second or A team playing in the Border League, which still contained a mixture of Scottish and English clubs. Most of the twelve other clubs in the Northumberland League were from just north of Newcastle in the Morpeth and Backworth districts (including a club still famous today, Blyth Spartans). Inevitably Berwick's travel expenses were considerably higher in this new league than in the Border League. More significant, however, was the fact that the travel costs of other clubs in the Northumberland League rose sharply, which triggered their sense of economic pragmatism.

Rangers played a large number of away games in the Northumberland League at the beginning of the 1904–05 season so that the difficulty with expenses of visiting teams arose around the half-way point. Average travel costs to Berwick for the other clubs were about £4 and in addition the players lost half a day in travel time. The Berwick club responded by offering financial assistance to the poorer clubs of 15 shillings (75p) towards travel expenses. Early in April 1905, Seaton Burn FC protested that 15 shillings was not enough and that the real cost of additional travel beyond Alnmouth was 35 shillings. The upshot of the conflict over travel costs was that three clubs refused to visit Berwick and the fixtures were not completed. By late April three clubs had tendered their resignations to the Northumberland League and other clubs were calling for Berwick Rangers to be asked to resign.

The annual general meeting of Berwick Rangers FC in June 1905 took place amid growing uncertainty as to the club's future. Given the opposition from some Northumberland League clubs, Rangers had already applied to the Northern Alliance (another English league) and an application to the North Northumberland League was being held in reserve. In direction Berwick was still looking towards England, which was confirmed by yet another proposal to affiliate directly with the (English) Football Association in London. The meeting noted that it was already too late to apply for the next season's FA Cup competition but the FA Amateur Cup could still be entered in August. The main advantage of FA membership was seen as the possibility of appealing to the FA over and above the Northumberland FA, and the main disadvantage as the cost of a guinea for membership. When the proposal to affiliate with the FA came to a vote the result was a tie, and the chairman cast his vote in favour. This decision was never acted upon because shortly after the annual general meeting Rangers learned that its application to the Northern Alliance had been unsuccessful.

Worse was to follow at the annual general meeting of the Northumberland League in July 1905. The league secretary commented that 1904–05 had been the worst season in the history of the league. Primarily this was due to the false step of accepting a club so far removed from the rest as Berwick Rangers. He pointed out that other clubs could not afford to pay heavy travel expenses. His solution was to propose geographical limits for the league, specifically that the northern extremity of the league be Alnwick (29 miles south of Berwick). The secretary honestly admitted that the resolution had been framed for the purpose of excluding Berwick Rangers.

The Rangers representative proposed an amendment that the league stay as it was. To assist the amendment Rangers made the generous offer of paying each visiting team 35 shillings, which was equivalent to twelve railway Saturday returns from Alnmouth (the station near to Alnwick) to

Berwick. Voting on the amendment went 7–5 against and Rangers were out of the Northumberland League. However, the club was invited to reapply and restate the offer at the vacancies meeting the next week. This Berwick did but the end result was the same with the door to the Northumberland League firmly closed. For the other clubs economic pragmatism dictated a league without Berwick Rangers.

On 10 August 1905 the *Berwick Journal* observed that Berwick Rangers seemed to be in rather a hole as to what to do for next season. It also reported that Rangers had applied belatedly to the Scottish FA, the East of Scotland FA and the East of Scotland League. Pushed to the brink, Berwick Rangers had taken a last chance on Scotland. One week later the paper was able to report that all three applications had been successful. In one leap Berwick Rangers abandoned English football and were to play competitively only against Scottish teams. Club officials stated that Rangers was severing its connection with English football because of the treatment meted out by the Northumberland League. Berwick Rangers has remained in Scottish football ever since.

Scottish football arrived very suddenly. By the end of August 1905 Berwick Rangers had beaten Highland Light Infantry 4–1 at home in the East of Scotland Qualifying Competition. Early in September the first appearance in the Scottish FA Qualifying Cup ended in a 3–3 draw at West Calder Swifts; the replay was won 2–1 in front of a crowd of 1,500. At the end of the first season in the East of Scotland League, Rangers finished second. The annual general meeting in July 1906 reported that the club had received no compensation from the three teams who refused to play at Berwick in the Northumberland League the season before, and that the Northumberland League had sided with the other clubs. Not surprisingly the decision to remain affiliated with Scotland was unanimous.

Nowhere else to go: Derry City into the Republic of Ireland

Any explanation of Derry City's move across the border has to be political. The escalating level of political violence in Northern Ireland between the Protestant majority and Catholic minority populations from the late 1960s led inexorably to the club's withdrawal from the (Northern) Irish League in 1972. Northern Ireland's second city is Londonderry to the English and the Protestant community but plain Derry to the Irish Catholics. Its population is overwhelmingly Catholic and the city is only a few miles from the border with the Republic of Ireland.

A more crucial geographical feature is the location of the club's ground. Brandywell is situated on the edge of the Bogside, the estate which is the central focus of Catholic republicanism. The ground is located within the confines of Free Derry, a no-go area to both the (Protestant) Royal Ulster Constabulary and the British military since 1969. Political pressure on Protestant clubs not to play at the Brandywell was to prove central to City's withdrawal from senior Northern Irish football.

The case of Derry City is not the first example of a political withdrawal from the Irish League. In 1949 Belfast Celtic (the leading Catholic club) resigned from the league because of crowd trouble at matches. Celtic quit senior football despite a phenomenal record of success as league champions on fourteen occasions and cupwinners eight times (see Kennedy 1989). Nor have such problems disappeared in Northern Irish football since the resignation of Derry City. Cliftonville, the remaining Catholic club in the Irish League, still cannot play home matches against Linfield, the Protestant unionist flagship, at their own ground Solitude, which is in the heart of Catholic West Belfast.

Two books covering the history of Derry City were published in the mid-1980s. Platt (1986) covers only the period up to the club's withdrawal from the Irish League in 1972, whereas Curran (1986) includes the rebirth of Derry City and the first season in the League of Ireland, 1985–86. This case study not only draws material from both books but also is based on interviews in August 1995 with three key informants: Kevin Mahon, assistant manager at Derry City 1995–96; Arthur Duffy, sports reporter for the *Derry Journal*; and Eddie Mahon, former Derry City goalkeeper and captain who was one of the consortium of four ex-players to approach the League of Ireland with a view to entering a Derry team in the league.

Derry City Football and Athletic Club was formed in 1928 and played in the (Northern) Irish League from 1929 until the club's resignation in October 1972. During this period City achieved occasional successes – champions in 1965 and cupwinners in 1949, 1954 and 1964. Political conflict between the Protestant and Catholic populations in Northern Ireland intensified in 1968, whence we can date the deterioration and demise of Derry City in Northern Irish football. Platt (1986) reports that in November 1968 the attendance at a match versus Coleraine suffered because of a civil rights demonstration on the same day.

The start of the 1969–70 season was disrupted by serious civil disturbances in Derry. An annual Protestant Apprentice Boys' march along the walls of old Derry, which overlook the Catholic Bogside, was regarded as a provocation by the Catholics and sparked prolonged violent confrontation. The political end result was the formation of the Derry Citizens' Defence Association to police Catholic Free Derry and the declaration of a no-go area for the Royal Ulster Constabulary (RUC) and the British army in the Bogside. For Derry City the effect was that the Brandywell was now in the frontline. Irish League games were suspended at the Brandywell on the grounds of inadequate policing (by the RUC).

A ten-week period ensued without a first team match at the Brandywell lasting from the Ards match on 9 August to Cliftonville on 18 October (a reserve team match was played on 27 September). A compromise involving the use of military police was agreed to enable the Cliftonville match and other subsequent games in 1969–70 to go ahead at the Brandywell. An exception was predictably the scheduled game in April against the arch Protestant rivals Linfield from Belfast. Fear of retaliation for attacks on Derry fans in Belfast was given as the reason for postponement by the security authorities. The match against Linfield was played eventually in May but at Coleraine, which is 31 miles to the east. A poor attendance meant that the money taken failed to cover the minimum payment required to an away team. Financial problems were adding to Derry City's political problems.

It was not until the seventh game of the 1970–71 season that Derry City was allowed to play at Brandywell. Conflict between the club and the Irish League was again heightened by clashes (both football and political) with Linfield. City was scheduled to play Linfield away in November 1970 at Windsor Park in Belfast, the national stadium for the Northern Ireland national team as well as Linfield's home ground. Although the security authorities declared the game safe, Derry City refused to play at Windsor Park on the grounds of danger to the club's players and supporters. The Irish League's ruling on this match led many to question its impartiality in relation to Derry City. Derry's reasons for not playing were understood and accepted by the league, yet the match was awarded to Linfield and City had to pay £300 compensation to Linfield. In cases where other (Protestant) clubs refused to play at Brandywell, there was no similar ruling from the league.

Linfield continued to haunt Derry City in the 1970–71 season. The clubs met in the semi-final of the Irish cup at a neutral venue. City won the match to proceed to the final but there was fighting between rival supporters at the end. Despite the sensitive relationship between the two clubs, the Irish Football Association (IFA) insisted that the final be played at Windsor Park – the home of Linfield. In the media the 1971 final has been described as the silent final: the attendance was only 6,000 and a mere 180 Derry City fans travelled by train to Belfast. Unsurprisingly City meekly lost 0–3 to Distillery.

Derry City began 1971–72 by playing home matches at Brandywell but the reprieve was to be short-lived. A match against Ards on 2 September was played with most of the approaches to the ground behind the barricades of Free Derry. On 11 September 1971 the Ballymena United team bus was hijacked and burnt out by local youths, an event comparable with what was going on throughout Northern Ireland at this time. Security clearance was granted for the next home game but other clubs now refused to visit Brandywell and the ground was banned by the Irish League. The 0–1 defeat by Ballymena proved to be the last (Northern) Irish League game played at Brandywell.

Coleraine came to Derry City's aid by offering the use of The Showgrounds for home matches for the rest of the season. This stop-gap solution increased financial pressures on City. For instance the October home match against Cliftonville attracted a crowd of 100 to The Showgrounds. Derry City was not the only football club displaced from its home ground by the political situation. Distillery was forced to abandon Grosvenor Park in West Belfast and groundshare with Crusaders at Seaview Park in East Belfast. Distillery remained at Seaview

Park until 1979 when New Grosvenor Park was inaugurated 9 miles south in Lisburn.

The 1972–73 season began with a few optimistic signs for Derry City. On 16 August a friendly match was played at Brandywell against Finn Harps, a team from Ballybofey, County Donegal in the Republic of Ireland. Moreover regular greyhound racing had recommenced at the Brandywell stadium with no security problems. Most important of all was a statement by the security authorities that Brandywell was as safe as any other ground in Northern Ireland. However, as Curran (1986) accurately states, the Irish League decided that it knew better than local security experts about the the position in Derry and the ban on Irish League matches at Brandywell remained in force. To counter the optimistic signs mentioned above, it should be noted that the infamous Bloody Sunday, when British soldiers opened fire on civil rights marchers and killed thirteen people, had occurred in Derry in January 1972. As a result relations between the Catholic and Protestant communities had become polarized even further.

Other clubs continued to refuse to play at Brandywell and the league insisted that Derry City's home matches be played at Coleraine. Derry's response was to throw down the gauntlet with a 'No Brandywell No Match' statement. Two home matches in September came and went unplayed, but City did play its away fixtures. What was to prove the club's last ever Irish League match on 7 October was ironically against Distillery, the other club unable to play at home.

In an attempt to resolve the situation, a special meeting was called for 9 October to consider a proposal by Portadown FC that Derry be allowed to play at Brandywell. The vote went 5–6 against with Coleraine abstaining. Four days later, on 13 October, Derry City resigned from the Irish League citing as the main reason the continued refusal to permit matches at Brandywell despite security clearance. On 24 October an article in the *Derry Journal* suggested for the first time that an eventual solution might lie with the League of Ireland in the Republic of Ireland.

Derry City spent the next twelve years in limbo unable to take part in senior professional football. A conscious effort was made to keep the name of the club going, by retaining the social club and by entering a team into junior football via the Northwest Saturday Morning League. IFA membership was maintained until 1985 along with an annual rejection of the club's application to rejoin the Irish League. The repeated rejections were handed out in the context of continued security clearance for football matches at Brandywell. Clearly other clubs did not want Derry in the Irish League.

As the limbo years wore on, a growing number of people felt that a city the size of Derry should have a senior professional football club whatever the political situation. The initiative was taken up by four former players including Eddie Mahon (one of our interviewees) and the Derry City captain in October 1972. In March 1984 they formed a new independent club under the name of Derry Football Club. To show that they meant business, a match was played at Brandywell between Derry

FC and Shamrock Rovers from Dublin, which attracted a healthy crowd of 4,000. The consortium first considered applying to join the Scottish League on the grounds that the Larne–Stranraer ferry provided cheap and accessible transportation to Scotland. Soundings were taken from the Scottish FA but the latter, fearing the exportation of 'the Northern Ireland problem', gave no encouragement to Derry FC.

Turning to the Republic of Ireland next, a press conference was held in Dublin to publicize the case of Derry FC. Several leading politicians and journalists attended the conference (Eamon Dunphy, the former international footballer and current journalist, was influential in this regard) but only one League of Ireland club, St Patricks Athletic. Worried by the possible success of the rival club, Derry City had asked League of Ireland clubs not to attend. A common view emerged that the kind of security problems associated with (Catholic–Protestant) Irish League matches would not arise in relation to (all-Catholic) League of Ireland matches.

Derry FC presented the case for inclusion to the League of Ireland annual general meeting in 1984 and met with some encouragement. However, the league wished to defer a decision until sounding out the views of the (Northern) Irish FA, within whose boundaries Derry is located, and also of UEFA. Fran Fields, the chairman of Finn Harps from nearby Donegal, played a central role in arguing Derry's case within the League of Ireland. As soon as there were signs of possible success for Derry FC, the issue was complicated by Derry City FC suddenly deciding also to apply for the League of Ireland. The increasingly delicate situation was progressed in August 1984 by an initial meeting between the League of Ireland and the Irish League, the outcome of which was an agreement to discuss the matter further after a period of deliberation.

Eventually the Irish League gave permission only for Derry City to apply for the League of Ireland as a special case. Under UEFA rules the League of Ireland is obliged to accept the decision of its neighbouring FA with jurisdiction over the place in question, and therefore at this point the application of Derry FC was doomed. In October 1984 Derry FC withdrew its application and the consortium effectively placed their resources behind the bid of Derry City FC. At the May 1985 League of Ireland annual general meeting, Derry City was duly elected into a new second division, actually called the First Division but located beneath a Premier Division.

By granting permission to Derry City to apply for the League of Ireland, the Irish League did not wish to set a precedent for other Northern Irish clubs. The nature of the special case was that the (Northern) Irish Football Association could not offer professional football in Derry because of the political conflict. Thus the club should be allowed to seek senior football across the border. The specificity of the Derry City case was confirmed in later years when the League of Ireland twice rejected applications from Donegal Celtic, which comes from Catholic West Belfast; it was ruled that senior professional football is already available in Belfast under the auspices of the IFA.

Derry City was reborn into the League of Ireland on 8 September 1985. A crowd of 8,000 saw City beat Home Farm of Dublin 3–1 at the Brandywell. The revived club unleashed a tremendous burst of enthusiasm in its first few seasons in the Irish League, not only due to the novelty value but also acting as an outlet for a repressed population in previous years. Initially Derry City was accompanied into the Republic for away matches by a travelling army of 3,000 fans, who were regarded as a breath of fresh air in League of Ireland football. Those who predicted trouble were disappointed as the supporters developed a reputation for good behaviour and a sporting attitude.

An interesting feature of the politics of football in this reborn era is that since 1985 there has been no official police presence in Brandywell and there have been no violent incidents at the ground. A policy of self-policing has been adopted: the presence of RUC in Brandywell is of itself liable to encourage violence. Success has been forthcoming also on the field of play with promotion to the Premier Division in 1987, the league and cup double in 1989, and cupwinners again in 1995. This success has brought entry into Europe as representatives of the League of Ireland. UEFA rules require a police presence at European matches. At Brandywell this situation has been diplomatically handled by stationing the police in the vicinity of the ground (one suspects just outside Free Derry) available to be summoned if necessary, but they never are.

What of the future? The peace process set in motion by the ceasefire of 1994 has led some to debate the possibility of a return to Northern Irish football. However, the majority of supporters are against a return for three main reasons: first, the fact that City was forced out of the Irish League by the other clubs still rankles; second, the decades of political conflict have nurtured deep-seated feelings of animosity which may take a generation or more to subside; and third, to play in the Republic is a political statement representing many fans' desire for a united Ireland. Some supporters refuse to attend even a friendly match against a team from the north.

Among local business people and club sponsors, there is less opposition to a return to the north. In economic terms the costs of playing in the north are lower. League of Ireland matches are played on a Sunday (unlike the Irish League on Saturdays) which is a difficult day for travelling long distances. Journeys to play in Cork or Cobh involve an overnight stay, which adds markedly to running costs.

Some envisage the continuation of the peace process leading to an All Ireland League combining the best teams from north and south. A higher profile and standard of play for the bigger clubs would provide increased income to offset the higher costs involved. Rugby Union and Gaelic Football have maintained All Ireland competitions despite the political division of the island. Opposition to an All Ireland League may come from the officials on both sides who have the most to lose in a united association. A cautious interviewee suggested 2010 for the All Ireland

League if the peace process is maintained. Should it not be maintained, an alternative option for Derry City would be to build a new stadium just over the border in the Republic thereby officially coming under the jurisdiction of the FAI.

Refugees on either side of the border: the case of Cyprus

The existence of refugee football clubs in Cyprus dates from the 1974 Turkish invasion of the island, which resulted in a *de facto* partition into the Turkish north (roughly one-third) and the Greek south (roughly two-thirds). In November 1983 the north declared itself a fully independent nation as the Turkish Republic of Northern Cyprus. However, thus far the fledgling state has been recognized only by Turkey and ignored by the rest of the world. As a result the *Kibris Türk Futbol Federasyoni* (Cyprus Turkish Football Federation) is similarly unrecognized by and ostracized from world football.

Conflict between the Greek Cypriot and Turkish Cypriot communities began to escalate towards the end of the period of British colonial rule (1878–1960). In 1954 militant Greeks founded EOKA (*Ethniki Organosis Kyprion Agonistan*) to fight for *enosis* (union with Greece). In 1955 EOKA began a campaign of violence which was directed at both the British military presence and the Turkish minority. Not surprisingly the Turkish Cypriot community responded in 1958 by forming TMT (*Türk Mudafaa Teskilati*: Turkish Defence Organization) whose aim was *taksim* or partition of the island between the two communities.

Repercussions from the political conflict on the island's football clubs first appeared in 1955. In response to the EOKA campaign the Turkish Cypriot clubs withdrew from the national league (comprising both Greek and Turkish clubs) and formed a separate league for Turkish clubs only. Even the most successful Turkish club, Chetin Kaya Turkish Sports Club, took this action because it considered its players and supporters to be in danger.

Full independence for the Republic of Cyprus in 1960 did not resolve the conflict between the two communities. The demand for *enosis* remained among certain sections of the Greek community. A bizarre expression of this tendency emerged in the football world with the (Greek) Cypriot league champions playing (the following season) in the Greek national league first division.

Olympiakos Nicosia were the first to do this in season 1967–68 and Apoel Nicosia were the last in 1973–74. In football terms the results were hardly spectacular. Out of the eighteen teams in the Greek first division the champions of Cyprus finished eighteenth four times, seventeenth twice and thirteenth once (Apoel in the last season).

The main political impact on Greek Cypriot football came with the 1974 Turkish invasion and resultant partition of the island. It is estimated that 165,000 Greek Cypriots fled to the south in the wake of the invasion. Among the refugees were the officials, supporters and players of several

Greek Cypriot football clubs from the Turkish occupied north. Hence the phenomenon of refugee football clubs was born in which clubs continued to exist and play at new locations across the partition from their home towns. Subsequent detailed material on this case study was obtained from a combination of official published sources and interviews with key officials and informants. Particular thanks are due to Adonis Procopiou of the (Greek) Cyprus Football Association, Olgun Üstün and Memdah Asaf Sohak of the Cyprus Turkish Football Federation, Paris Menelaou, a freelance journalist, Haris Christoforou of the *Cyprus Mail*, Yiannakis Papatheodorou, the general manager of Anorthosis Famagusta, and Diofantos Chrysostomou, the president of Nea Salamina Famagusta.

Table 5.1 documents the number of refugee clubs in the leading divisions of Cypriot football. There are refugee clubs on both sides of the partition, which is policed by the United Nations and has taken on an increasing air of permanence since the mid-1970s. For each refugee club both the original home and the current location are listed.

To the south, the official Greek Cypriot league recognized by UEFA contains three refugee clubs in the first division, four in the second division, and three in the fourth division. Most famous are the two clubs from Famagusta – Anorthosis the 1994–95 league champions and Nea

Table 5.1   **Refugee clubs in the leading Cypriot divisions**

A Greek clubs playing in the south

Division	Name of club	Original home	Current location
1	Anorthosis Club	Famagusta	Larnaca
1	Nea Salamina	Famagusta	Larnaca
1	Ethnikos Akhna	Akhna	Akhna
2	Dighenis Akritas	Morphou	Nicosia
2	Doxa	Katokopia	Peristerina
2	PAEEK	Kyrenia	Nicosia
2	Ethnikos Ashas	Asha	Strovolos
4	AEK	Kythrea	Aglangia
4	Asil	Lysi	Larnaca
4	Heracklis	Yeroklakkou	Strovolos

B Turkish clubs playing in the north

Division	Name of club	Original home	Current location
1	Dogan Türk Birligi	Limassol	Kyrenia
1	Gencler Birligi	Limassol	Famagusta
1	Türk Ogaci Limasol	Limassol	Kyrenia
1	Baf Ülkü Yurdu	Paphos	Morphou
2	Y Bogazici	Alaminos	Famagusta
2	Binatli Yilmaz	Paphos	Morphou
3	Beyarmudu	Dhekelia	Famagusta
3	Pile	Pyla	Famagusta

Salamina the 1990 cupwinners. The settlement of Akhna is divided by the partition and the Greek football club Ethnikos has moved ground from the Turkish north to the Greek south.

To the north the unofficial Turkish Cypriot league (unrecognized by UEFA) includes four refugee clubs in the first division, two in the second division, and two in the third division. The two most successful refugee clubs have been Dogan Türk Birligi SK (champions six times) and Baf Ülkü Yurdu SK (champions four times).

On both sides of the partition the governments have actively subsidized the continued existence of the refugee clubs. In the south, the Cyprus Sports Organization has given support to refugee clubs for the construction of a new stadium, a new stand or a new social club. A political decision was taken to assist the refugee clubs as political symbols of lost towns and villages to the north of the partition. Subsidies for new stand construction from the Cyprus Sports Organization constitute 50 per cent of funds for refugee clubs compared with 33 per cent for other clubs.

Although the Greek Cypriot government has aided refugee clubs in general to survive, relative success in football terms is based more on economic factors. Anorthosis Famagusta have been the most successful of the refugee clubs in the south thanks to their wealthy backers. Prior to the 1974 invasion, Anorthosis was a wealthy club with sponsors involved in the Famagusta hotel and tourist businesses. The tourism-inspired financial revival in the south enabled many of these families to recover their wealth and Anorthosis benefited as a result. By contrast Dighenis Akritas from Morphou was sponsored by the owners of the surrounding citrus orchards and strawberry fields. It was not possible to re-establish these forms of enterprise in the south and along with its sponsors, Dighenis Akritas has descended in recent years to the second and third divisions.

Most of the support for refugee clubs in the south comes from refugees from the north and their offspring, who maintain the family tradition. Similarly, most of the sponsors are business people from that particular home town or village. Only Anorthosis has attracted significant new support in Larnaca because of its recent success. Nonetheless the registered members of Anorthosis reflect the predominance of former refugees from Famagusta spread throughout the south: 40 per cent of members are from Larnaca, 35 per cent from Limassol and 10 per cent from Nicosia.

A distinctive feature of football in the Greek south is that only the refugee clubs own their stadiums. All the other clubs play in one of the many municipal grounds, which are shared by teams in the town. The refugees do not feel themselves to be fully part of the municipality and therefore prefer to have their own identity in their own stadium. Furthermore, even without the refugee clubs there is pressure on the municipal pitches owing to the number of teams playing on them each weekend.

Anorthosis Famagusta was the first club to have its own private stadium in Larnaca in 1981. The Stadion Antonis Papadopoulos has been

expanded to a 9,400 all-seater arena. Famagusta's other refugee club –
Nea Salamina – opened its own stadium in Larnaca in 1990. Stadion
Ammokhostos (Greek for Famagusta) has a 5,000 capacity and is located
only 1 kilometre from the Anorthosis ground. Asil Lysi also has its own
Stadion Kamares in Larnaca. PAEEK of Kyrenia opened a new ground
in Nicosia in 1994.

In the Turkish Republic of North Cyprus, the economy has been less
developed since the partition. As a result all the football clubs are
amateur and all the stadiums are municipally owned. In addition, both
the country and the football federation are recognized only by Turkey.
Football isolation on the island is relieved occasionally by matches
against Turkish amateur teams.

Despite these disadvantages, the government in the north has, like its
counterpart in the south, provided government aid to refugee clubs. The
Ministry of Sport subsidizes improvements to facilities at grounds and
the purchase of equipment such as nets and balls. Also, some promising
footballers are employed in government services in order to assist their
development. Finally, refugee clubs may seek financial assistance from
the national lottery.

One of the most poignant effects of the political conflict in Cyprus on
football has been the isolation and forced relocation of Chetin Kaya
Turkish Sports Club in Nicosia. Chetin Kaya TSC had a highly
successful period in the early 1950s becoming the only Turkish club to
ever win all Cyprus trophies. Given that the Turkish minority comprised
less than 20 per cent of the population at the time, the club's performance
in winning the league championship in 1951 and the cup twice (in 1952
and 1954) was impressive.

Many of the older generation of players and supporters talk with great
fondness of the epic encounters between Chetin Kaya and the leading
Greek clubs such as Apoel Nicosia and AEL Limassol. The commencement of EOKA's campaign of violence in 1955 resulted in Chetin Kaya
and other Turkish clubs retreating into a league for Turkish clubs only.
In this small pond Chetin Kaya has had its successes as league
champions five times and cupwinners twelve times but they were
achieved in isolation from the wider football world of European
competition.

A further problem for Chetin Kaya has been the location of the club's
ground on the frontline between the two communities in Nicosia. The
club had to abandon its traditional ground in 1963 because of the dangers
of sniper fire for both players and spectators. Currently the overgrown
ground is located within the United Nations buffer zone in Nicosia.
Along the only crossing point in Nicosia between the divided communities is (to the left of the road heading north) the high-rise Ledra Palace
Hotel, which serves as the United Nations headquarters and accom-
modation. To the right of the road beneath the old walls of Nicosia lies
the former Chetin Kaya ground. Some United Nations personnel use the
overgrown terraces for jogging.

The highest profile achieved by the refugee clubs in European football has undoubtedly been the appearance of the two Famagusta clubs in European competitions. Nea Salamina won the cup in 1990 and therefore represented Cyprus in the European Cup Winners' Cup in 1990–91 losing both home and away legs to Aberdeen (representing Scotland). In 1995 Anorthosis Famagusta won the league championship and entered the European Cup in 1995–96 to encounter another Scottish opponent, Glasgow Rangers. This tie was much closer with Rangers winning 1–0 on aggregate.

The two Famagusta clubs playing in Larnaca have a shared refugee status but also exemplify a political contrast of a different kind. Nea Salamina is left wing in political orientation and its current president, Diofantos Chrysostomou, is a communist deputy in the House of Representatives. Greek Cypriot society was sharply polarized into left and right by the civil war on mainland Greece in 1948. Nea Salamina was founded in that year in opposition to the right-wing Anorthosis Famagusta. Similar splits occurred in other towns in 1948, most notably left-wing Omonia Nicosia formed as a breakaway from right-wing Apoel Nicosia, and left-wing Alki Larnaca founded to counter right-wing EPA Larnaca. For a period of five years until the 1953–54 season separate right-wing and left-wing leagues operated – such was the strength of the passions generated.

These political divisions although still in existence are now taken less seriously. As Greek Cypriot football has become more professional with increasing sponsorship money, so the political element has decreased in importance. Nea Salamina currently operates an open membership policy with no restrictions. Most of the club's 500 full members are left-wing in orientation but there are notable exceptions. Significantly, most of the members originate from Famagusta rather than the current location Larnaca.

Despite the political divide, Nea Salamina enjoys good relations with Anorthosis: both are refugee clubs from Famagusta. Nea Salamina regard the club (social and football) as playing an important role in keeping refugees close to their home town and connecting the next generation of children with Famagusta. The good relations between the clubs were confirmed by Anorthosis allowing Nea Salamina to share its new stadium for a five-year period up until 1990. Prior to this Nea Salamina played at various grounds in Limassol, Larnaca and Dherinia, and afterwards the club moved into its own new Stadion Ammokhostos; this cost 330,000 Cyprus pounds, 30 per cent of which was covered by government subsidy.

In contrast to Nea Salamina, Anorthosis is right wing in political orientation with wealthy backers including the president Kikis Constantinou, who is a luxury hotel owner. The club was founded in 1911 and initially its main activity was cultural, including running a famous mandolin group. Gradually sport became more important; in addition to football the club currently has successful men's and women's volleyball teams. The Anorthosis logo is a phoenix rising from the ashes, an image redolent with political symbolism. Some of the club's members were formerly EOKA leaders including Antonis Papadopoulos, after whom the new stadium is named. Unlike Nea Salamina, membership of Anorthosis is not open but status based. Qualification rules are complex and a prospective new member must be sponsored by some of the current 1,300 members. Anorthosis remains a powerful social and political club and maintains social clubs in Limassol and Nicosia as well as Larnaca.

Anorthosis views the role of the club as keeping members and Famagusta close together, acting as a symbol of refugees from Famagusta. An official club brochure states that 'the club and its supporters together with the citizens of Famagusta became refugees within their own country' after the 1974 invasion. Inside the ground on a whitewashed wall above the entrance to the changing rooms is a mural depicting the partition of the island of Cyprus with blood dripping from the borderline. A Turkish knife is stuck into the borderline and points down, presumably unintentionally, to the referee's changing room!

Officials of Anorthosis regard the sporting teams (football and volleyball) as important in enabling the name of their home town (with its Greek connotation) to be heard throughout Europe. Hence the delight at the club's two matches against Glasgow Rangers in 1995, which were shown on television all over Europe. The impression given was that this was more important than actually winning the tie.

In the years following the Turkish invasion, Anorthosis led a nomadic existence playing home matches in Akhna 1974–75, Limassol 1975–76, Nicosia 1976–77, Akhna again 1977–79, the Zenon (municipal) stadium in Larnaca 1979–81, before settling into the Antonis Papadopoulos stadium in Larnaca in 1981. The latter was the first privately owned stadium in Cyprus and remains to this day the most impressive of its kind on the island. The total cost to date of developing all four sides of the ground is 1 million Cyprus pounds, one-quarter of which has been met by government subsidy.

Despite the difficulties encountered since 1974, Anorthosis Famagusta has recovered to re-emerge as one of the leading football clubs in Cyprus. Prior to the invasion Anorthosis had been league champions six times. During the nomadic years of frequent ground changes, the club managed to remain in the first division. Once a permanent base was secured, the next priority became development of the stadium and its facilities. The final stage which involved investing in players for the football team came to fruition with the league championship in 1994–95. Nevertheless the ultimate aim remains to return to the home town of Famagusta and to the original club ground, the GSE Stadion. The same objective could be attributed to all the refugee clubs, particularly in the south, but the stability of the partition as years go by makes this unlikely.

Football as Extension of the State

Red Star Dynamo Lokomotiv Torpedo FC: Football in Eastern Europe

The most important cleavage in world politics in the twentieth century was undoubtedly that between the communist bloc under the leadership of the former Union of Soviet Socialist Republics and the Western capitalist bloc under the leadership of the United States of America. Following the Russian revolution in 1917 and the ensuing civil war, the Soviet Union was founded in 1922. The new socialist political and economic system was a direct challenge to the capitalist economic system and the multi-party politics of the West. All aspects of Soviet society were to be radically transformed, including sport.

After the Second World War the Soviet Union expanded its sphere of influence into Eastern Europe. The established Soviet political and economic model, including the socialist organization of sport, was imposed on the new communist states in Eastern Europe. This iron curtain across Europe was to last until the year of Eastern European 'revolutions' in 1989. More than forty years of Eastern European football were played under the socialist model of sport. Football was both a part of, and a reflection of, the socialist state.

Included in this category were Czechoslovakia, Hungary, Poland, Romania, Bulgaria, Yugoslavia, Albania and the former German Democratic Republic (now part of a reunited Germany). Since 1989 Czechoslovakia has split into independent Czech and Slovak republics, and Yugoslavia (though still in existence) has lost control of the breakaway republics of Croatia, Slovenia, Macedonia and Bosnia-Hercegovina. Furthermore, there are now fifteen independent republics instead of the Soviet Union.

During the period of communist control, what the countries of Eastern Europe had in common in politico-economic terms was their adherence to some form of state socialist society. Among the main ingredients of such a society were a system of central planning of all aspects of the economy (including facilities for sport and the wages of full-time sports players); a meshing of the ruling communist party and the state such that all manner of appointments were subject to political influence (including officials in sports organizations and football clubs); an official ideology espousing the historical role of the proletariat and the predominant position of working-class organizations (including the linking of football clubs – and sports clubs in general – to party and worker organizations).

Football in Eastern Europe before socialism

Prior to the Russian revolution, football had made an appearance in Tsarist Russia. It was first played in the 1880s but its development was retarded by a combination of political circumstances and the harsh winter climate. Two English brothers, Harry and Clement Charnock, formed a team at the Morozov cotton mills in Orekhovo in 1887. The team played in a set of Blackburn Rovers shirts imported from England. By 1906 the club was renamed Orekhovo SK and later, as part of the socialist reorganization in 1923, became Dynamo Moscow.

Football in Tsarist Russia was predominantly a pastime for the privileged classes, although an entrance was made onto the international stage in 1912. The October Revolution in 1917 and the ensuing civil war postponed further development of organized football before leading to a restructuring along socialist lines. Although there had been city leagues in St Petersburg and Moscow at the turn of the century, there was no national league in the Soviet Union until 1936.

Elsewhere in Eastern Europe, football had a longer period of independent development prior to the communist era and in some cases even predates the existence of some of the present day nation-states. As a result of this earlier development, the imposition of socialist organization of sport represented a more profound break with existing football traditions. Football was introduced to the Habsburg empire in Central Europe initially in Vienna by English expatriates in the 1890s with the first recorded match in 1894. The game spread quickly to Budapest and Prague such that the three cities became the first focus of organized football in central Europe. British coaches were influential in the period prior to the First World War such as Edgar Chadwick, formerly of Everton, in Prague.

Hungary and Czechoslovakia (Bohemia before the First World War) were early in founding a football association (both 1901), affiliating with FIFA (both 1906) and competing in international matches (1902 and 1903 respectively). Some of the earliest Hungarian teams were in fact football sections added to gymnastic clubs in the 1890s, for example Ujpest TE and MTK in Budapest. The Hungarian League began quickly in 1901, though all the teams in it were from Budapest until 1926. Immediately prior to the First World War, Hungarian football was already semi-professional.

Towards the end of the nineteenth century, similar beginnings were evident in Bohemia with the setting up of football sections of multi-sport clubs in Prague. The two leading football clubs to this day were formed in this way – Sparta Prague in 1894 and Slavia Prague in 1896. A league for Prague clubs began in 1896 but the Czechoslovak League did not appear until 1925. Even then the league was dominated by Bohemian clubs with no Moravian club participating in the first division until 1933 and no Slovak club until 1935. During 1939–44 Slovakia (an independent state allied to Nazi Germany) played international matches and ran its own national league. Both recommenced recently in 1993.

Both Hungary and Bohemia were included on the itinerary for England's first ever foreign tour in 1908. Both were defeated – Hungary 7–0 and Bohemia 4–0. This early development of organized football and allied international success ultimately led to both countries introducing professional football in the 1920s – Czechoslovakia in 1925 and Hungary in 1926. Professional footballers from both countries were much in demand in the inter-war period and their export became a lucrative business. For instance, playing in the French League during the period 1932–39 were fifty-nine Hungarians and forty-three Czechoslovaks, totals bettered only by English and Austrians. The growing prowess of both national teams was demonstrated by the England tour of 1934. Both of them defeated England 2–1.

After a century of partition into areas controlled by Austria, Prussia and Russia, Poland was re-established as an independent state in 1918. Football developed initially in the Austrian part largely because any form of popular organization was regarded with political suspicion in the Russian and Prussian domains. As a result Kraków became the pioneer of Polish football. Two of the oldest surviving clubs originated here, namely Cracovia and Wisla Kraków, both in 1906. In the Tsarist part of modern Poland, Lódz displayed the first stirring of football activity. Here some Englishmen involved in manufacturing created the first team. To this day two of the leading clubs are from Lódz, LKS being formed in 1908 and Widzew in 1910. After the renewed political independence of Poland, organized football developed rapidly with the founding of the Polish FA in 1919, introduction of a national championship in 1921 and the first international match in the same year.

Foreign workers in Bucharest introduced football into Romania in the 1890s. The main nationalities involved were British, Belgian, Dutch and German. By the turn of the century, teams had been formed at the Colentina textile works and the Standard Oil Company of Ploesti. At this time, football in Romania was played and organized mainly by foreigners. The first national champions, Olimpia Bucharest in 1910, had several British players in their team. Only after the First World War did Romanians take over the game. Romania's late affiliation with FIFA in 1930 and instant entry in the inaugural 1930 World Cup in Uruguay (one of only four European countries to attend) were the direct result of King Carol's passion for football. The king personally picked the players for the World Cup and also 'arranged' time off work for them with their employers.

Football is reputed to have been introduced into Bulgaria by a Swiss physical education teacher in Varna. As a result Varna became the hotbed of Bulgarian football in the early years. The oldest surviving clubs date from just before the First World War such as Botev Plovdiv and Cherno More Varna 1912, Slavia Sofia 1913 and Levski Sofia 1914. Organized football in Bulgaria was finally established in the 1920s. A Sofia league began in 1921, followed by a national championship in 1925 and a fully fledged national league in 1937.

In other parts of the Balkans, football's development was arrested by political conflict in the region, which culminated in the First World War. Yugoslavia as an independent state was not created until 1919. A football association was formed immediately, and a national league followed in 1923. The oldest club (now in Croatia) is Hajduk Split, formed in 1911. Hajduk refers to local resistance fighters against the Ottoman Empire. Organized football did not develop in Albania until 1930, and lasted only until 1938 when Italy invaded and annexed the country.

Political importance of football in Eastern Europe

Sport was accorded a high profile in the communist bloc. The political importance of sport lay in its potential for demonstrating the superiority of communism over capitalism by winning more trophies. Superiority must however be guaranteed. For a long while the Soviet Union pursued an isolationist policy in relation to international football competitions. Their first appearance in Olympic football was not until 1952 and they did not enter the World Cup until the qualifying tournament for 1958. Predictably a political explanation lay behind this. The Soviet Union did not wish to enter the world arena until it felt confident of performing successfully and indeed had a good chance of winning trophies. The World Cup quarter-finals were reached at the first attempt in Sweden in 1958.

In the other countries of Eastern Europe, the national team has played an important role in national consciousness from the very beginning of football. In the inter-war period, many of the countries of Eastern Europe were either new or reconstituted nations. As such football provided an opportunity for crystallizing nationalist sentiment in an era before the penetration of modern mass media. Also many of the early international matches in the region tended to be against near neighbours, thereby stoking the flames of popular nationalism.

The national football teams retained a prominent position in the hearts and minds of the nation during the communist years. Support for the national team could easily be construed as support for the regime. Moreover international sport was a key arena in which to demonstrate the strength and superiority of socialism. It is for this reason that the Olympic Games football competition was taken so seriously by the communist countries, leading to a period of complete dominance from 1952 to 1976. Among the attributes advocated and adhered to by Eastern European teams of the early communist period were an ethos of good sportsmanship (thereby demonstrating the pre-eminence of socialist man) and an emphasis on teamwork (thus confirming the superiority of collectivism). The national legends at this time were more likely to be teams rather than individuals.

The strength and invincibility of Dynamo Moscow in 1945 provided the first legendary team to emerge under communism. In order to celebrate allied victory over Nazi Germany, the Russian team came on a tour of Britain in November 1945. This visit occurred during a long period of Soviet isolation from international competition which made them an unknown quantity. Four matches were played, of which Dynamo won two and the other two were drawn. The quality of the Russian play impressed the many spectators who flocked to see them. About 82,000 saw the first game, a 3–3 draw with Chelsea, and 45,000 witnessed the 10–1 demolition of Cardiff City. The 4–3 win over Arsenal was watched by 54,000 and a further 90,000 attended the 2–2 draw with Glasgow Rangers. After the impressive display against Cardiff, the Russians were regarded in the press not as a football team but as a machine. Their style of play was to British eyes unusual, based on accurate passing along the ground, subtle interchanging of position and above all else teamwork. The mystique was heightened by their bizarre (at the time) kit including long baggy blue shorts with a white rim at the base. The legend was enhanced by the circumstances of the victory over Arsenal, who fielded England's star winger Stanley Matthews as a guest player. This match was played at Tottenham Hotspur's White Hart Lane ground in a veritable pea-souper fog (of the kind now seen only in Hammer horror films) and controlled by a Russian referee and two Russian linesmen, who policed a half each but both on the same side of the pitch. Upon their return to the Soviet Union all the members of the team were made Heroes of the Soviet Union.

In the first half of the 1950s, the Hungarian national team provided the second legendary team. Known as the 'Magic Magyars', Hungary lost only one game in almost six years covering a total of forty-eight games. Its misfortune was that the one defeat came in the 1954 World Cup final against Germany, a team it had already beaten 8–3 in an earlier round of the tournament. However, the run of victories did include winning the 1952 Olympic gold medal. Undoubtedly the status of this Hungarian team was increased by its performances against England. In November 1953 Hungary dispelled the myth of English invulnerability by winning 6–3 at Wembley, the first home defeat for England against foreign opposition. Next year in Budapest the difference in quality between the two sides was confirmed emphatically in a 7–1 scoreline. In terms of playing style the Hungarians combined individual brilliance with collective skills, relied on finesse rather than force to dominate a match and introduced the tactical innovation of the deep-lying centre forward. Sadly the 1956 Hungarian uprising against Soviet domination led to the breakup of the side with three of the leading players (including perhaps the best of them all Ferenc Puskas, the 'galloping major', who played for the army team Honved) defecting to the West.

In the communist era, the presentation of sport in the press and media comprised only officially approved coverage, including strong support for the national football team in the hope that success on the field would reflect beneficially on the regime. All Eastern European socialist republics had a national daily sports paper (such as *Ceskoslovensky Sport* in Prague and *Nep Sport* in Budapest) in which football was given a high profile. An interesting feature of the coverage during this period was the complete invisibility of defected sports stars, including footballers, in the national press. Even where such individuals were highly successful in the West, their performances were never mentioned.

Sport's high status in the communist era is exemplified in the set of national stadiums constructed in the 1950s (Prague is the exception to this with Strahov dating back to the 1930s). Most of them remain large all-seater venues perhaps lacking in Western comforts but certainly grand in scale. The most important are Budapest's Nepstadion (72,000), Sofia's Vasilij Levski Stadion (55,000), Bucharest's 23 August Stadionul (65,000), Chorzow's Slaski Stadion (70,000) and Moscow's Centralny (formerly Lenin) Stadion (100,000). The independent republics of Ukraine and Georgia have large all-seater national grounds in Kiev (100,000) and Tbilisi (74,000) respectively.

Total state control of sporting activity resulted in regular political interference in the organization of the national team. In some respects this situation was to the benefit of the national team, which could demand all the players and resources desired. The common scenario in the West of disputes between leading clubs and the national team over the availability of players was just not an issue in the East. The club versus country debate was always decided in favour of the national team.

An extreme example of interference in national team selection and administration occurred in the Soviet Union in the mid-1970s. After Dynamo Kiev became the first Soviet club side to win a European club trophy, the authorities declared that the club's players *en masse* were to become the Soviet Union national team for the next two years. This experiment was ultimately unsuccessful in that the pressures of appearing as both a club and a national side took their toll on the players' performance. In a similar vein, the Romanian FA installed the under-18 national team in the first division championship as Viitorul Bucharest for two seasons from 1961 to 1963. Many observers have argued that the achievements of the Soviet Union national team have not matched its undoubted potential. In the World Cup the Soviet Union never progressed beyond the semi-final stage, which was achieved in England in 1966. However the Soviet Union had a strong record of success in the other major events. It struck Olympic gold twice in 1956 and 1988, won the first European championship in 1960 and was runner-up in it three times (1964, 1972 and 1988).

The rest of Eastern Europe has a distinguished football pedigree, with a record of success in the World Cup, the Olympics and the European Championship. It has provided the runners-up in the World Cup final four times (Czechoslovakia and Hungary twice each), the winners of the Olympic football gold seven times and the silver nine times, plus one victory and three runners-up in the European Championship. Czechoslovakia and Hungary were among Europe's football elite in the inter-war period; they have also had their successes under communism. Both countries fall within the Donauschule tradition (along with Austria) of football with an emphasis on passing and high technical skill.

On two occasions Czechoslovakia has reached the World Cup final only to lose both times. In 1934 it lost in extra time to the host nation Italy after spurning chances to clinch the match in normal time. Its second final in Chile in 1962 was lost 1–3 to the great Brazilian team including Pele. Czechoslovakia has won the Olympic gold in 1980 and lost in the final twice – 1920 and 1964. In the former case it was never awarded the silver medal after walking off the field against Belgium (the host country) before the end of the match when 0–2 down. Czechoslovakia's other notable triumph was to win the European Championship in 1976. It is generally agreed that there have been three great Czechoslovak national sides: the 1930s team (World Cup finalists in 1934), the early 1960s team (World Cup finalists in 1962 and based heavily on the army team Dukla Prague) and the 1976 European champions.

Hungary has an identical World Cup record to Czechoslovakia in the sense of reaching but losing two World Cup finals. The 1938 final was lost to the World Cup holders Italy and in 1954 the 'Magic Magyars' surprisingly lost to Germany. Hungary also has a good record in Olympic football, winning the gold three times (1952, 1964 and 1968) and the silver in 1972. There have been three great Hungarian national sides: the first was immediately prior to the First World War and the second in the 1930s reached the World Cup final. The last great Hungarian team was the 'Magic Magyars' of the 1950s. Since the mid-1970s Hungarian football has fallen below its previous high standards and as yet the decline shows no sign of abating. Failure to qualify for USA 1994 was known early in the qualifying competition.

Yugoslavia has reached the semi-finals of the World Cup on two occasions, once before communism (1930) and once during (1962). Yugoslav successes include being Olympic runner-up three times, runner-up in the European Championship in 1968 and semi-finalists in the European Championship in 1976. By contrast, Albania has been singularly unsuccessful in never qualifying for the final stages of the World Cup or European Championship.

Three countries in Eastern Europe – Poland, Bulgaria and Romania – have seemingly benefited from the communist reorganization of football.

Poland achieved little in the way of football success in the pre-communist period. The one great Polish team emerged in the 1970s; it came third in two World Cups (1974 and 1982), won the Olympic gold in 1972 and the silver in 1976. Following the team's last success of 1982, many players moved to the West. The Poles were runners-up in the 1992 Olympics.

Bulgaria benefited from improved training facilities and technical standards under communism; its only major success, however, was to win the Olympic silver in 1968. Bulgaria achieved its best run in the World Cup by qualifying for four consecutive final tournaments between 1962 and 1974. Since 1989 Bulgaria achieved its best ever performance in the World Cup by reaching the semi-finals in 1994.

Romania's overall standard of play improved under communism, although the national team has had no major successes in international football. Romania has qualified for the final stages of the World Cup on five occasions, but three were in the early days of the competition in the 1930s. During the same period they won the Balkan Cup more times than any of their neighbours. The biggest triumph for Romanian football under communism was by the club side, Steaua Bucharest, which won the European Champions' Cup for clubs in 1986. Like Bulgaria, Romania's best ever performance in the World Cup was in 1994, when it reached the quarter-finals.

Socialist organization of sport

Total reorganization of sport along socialist lines was undertaken in the Soviet Union in the 1920s; this then became the role model for the other communist countries of Eastern Europe after the Second World War. The new sports structure emphasized the historical role of the working class and was based on multi-sports clubs for worker organizations. Sport was seen as part of the cultural emancipation of the working class. Most of the key elements in the socialist organization of sport remained intact until the late 1980s in Eastern Europe.

The communist model of sport was opposed to professionalism, which was associated with decadent capitalism. Top-level players were not professionals, but were registered as employees of the organization which sponsored their club. In practice they trained and performed as full-time 'professional' sportsmen. The Union of European Football Associations (UEFA) classified Eastern European players in a hybrid category as neither professionals (in the commercial sense) nor amateurs (in the part-time sense). In 1988 UEFA altered the status of footballers in Czechoslovakia and Hungary to full-time professionals, returning them to the same position as the inter-war period.

Football clubs under communism were usually part of multi-sports clubs, which were sponsored by a factory, enterprise, ministry or trade union. Many of the leading clubs were sponsored by heavy industrial enterprises such as chemicals, steel and engineering. In Czechoslovakia, Banik Ostrava was sponsored by the miners' trade union and Plastika Nitra by a plastics factory; in Hungary, Tatabánya was backed by a coal-mining company and Raba Györ by a locomotive manufacturer; the Lokomotiv clubs in Moscow, Sofia, Plovdiv and Dresden were sponsored by the rail workers' union and Torpedo Moscow by car workers.

A major feature of the Eastern European leagues was the presence of powerful clubs funded by the army. The original was CSKA Moscow (previously CDKA and CDSA). Some of the army clubs were new creations, going straight into the national first division such as Dukla Prague (originally ATK), Steaua Bucharest (previously CCA), CSKA Sofia (originally CDNA) and Red Star Belgrade. Others were transplanted into existing clubs. Legia Warsaw was founded in 1916, but became the army club only after the Second World War. In Budapest the army club Honvéd took over the ground and identity of AC Kispest.

Compulsory national service gave the army clubs the pick of young players, and talented individuals were induced to remain in the army by an attractive offer to do nothing other than play football full-time. Not surprisingly the army clubs tended to be the most successful: CSKA Sofia was champion twenty-seven times during the communist era, including nine consecutive years 1954–62; Steaua Bucharest won the Romanian championship fourteen times, including a run of five consecutive wins 1985–89; Dukla Prague was champion eleven times, including four consecutively 1961–64; by 1989 Red Star Belgrade had been Yugoslav champions sixteen times, and Honvéd Budapest had been Hungarian champions twelve times.

The second best bet to win the various national championships was the team sponsored by the security ministry/secret police. Dynamo Moscow founded in 1923 was the first such club. Other Dynamo (or Dinamo) clubs appeared later in Bucharest, Dresden, Zagreb, Tirana, Kiev, Tbilisi, and temporarily in Sofia and Prague. In Budapest the former Jewish club before the Second World War, MTK, became the secret police team for a while. Championships won by the Dynamo/ Dinamo clubs up to 1989 include Tirana fourteen, Bucharest thirteen, Kiev twelve, Moscow eleven and Dresden eight.

The political climate in the socialist republics of Eastern Europe could often be gauged by the names of the football clubs. During the 1940s and 1950s new ideologically sound names were imposed on the major clubs. In Bulgaria, Levski Sofia (named after a national hero in battles versus the Turks) had to spend the period 1949–56 as Dinamo Sofia, and Slavia Sofia (six times champions before communism) endured two years as Strojtel and five years as Udarnik. In Czechoslovakia, Bohemians Prague were named Spartak Stalingrad from 1951 to 1961, Slavia Prague became Dynamo Prague from 1953 to 1965, and Sparta Prague were known as Spartak Sokolovo from 1953 to 1965. The fans, of course, continued to call the clubs by their traditional names. The three Prague clubs reverted to their pre-communist names in 1965 at the beginning of the 'Prague Spring'.

In Hungary, the liberalization of 1956 prior to the October uprising enabled leading clubs to return to their original names. MTK Budapest had three different names between 1949 and 1956, and Ferencváros had endured periods as EDÖSZ (the food industry workers' trade union 1949–50) and Kiniszi (a Hungarian hero 1950–56). The years between 1954 and 1956 also witnessed a period of liberalization in Poland. Twelve first division clubs discarded their imposed socialist name and reverted to their previous name, as did second division Cracovia – Poland's oldest surviving club.

The communist authorities interfered with club football in Eastern Europe in other ways. In Bulgaria during the 1968–69 season the government ordered six mergers involving football clubs. The two most famous were in Sofia with the merging of Levski and Spartak, and Slavia and Lokomotiv. The latter fusion lasted only until 1971 due largely to opposition from the fans, whereas the separate name of Levski was re-established in late 1989 during the social revolution. More seriously, in Romania two previously small clubs associated with the Ceauşescu family (FC Olt and Victoria Bucharest) were remarkably successful until the overthrow of the regime and their resultant forced demotion.

Political control extended to restrictions on the transfer abroad of football players in contrast to the free market situation in the inter-war period. Transfers operated within strict limits. Footballers could move to the West only after reaching the age of 30 and if they had served the national team with distinction. Although full-time footballers were relatively well off in Eastern Europe, the gains to be made were far greater in the West.

Given the clear association between certain clubs and central institutions in the state, the possibility arose of opposition to the regime focusing on other clubs. Rapid Bucharest in Romania and Ferencváros in Hungary both attracted supporters disaffected with communism. Spartak Moscow became known as the people's team, because the club was not associated with a single part of Soviet society. Several clubs in the Soviet League came to represent nationalist ambitions in opposition to Moscow, for example, Ararat Yerevan in Armenia, Netfchi Baku in Azerbaijan, Dynamo Tbilisi in Georgia, and Zhalgiris Vilnius in Lithuania.

Changes in the late 1980s in response to *perestroika* and *glasnost*

A series of major organizational changes began in Eastern European football towards the end of the 1980s, most notably professionalization of the players, independence for the football authorities and football clubs from the state, a switch from traditional socialist sponsorship to more commercial forms, and the lifting of restrictions on transfers to the West. Taken together this package of reforms provided both new opportunities and new problems for football clubs and players. Successful players and successful clubs benefited but ordinary players and ordinary clubs faced a bleak future in the 1990s.

Younger players were transferred to the West in response to Gorbachev's policy of *glasnost*. This trend started with Alexander Zavarov's move from Dynamo Kiev to Juventus of Italy at the age of 27 for £3.2 million in the summer of 1988. The *glasnost* policy of permitting official transfer to the West can be seen also as an attempt to stem the flow of unofficial defections. The most notorious case in Czechoslovakia in the 1980s was the joint defection of Ivo Knoflicek and Lubos Kubik from Slavia Prague while on tour in former West Germany. After several months in hiding around Europe and a fruitless attempt to sign for Derby County in England, both returned eventually to Prague to negotiate compromise deals which took them to St Pauli (West Germany) and Fiorentina (Italy) respectively.

As with Hungarian society as a whole, Hungarian football experienced more gradual change over a longer time period. The first steps towards professionalism were taken in 1979 and official approval was granted in 1983. In 1989 the Football Association became independent of the state and freedom of contract was granted to the players. Similarly, many of the changes in Czechoslovakia took place before the 'velvet revolution' of 1989, largely in response to pressures for change from within but also influenced by the general context of *perestroika*. However, it was not until 1990 that players obtained freedom of contract and the Football Association became independent.

A series of problems in the 1980s highlighted the urgent need for change in Eastern European football. One recurring theme involved the payment of unofficial illegal bonuses to top up players' inadequate wages. Czechoslovakia provided an example of this with a financial scandal at first division Bohemians Prague. The president, secretary, treasurer and twenty present and past players of the club stood trial on charges of corruption and embezzlement. Several officials were imprisoned but then released as part of the general amnesty following the velvet revolution.

Match-fixing on behalf of a betting syndicate or in order to influence promotion or relegation issues was a further source of corruption. Hungary's major scandal of the early 1980s involved 499 players, officials and organizers, some of whom were given prison sentences. Further examples of match-fixing were evident towards the end of the 1982–83 season in Bulgaria and the 1986–87 season in Poland.

Modern football hooliganism spread to Eastern Europe in the mid-1980s. Supporters of the leading clubs were most likely to attract hooligan gangs, such as at Sparta Prague in Czechoslovakia and Ferencváros in Hungary (see Figure 6.1). Serious hooligan violence in Czechoslovakia began on the last day of the 1984–85 season, when Sparta fans broke train windows, slashed seats and threw bottles on the way to Banska Bystrica in Slovakia. Thirty fans were arrested and the authorities announced that they would not tolerate 'the manners of English fans in our sports'. So concerned were the authorities that they commissioned a documentary film on Sparta fans travelling to an away match entitled *Proc?* (Why?). However, officials admitted that the film had resulted in more widespread copying of spectator violence, even among crowds leaving the cinema after watching the film.

Coping in the post-communist world

One of the most visible effects on world football has been the breakup of the Soviet Union into fifteen independent republics. Ten are members of UEFA – Russia, Ukraine, Belarus, Estonia, Latvia, Lithuania, Moldova, Georgia, Armenia and Azerbaijan. The other five – Kazakhstan, Kirghizstan, Tadjikistan, Turkmenistan and Uzbekistan – are affiliated with the Asian Football Confederation. Other new members of

*Fig 6.1   As the communist regimes liberalized, so the English 'disease' of football
hooliganism spread to Eastern Europe. Ferencvaros fans took a leading role in
Hungary*

UEFA are the Czech Republic and Slovakia (former Czechoslovakia) plus Croatia, Slovenia, Macedonia, and Bosnia-Hercegovina (former Yugoslavia).

Since 1989 the traditional socialist structure has been dismantled and sport in the post-communist era has experienced a difficult transition to a market rather than a state environment. Although Eastern European football retains an imprint of communist rule and its distinctive organization of sport, the major economic, political and social changes have inevitable repercussions for football in these countries.

There have been more name changes since 1989. Three trends are discernible. First, there is a return to original names. In Budapest, the army club Honvéd has replaced the soldier on its badge with a lion, the emblem of AC Kispest, which previously played at the ground; the club's name is now Kispest-Honvéd. In Bulgaria, Trakia Plovdiv has reverted to Botev Plovdiv, its original name in 1912. The second trend is dispensing with names associated with the old communist regime. In the Czech Republic, Ruda Hvezda (Red Star) Cheb has switched to Union Cheb, and in 1992 Dinamo Zagreb became Croatia Zagreb. Third, names are changed to match that of a new sponsor. In the Czech Republic, Zbrojovka Brno became Boby Brno. In Hungary, Videoton became Parmalat.

Large-scale state financial support has been removed from both the national team and the leading clubs. The resultant financial crisis means that football must quickly learn to adapt to the new economic reality. The move from state socialism to market capitalism has also resulted in severe economic pressures on the general population, including football spectators. Policies have often involved prices doubling (at the very least) with wages remaining constant. In football, there are higher admission charges and a resultant decline in attendances at matches. For instance, average attendances at football matches in the Czech Republic have more than halved since the mid-1960s. The first division average for Czechoslovakia in 1965–66 was 11,910, but was around 5,500 in the early 1990s. Reduced crowds exacerbate the financial crisis, especially for those clubs without new sponsorship and for the players.

Smaller clubs were the first to be hit by the new era of financial independence from the state. In Hungary, the number of multi-sports clubs decreased in 1988–89 by 8 per cent and the membership of clubs declined by 19 per cent. In Czechoslovakia, 16 of the 593 registered football clubs closed down in 1990–91 because of financial problems.

Many of the problems under communism have continued. Bribery and corruption are rife among the newly commercialized football clubs of Eastern Europe. On the last weekend of the 1992–93 Polish season, the two contenders for the first division championship both contrived large wins, Legia Warsaw by 6–0, and LKS Lódz by 7–1. After an investigation, the championship was awarded to third-placed Lech Poznan. Towards the end of the 1994–95 season in the Czech Republic, allegations surfaced of referees taking bribes. Much was made in the press of Sparta Prague's successful late run for the championship, during which Sparta was awarded six penalties (while conceding none) and had seven opposing players sent off (compared to Sparta's none). In March 1996 the Romanian Football Association officially admitted that corruption and match-fixing permeated the national league.

It is in the former Soviet Union that football scandals have been most prominent. In 1995–96 the Ukrainian champion, Dynamo Kiev, was thrown out of the European Champions League for attempting to bribe the referee against Panathinaikos of Greece. Dynamo has built a profitable business empire in collaboration with the local mafia since the introduction of market forces (see Kuper 1994). Elsewhere in the Ukraine, the president of Shakhtor Donetsk was killed by a mafia bomb at the stadium in 1995.

Not all Eastern European clubs have been abandoned by their traditional sponsors. Steaua Bucharest continue as the army club in Romania, although the club's persistent dominance is probably due more to making money through transferring players abroad. In Poland, Hutnik Kraków remain sponsored by the state-owned local steelworks, and Zaglebie Lubin by the state-owned local copper-mine. Where privatization has not taken place, the traditional pattern often still prevails.

Some of the leading Eastern European clubs have negotiated major sponsorship deals with Western firms in the post-communist era. In Czechoslovakia, the best supported team, Sparta Prague, was the first to secure a deal in August 1990 involving shirt advertising in return for sponsorship from Opel. Minolta of Austria sponsor the team from Nitra; this change of sponsor deprives us of one of the most evocative names in European football, that of Plastika Nitra. In Hungary, the best supported club, Ferencváros, obtained a lucrative sponsorship deal with a French construction company (Bras) in 1990, but the deal ended after only one season. Another Budapest team, Kispest Honvéd, was backed by a Belgian businessman (Louis De Vries). Parmalat, the Italian dairy produce corporation, sponsors both Dynamo Moscow and Parmalat FC from Székesfehérvar in Hungary.

Several clubs in Eastern Europe are sponsored by a wealthy entrepreneur, often an expatriate made good in the West. In September 1991, Slavia Prague was taken over by Boris Korbel, an American multi-millionaire of Czech origin. He was to finance the reconstruction of its stadium, which has been left uncompleted by his recent disappearance from the scene. Further examples in the Czech Republic are Petra Drnovice (a village team promoted to the first division by the funding of Jan Gotwald) and Boby Brno (sponsored by a former ice hockey player). In Hungary, entrepreneur Jozsef Stadler converted village team Akasztó into a first division club renamed FC Stadler with its own 21,000 capacity new stadium. At the time of writing both the club and Stadler himself are under fiscal investigation.

One of the most bizarre developments in post-communist football surfaced in Poland in 1995. Two financially troubled first division clubs sold their places to lower division clubs, which had financial backing. Money from entrepreneur Pan Krzyzostoniak enabled Lechia Gdansk (relegated to the regional third division at the end of 1994–95) to merge with Olimpia Poznan and take up the place in the first division. Home matches in the 1995–96 season were played in Gdansk, which is 300 kilometres from Poznan. Similarly, Sokol Pniewy sold a first division place to second division GKS Tychy, which is 400 kilometres away.

At the beginning of the communist era, some new football clubs were created and immediately placed in the first division, while certain 'bourgeois' clubs were discouraged, and as a result fell into decline. Post-communism has led to a reversal of history in some cases, for example army club Dukla Prague never received popular support despite regular successes, because the club was associated with the communist regime. In 1988 Dukla finished second in the Czechoslovak League, but by the mid-1990s the club had been relegated twice to the level of the Czech regional third division. By contrast Viktoria Zizkov, a popular club from a working-class district near the centre of Prague (and Czechoslovak champions in 1928), disappeared under communism into the depths of the regional third and fourth divisions. Even when playing at this level, Viktoria often had larger crowds than first division Dukla. By 1993 Viktoria had returned to the Czech first division.

In post-communism there is strong economic pressure on leading players to move to the West. The flow of transfers from Eastern Europe accelerated after the 1990 World Cup finals in Italy. Seventeen of the Czechoslovak squad of twenty-two players moved to the West and most of the Romanian squad were transferred abroad after the finals. In comparison to ordinary workers in Eastern Europe, professional footballers remain well-off but the austerity policies introduced by many governments are imposing hardship at all levels of society. Hence the solution for the best players is to seek a transfer abroad (i.e. to the West) in order to secure a higher standard of living and Western currency.

In December 1990 there were over 200 Hungarian footballers officially playing abroad. Around three-quarters of them were playing in the Austrian regional third and fourth divisions. These players are semi-professionals, who live in Hungary and cross the border each weekend to play for Austrian teams in return for match expenses. Austrian match expenses are very desirable as they are higher than a full-time salary in Hungary. In October 1990 there were 170 Czechoslovak footballers officially playing abroad. Around two-thirds of them were located with lower division teams near the border in Germany and Austria. As with Hungary, these players are semi-professionals who continue to live in their home country. The largest outflow of players has been from Croatia with more than 1,500 leaving to play elsewhere between 1992 and 1996.

The only chance of persuading leading players to remain in their home country lies with leading Eastern European clubs with substantial Western sponsorship deals. Even these clubs cannot compete with offers from Italy, Spain, England, Germany and France: these countries stand at the apex of the new international division of labour in football (especially Italy, Spain and England), while Eastern Europe provides a new source of cheap labour. From the point of view of the national teams, the migration of leading players abroad is a mixed blessing. These players are refining their skills in the best leagues and among the best players in the world (e.g. in Italy), but the main problem is then obtaining their release for international matches. Whereas FIFA can insist that players are released for World Cup matches, this is not the case for international friendly matches. Successful teams are built and team spirit forged in these friendly matches.

Is there a future for football in Eastern Europe? Although the current transition period is a difficult one, there are reasons for optimism. There is a long history of football success in the region and young players are still emerging with 'natural' ball skills as well as high technical ability. Bulgaria, Romania, Russia, Croatia and the Czech Republic all qualified for the finals of the European Championship in England in 1996, and the Czech Republic lost in the final against Germany after extra time. Perhaps more significantly a club side, Slavia Prague, reached the semi-final stage of the UEFA Cup in 1996.

Don't shoot me, I'm the *presidente*: football and politics in Argentina

In Argentina sport and politics are inextricably linked. Football is an extension of politics. It is part of the political system and anything that begins as sport rapidly becomes politicized (Romero 1994: 18). Historically, there are grounds to claim that football is the social model around which the political system has been constructed. This chapter outlines how these ties were established, the form in which these links are maintained and the reasons why the relationship between football and politics is likely to continue in the foreseeable future. This will involve analysing the motivation for the relationship on the part of the main players in the structures of football in Argentina, namely the state, the Argentine Football Association, the clubs and the fans. The role of businesses and, to a lesser extent, the media are interrelated to the above and will be examined in their appropriate context.

Formation of early football clubs in Argentina

Football was first introduced into Argentina via the port area of Buenos Aires where the English, known locally as *los ingleses locos*, played among themselves (Bayer 1990), before spreading inland via British railway workers who worked for English companies in Argentina during a period of extensive railway construction. The British had the physical space in which to play and were encouraged by their employers. This explains why many football clubs were originally based along railway lines and were commonly named after them (e.g. Central Argentino in Buenos Aires; Central Norte in Tucumán; Andes Talleres in Mendoza; Pacífico in Bahía Blanca; Rosario Central in Rosario which was originally called Rosario el Central Argentine Railway Athletic Club).

The first football club, Buenos Aires Football Club, was formed in 1867 as a spin-off from Buenos Aires Cricket Club and the first match on record took place between Colorados and Blancos on 20 June 1867 (*El Gráfico* 1993). Inspired by the 45,000 British nationals who were living in Greater Buenos Aires at that time, and also by the companies that these Britons worked for, several other football clubs were established and in 1891 a football league began. This was just three years after the (English) Football League and earlier than any other European league championships.

New football clubs established around the turn of the century played an important role in the social and political life of the *barrio* (neighbourhood) where they were based (Scher and Palomino 1988). It has been claimed that they contributed towards the integration of a young immigrant population into Argentine society (Archetti 1994). The earliest clubs consisted of predominantly, and usually exclusively, British members. Names of the clubs were usually in English and some Argentine clubs still carry the legacy of English names.

One of the most successful football clubs at the start of the century began as the English High School team. The person responsible for this team was a Scot, Alexander Watson Hutton, who was later to become the first president of the Association Argentina Football League, established in 1893. English schools played an important role in spreading the popularity of football in Argentina and many clubs began as a school or college team.

Creolization of the sport was essential if it was to be accepted and adopted by the native Argentine population. As this process took place, there arose some friction between the English clubs and native Argentines. The integration of Argentines into some, traditionally English, clubs was resisted, leading to the establishment of new clubs where Argentines were welcome. Such clubs included Argentino de Quilmes (1899), an Argentine-friendly counterpart to Quilmes (1897), Estudiantes (1898) and Independiente Football Club (1905), formed in protest at being excluded from its company's football team. Part of the creolization of football (its integration into Argentine society) involved the castilianization of the names of clubs. The English High School team changed its name to Alumni and Independiente Football Club became Club Atlético Independiente.

At the beginning of the twentieth century most of the clubs we recognize today were established. In 1901 River Plate was founded. Near the railway station Ferro Carril Oeste, Argentinos Juniors was founded. Racing was another club which owes its origins in 1903 to a railway station, in Avellanada. Boca Juniors was based in the Genovese *barrio* alongside the port in Buenos Aires; the name chosen when it was formed in 1905 is itself revealing. It rejected other names such as Italian Stars and Children of Italy because it felt a strong identity with its *barrio* (*El Gráfico* 1993). Boca, meaning mouth of the river, establishes the club's identification with its port on the River Plate, and Juniors, as the players now considered themselves to be children of that place, rather than immigrants. So in football's formative years, the roots of the clubs developed to become closely linked to their local communities.

Establishment of structures that integrate football and politics

Of crucial importance to the subsequent development of football in Argentina is that it preceded democratic politics. Universal manhood suffrage was not approved until 1912 and the first democratic election took place in 1916, by which time forty-six of the leading professional clubs involved in the restructuring of the sport in 1985 were already in existence. Newly formed political parties who had no adequate organization of their own used the infrastructure of football and its neighbourhood-based clubs. Both football and politics, therefore, were organized in a similar manner within the community.

In order to fully appreciate the role of politics in Argentine football, it is necessary to understand the relationships between the four main elements of its organization – the state (represented by politicians), the Argentine Football Association, the clubs and the fans. There are also other, closely related elements such as businesses and local communities that figure in the structures, which will also be considered.

The links between these four key players are complex. Sufficient motivation was present on the part of all parties to ensure the continuation of a relationship that has survived most of this century and will continue into the next. In theory, Argentine football has a hierarchical structure that shares the pattern of structures of many other institutions. The Argentine Football Association (AFA) is responsible for the running of football and is answerable only to the state. The clubs, whose chairmen and directors double as politicians, are governed by the Football Association's structures and rules. Traditionally in many countries, the fans have little power in the formal structures of football, but in Argentina because of the unique ties between politics and football, the role of the fans is of utmost importance in the running of a club, and to a politician's career (to this day rival political lists appear in club elections). It was during the 1920s and 1930s that the relationship between these four elements of the football hierarchy became established.

During their early years many clubs were financed by benefactors, received donations from supporters and sponsorship from local businesses. As the immigrant population integrated into Argentine society, so football became widespread. This was not a smooth process and between 1912 and 1926 football's ruling body split on two occasions (1912–15 and 1919–26). Shortly following the creation of the unified *Asociación Argentina Amateur* in 1926, footballers joined forces and voiced their frustrated desires to become recognized sportsmen with freedom of contract. They reviewed their positions as employees, established a players' union and went on strike in April 1931.

Regarding the political situation, this was a difficult time in Argentina. Hipólito Irigoyen's government fell in 1930 as General José Félix Uriburu led the revolution which brought about a deep transformation of the state and society and represented the commencement of an unstable political situation that has lasted ever since. Intense social and economic changes involved an expansion in urban areas, especially in the population of Buenos Aires, and the rise of the working classes in an industrial era. This was to be an important market for football, and football was to become a useful medium by which the state could control the population.

The state wanted football to fulfil the function of distracting the population from these everyday problems and disturbing political issues. 'Football distracts ·people, excites them, makes them forget about everyday problems – problems that are many and very serious' (*El Gráfico* 1993). It was crucial, therefore, to the authorities that football acted as a social drug.

Partly because of this opportune timing as far as the footballers were concerned, the players' strike of 1931 was successful and brought about the legalization of professional football, via the creation of a new institution, the *Liga Argentina de Football*. A professional league championship emerged incorporating teams from Buenos Aires and La Plata.

The immediate consequences of the professionalization of football entailed an increase in attendances, intensified competition between the clubs and heightened rivalry between spectators, particularly between Boca and River who had both been accustomed to success while they played in different leagues during the 1920s. Big-name signings followed, sparked by River's acquisition of Bernabé Ferreyra in 1932, as the clubs enjoyed a short boom period of expansion and relative wealth. Indeed, River rapidly became a very rich club. Until then it had lived in the shadow of the crowd-pullers of Boca and Racing.

Popularization of football coincided with the spread of mass media. The press and radio contributed to the diffusion of the sport – and to its exploitation in controlling and manipulating the masses during a period of political instability. Motivation for state involvement in the *Liga Argentina de Football* and in the running of clubs is clear. Government officials realized the potential of using football for political propaganda. It was advantageous to the state to establish a relationship, albeit indirect, between itself and football fans. As in Franco's Spain (see chapter 3), football fulfilled a role of encouraging the population to take their minds off everyday, political issues. Later also, in 1966, during the dictatorship of General Juan Carlos Onganía, up to six football matches were televised a week and clubs were recompensed to make up for loss of revenue in attendances (Fernández Santander 1990).

Football clubs provided politicians with a shop window; the motivation which helps explain the close links between football and politics in Argentina in the 1930s remains the same today, thus ensuring the continuation of such relationships. Directing a football club, supporting the club through some other activity, or simply attending a football match provides politicians with the opportunity to become known by a large public, facilitating networks for political canvassing and encouraging the loyalty of the local community. It is usual for the names of politicians to appear on lists of honorary *socios* (supporters or club members) of most clubs and it has gradually become a normal way of creating political propaganda. It is common practice during presidential elections at football clubs, for rival political opponents to stand as candidates and run campaigns against one another thereby merging the structures of football and politics.

Many businesses decided to become involved in football too, not only for its potential for advertising, but also so that businessmen (the system involves exclusively men) could use football as a stepping-stone to a political career. It created a positive image if one appeared to have an interest in the local football team. Politicians like to appear in touch with the people this way. Even today, President Carlos Menem appreciates the value of being seen attending football matches.

It was already evident how the social function of football was vital in its origins, but for the reasons outlined above its political function became more intense and more overt once the sport was professionalized. In 1934, the Argentine Football Association changed its name once more and became the *Asociación de Fútbol Argentino* (AFA), as it remains today. Throughout its history the links between successive chairmen (*presidentes*) of the AFA and the state have been strong. During dictatorships, a state administrator has been appointed to run the AFA and at other times those officials who have been elected have usually had close relationships with the ruling government. Official links between state and football are via the AFA. It is the AFA *presidente* who represents football at a higher level.

It was common for AFA *presidentes* to have served in politics at some time in their careers and several held national positions in politics. Of the twenty-nine different AFA chairmen between the establishment of the institution in 1934 and the present day, a third have been appointed as government officials during periods of state intervention and many others who have been elected have had links with political parties or held a position in government at some stage of their careers. Conversely, their political links meant that as long as there was no change in the political power structure, they held a relatively stable position. Even when changes did take place, abilities to swap allegiances sometimes ensured survival – Colombo (1956–65) and Grondona (1979–present) survived at the end of dictatorships and Valentín Suárez presided over the AFA under both civil and military regimes, being elected *presidente* (1949–53), and appointed as *interventor* or administrator (1966–68). Several have been members of the political party *Unión Cívica Radical*, including the AFA's first chairman Tiburcio Padilla (1934–35), Pedro Canaveri (1946–47) and the AFA's two longest serving chairmen, Raúl Colombo (1956–65) and Julio Grondona (1979–present). During periods of intervention, some of the *presidentes* were also members of the Peronist *Partido Justicialista*.

Never have the state and the AFA been more closely tied than in the 1940s when the AFA chairman, Ramón Castillo, was the son of the President of the Republic. During the dictatorship of Juan Domingo Perón (1946–55), Oscar Nicolini, Cayetano Giardulli, Valentín Suárez, Domingo Peluffo and Cecilio Conditti were all government officials who ran the AFA. No government has failed to get involved in AFA business and no AFA presidency has failed to seek government support (Scher and Palomino 1988).

Typically, the head of the AFA has three areas of experience – links with politics, business and having served an apprenticeship in football, often involved in the running of a club. This practice continues today: the AFA chairman, Julio Grondona, is a member of *Unión Cívica Radical*, an important businessman in the steelworks and *ex-presidente* of Independiente football club. Unlike in Franco's Spain where government officials who had little or no interest in football were appointed to run the sport, it was not unusual under dictatorships in Argentina for the head of the AFA to have a keen interest in football.

It has always been in the interest of football clubs to exploit the government's desires to enhance the profile of football. In 1938 state subsidies were allocated in the form of special grants which enabled clubs to rebuild or upgrade their stadium or even to build a new one (for example River Plate in 1938 and Boca Juniors in 1940) and it is not uncommon in the history of Argentine football for the state to bail clubs out of financial straits and save them from bankruptcy.

State intervention in football reached a peak during the period of Peronism (1946–55). Although football was tightly controlled, it benefited in that policies were directed at expanding the appeal and strengthening the infrastructure of the sport. Perón undertook responsibility for sport as a mechanism of national integration via the socialization of the youth and used football as political propaganda. Also, as in Spain, it was important to export a positive image of the country and football was promoted in order to do this. Sporting success was equated with Peronist success, and medals achieved under Perón were named *medallas peronistas* (Peronist medals). In return for such support the AFA supported Perón as presidential candidate.

Perón himself was reputedly enthusiastic about football and attended matches frequently. He always appeared at important national matches. His wife, Evita, patronized the Evita Youth Championships in the 1950s during which football was used as part of the country's health programme for children (it was compulsory for all participants to pass a health check before entering the competition). Undoubtedly, these championships served to win over many youths to Peronism.

Clubs used their connections with power in order to develop. Links between state and clubs strengthened. Directors and *presidentes* of the football clubs themselves were, and still are, usually rich business people or politicians. It became normal practice during the Peronist period for football clubs to have a *padrino* (a godfather or patron) within government, that is, there were occupants of high positions of power who looked after the interests of a particular club. They had no official status as such, but many clubs looked to the support of their *padrinos*, who often doubled as directors at the club too, when they were in trouble or difficulties.

With the steady rise in popularity of football, clubs continued to outgrow their stadiums. The state still supported their redevelopment: Huracán, Racing and Vélez opened new stadiums in 1947, 1950 and 1951 respectively. Racing accomplished a particularly favourable negotiation via their *padrino*, Ramón Cereijo, the government Treasurer at the time.

Motivation for ties between state, the AFA and clubs is high. The state does what it can for football, via the AFA. As the AFA is usually run by government officials or supporters, they toe the party line and obedience will ensure they remain in post. The state hopes to benefit by exploiting football as a social drug, and/or as a vote-winner in times of democracy. Individual politicians, the *padrinos*, do what they can for individual clubs; it enhances their profile and status in society. Clubs benefit by having someone in power who will support them so it is in their interests to support, in turn, the person who is representing them.

The role of fans in football and politics

The final key player in the game involves the fans. The fans play an important role as they are the people who constitute the masses, the voters and the consumers. Their presence explains why everyone else wants to become involved in the sport. One of the prime reasons why the state originally became interested in football was to control the masses, to structure and define social identities and to reinforce national sentiments when international football became more important. The state therefore targeted football as being a place where the masses could and would gather and channel their frustrations; football's political role remains of prime importance. In more recent times, the fans have become essential to clubs, and to the economy of the state, in their role as consumers.

Since the industrialization of football in the late 1950s and in the 1960s, when football began to be run as a business, pressures on clubs to be successful have intensified. They had spent massively on players and on constructing large stadiums and needed loyal support by fans to maintain a steady income. This came at a time when attendances at football matches were declining. Argentina's poor performance in Sweden in 1958, in its first World Cup since 1934, brought shame and embarrassment to the nation. Argentines were victims of their own publicity and had believed they played the best football in the world until this disastrous World Cup; they had to rethink their ideas as confidence plummeted. This coincided with the emergence of alternative methods of occupying leisure time, such as the diffusion of television. Crowds drifted away from football.

It became increasingly obvious that income from the gates would not suffice to cover the costs of running a football club. Although most clubs traditionally enjoyed the financial backing of someone in the local business community, they were aware of the importance of the results on the pitch which determined success. Success guaranteed fans and publicity, and it is the fans who constituted the consumers that businesses hoped to attract via their advertising and sponsorship. Thus the phenomenon of *fútbol-espectáculo* (football-spectacular) was born. The clubs were run as businesses (originally the term was *fútbol-empresa* or football-business) and the aim was to attract the public. The two main protagonists in the *fútbol-espectáculo* were the *presidentes* of the two largest clubs in Argentina – Liberti, of River Plate, and Armando, of Boca Juniors. They invested huge amounts of money in their clubs, made big-name signings to attract the crowds and expected success. Of course, the income of a club depends partly on its success on the pitch, which led to corruption and violence in football to control results (Romero 1994).

It is difficult to specify exactly when violence in Argentine football began. Early evidence of violence in the 1930s suggests it was apolitical in nature, largely related to events that took place on the pitch, and directed towards players and match officials. (For further details on football violence in Argentina see Duke and Crolley 1996.) It is a much more organized violence, however, that characterizes Argentine football today. The existence of structures (described above) which linked football and politics, coupled with an increased awareness in the late 1950s and 1960s of the importance of results, meant that there was a temptation to manipulate violence by interested parties. Romero (1994) has claimed that the style of violence in Argentine football is as distinctive as the style of football. Much (though by no means all) of this organized violence is politically motivated. It has been difficult establishing exactly when this type of organized violence began, but it has been reported that the term *barras fuertes* was used in 1958 to refer to groups of violent football fans who appeared to be organized in a formal manner. However, it is usually considered to be around 1966, the year of the military coup in Argentina, when *barras bravas* (which translates roughly as 'the fierce opponents'), the main exponents of football violence today, appeared on the scene and the murder in November 1967 of Hector Souto, a Huracán fan, marked the beginning of the era of the *barras bravas* and the institutionalization of violence. There followed a huge escalation in violence in football.

In many ways, the emergence of the *barras bravas* represented the militarization of football support. They have a strict hierarchical structure which has a leader at its helm. Most of the group members will be aged between about 20 and 25, with the leaders frequently over 30. Members are recruited and set a series of trials to test their commitment and strategies. It is common for core members to be full-time professional militants and not, therefore, be in conventional employment.

Political motivation provides the key to the reasons which explain most of the activity of the *barras bravas*. They have connections with someone involved in the running of their club, often a particular candidate for club chairman, for example, who needs their support. They might also take part in political demonstrations, perhaps in support of their *padrino*. They are keen to engage in political activity in return for some form of payment, often the funding of transport so that they can attend away matches, or the gift of match tickets which can be sold at a healthy profit on the black market.

This understanding goes beyond football at club level and penetrates the AFA. Leading *barras bravas* were provided with both match tickets and air fares in 1986 in order to maintain the backing and cooperation of the *barras bravas*; this also ensured vocal support for Argentina in the World Cup in Mexico. During the 1994 World Cup in the USA, it has been estimated that $150,000 were spent on tickets for *barras bravas*, many of which were sold on the black market at three times their face value (Romero 1994). It is a practice which has only recently been brought to question following media outrage at the extreme violent behaviour of *barras bravas* with the apparent approval of clubs who continue to fund them, yet it has happened for many years. There is evidence of fans receiving payment for travel costs as early as 1962 (*Clarín* 19 December 1990) and it has been estimated that in 1965 around half a million dollars was spent by clubs in one season on tickets for *barras bravas* (Romero 1994).

Types of activities carried out by the *barras bravas* can be categorized as either overt or covert. Overt violence is the type that is carried out against rival fans and usually takes place within the football context, before, during or after a match. Motivation is not always political (a complex network of allegiances and rivalries between fans exists in Argentina), but *barras bravas*, or *los muchachos* (the boys) as they are sometimes known, do not normally attack at random. They are highly organized groups.

Overt violence is also directed at players, managers, directors and referees. These attacks are rarely random but are carefully planned and have a clear motivation. In May 1988, a San Lorenzo player was seriously injured as the result of an attack by *barras bravas* in the changing room in Córdoba. In February 1993, Daniel Passarella, then River manager, was beaten up by a faction of River *barras* (Kuper 1994).

Another angle to the politicization of overt violence in Argentine football centres around the relationship between police and fans. The police were blamed for the death of Adrián Scassera at a match between Independiente and Boca Juniors on 7 April 1985 (Scher and Palomino 1988), and thirty-five Vélez fans were injured when fighting broke out between police and fans in 1992 (*Clarín* 10 June 1992). According to Romero (1986), police are responsible for 68 per cent of football-related fatalities. The role of the police in Argentine society is significant here. They have a long history of violence against the people, often on behalf of a repressive state. They are seen as agents of the state. It is not unknown for *barras bravas* to unite when faced with police hostility and to become allies. One famous example is when rival fans from River and Argentinos Juniors joined forces in protest, chanted obscenities and gestured aggressively as police attempted to arrest two youths in Monumental in May 1983. As the Chief of Police commented after the match, 'People see a police uniform as a reflection of the country. They immediately think of those who disappeared under the dictatorship, of the Malvinas, of economic problems' (*El Gráfico* 7 June 1983).

Except when undertaking political activities, *barras bravas* do not carry out overtly violent actions against each other outside the football context, despite being fully aware of each other's meeting places. This is not always the case for some of their other activities. Covert activities carried out by the *barras bravas* are crucial to the internal structures of football. These operations involve blackmail and are carried out on behalf of the directors or club chairmen. The victims are usually the players: it is not uncommon for club chairmen to sort out their problems on the pitch via the *barras bravas*. If they want to get rid of a player (or sometimes a manager), it is easy for them to pay for the organized groups of fans to gain information on his private life and then to blackmail him. So the *barras* make sure it is their responsibility to know all about which players are taking which drugs (they might even be involved in supplying them) and all about their sex lives.

So these are the two covert methods the *barras bravas* control to threaten players or managers – either they can blackmail them with the information they have obtained or they can destroy them inside the stadium. Chants at football matches have little or nothing to do with events on the pitch. If the *barras bravas* chant abuse at a player when his contract is due to be renewed, it makes it much easier for the chairman to lower the conditions of his contract or it can even provide the club with the excuse to get rid of him. *Barras* are prepared to do this, if they are offered the right price.

This, of course, gives the fans a high degree of control over a player's career and consequently his livelihood so the players, in turn, try to keep the *barras* sweet. It is in their interests to do so. This provides another source of income for the fans. If the players are not intimidated by threats and do not respond to the *barras bravas*, they can also expect punishment. The threat of punishment is usually enough to see that the *barras bravas* achieve their objective. It is not uncommon for those who do not succumb to warnings to be physically attacked or shot! As players, directors and chairmen are aware that the threats are not empty, intimidation is indeed effective. There have been many examples during the late 1980s and early 1990s – Hugo Gatti was intimidated until he eventually left Boca. Yudica, manager of Argentinos, failed to listen to the advice of the fans in his team selections, refused to yield to pressures when his safety was threatened, his complaints to directors about being harrassed were ignored and eventually he was replaced by Veira. In a similar fashion, *barras bravas* were reportedly instrumental in removing Areán from San Lorenzo.

It is rare in Europe for the activities of violent groups of fans to enjoy the backing and open support of their club as they do in Argentina. (Exceptions such as Silvio Berlusconi at AC Milan and Jesús Gil y Gil at Atlético de Madrid are rare.) This is partly because of the historical and political links of football, but is perpetuated by the internal structure of football clubs in which it is the *socios* (members) who elect the club *presidente*. Electoral politics still, therefore, play a leading role in the organization of Argentine football clubs. It is because of the functions of electoral politics that the *barras bravas* become implicated in covert activities and are an essential cog in the workings of a club: clubs are frequently accused in the media of protecting the *barras bravas* and encouraging their violent activities (*La Prensa* 8 May 1994). In exchange for their political activity, the *barras* receive some form of payment. There have been suggestions that in addition to funding away trips and providing match tickets, some clubs are laundering drugs money. Allusions and indirect references to the infiltration of the drugs scene into football have been made tentatively on many occasions, not least by Vélez's *vicepresidente*, Francisco Antonio Pérez in 1988 who acknowledged that the football ground was being used for drug-trafficking (*Página 12* 27 November 1988). Concrete evidence concerning the role of Colombian drug cartels in two second division clubs has not been enough to stimulate a thorough investigation on the part of the authorities.

The football club in Argentina has a social function that goes beyond that of running a football team. It encourages support and rewards the fans' loyalty by providing other facilities for the local community. Even at the smallest clubs, other sports teams, and not just football, are run for members of the local community of all ages and both sexes. Special social events are often held for women and their involvement is encouraged. At large clubs, the responsibilities of the club extend far beyond the football team. Promising footballers might be invited to undergo their education at the club schools which opened in the 1970s; at Boca a library is situated within the stadium itself. *Barras bravas* themselves can fulfil a positive function in society and sometimes turn their attentions to organizing charitable events.

Recently, *barras bravas* have themselves made their way via the ballot boxes to occupying important posts in various institutions – one is the *vicepresidente* of a first division football club. Sometimes, a whole group will put itself forward in opposition to a particular candidate in club elections. One *barra* leader became elected chair of a leading trade union.

Connections with trade unions also date back a long way. In 1973 Quilmes enjoyed reinforcements from their allies on one occasion from Nueva Chicago in a match against Banfield in Avellanada. Members of one of the most powerful trade unions in Argentina were present among the *barras bravas* (*Página 12* 3 May 1991). Indeed, political activities of the *barras* are such that these can be given priority over their role as football fans. For example, Boca *barras bravas* gather immediately behind the goal at one end of the ground in the first tier; this area can be relatively empty during some games on occasions leading up to elections when members go campaigning. (See Figure 7.1 – this photo was taken during the final stages of an electoral campaign so there are gaps in the section where the *barras bravas* usually gather: their services were required elsewhere.)

Support for the *barras bravas* comes from higher up too. During the 1978 World Cup finals held in Argentina, when the state wanted to project a positive image of the country to the rest of the world, they feared the *barras bravas* would ruin it. The leaders of the *barras bravas*

Figure 7.1   The Boca end at La Bombonera, Boca Juniors Stadium. The match took place during an electoral campaign and the barras bravas *were called to political duties elsewhere, hence the gaps in the centre of the middle tier*

were called together by the military dictatorship and a truce was established so that they would instigate no violent incidents for the duration of the finals. It is significant that cooperation was achieved, and also revealing that despite huge public outcry at violence in football, so little has been done to eradicate it. It is only recently that the government has begun to make attempts via new anti-violence laws passed in May 1985 and March 1993; even now the judicial system is criticized for its leniency and for its failure to prosecute offenders.

Politicization of the 1978 World Cup finals

It was following the military coup of 1976, and the subsequent establishment of a dictatorship, that the government became openly involved in football and the links between football and politics were most visible. The World Cup was to be the world's window into Argentina and the regime invested huge amounts of money to promote the national image. The country's infrastructure was improved. Road networks and the public transport system were developed; new stadiums and a television centre were built. Some complained that the funds could have been better spent on much-needed hospitals, housing and schools.

The costs of these developments, along with those strongly rumoured to be spent on financing bribes (which influenced Argentina's 6–0 result against Peru) meant that the debt of the World Cup was to last many years. Following rumours of corruption in the financial side of the World Cup, attempts were made in 1978 by an appointed official, Alemann, to investigate the allegations. These efforts were thwarted when a bomb went off at Alemann's home. The debt of the World Cup 1978 was never given an exact figure.

It was essential during this World Cup to present an image of Argentina as a country free of problems which had a government who enjoyed the support of its people. Kuper (1994) describes the lengths to which the state attempted to hide internal divisions and to present this image of a united nation by erecting and painting a wall to hide the slums behind, by silencing the media and removing anyone who was considered a potential threat to the regime out of the city. The Argentine press was even ordered not to print anything critical about the national team (Scher and Palomino 1988).

President Videla himself presided over the opening ceremony and gave a moving speech on peace, friendship, human relationships and living together in harmony. All this in the same country which was violating human rights, was responsible for the 'disappearance' of thousands of its subjects and where military dictators used buildings just a few blocks from where this speech took place for torturing those who refused to submit to the dictatorship.

When Argentina won the World Cup final against the Netherlands, for politicians this equalled a success for the dictatorship. As in Franco's Spain when Real Madrid achieved great victories, the triumphs of the Argentine football team belonged to all Argentines: it was victory for the country. The Dutch refused to attend the closing ceremony in a gesture that was interpreted by the Argentine media as a demonstration of sour grapes after losing the final. What is more likely is that the Dutch wanted to make a politically motivated gesture against repression in Argentina.

President Videla's concerns to exploit the World Cup were such that he contracted a US company which had worked in advertising to promote the government's image during the build-up to the World Cup finals. The World Cup organizing body, called the EAM'78 (*Ente Auquártico Mundial* 1978), worked on the basis that what was good advertising technique for a product would also be good for the country's image and Argentina would be portrayed in a favourable light all over the world. The main person responsible for the organization of the World Cup was Carlos Alberto Lacoste, vicepresident of the EAM'78. President of the institution, General Omar Actis, was assassinated in August 1976. Strong rumours at the time suggested that Lacoste was responsible for the assassination and his motivation lay in the fact that he and Actis disagreed in some fundamental principles about how to organize the World Cup. Actis' successor, Antonio Luis Merlo, appeared to be far more manageable and Lacoste was allowed a high degree of freedom in his actions.

After the World Cup finals, Lacoste was financially rewarded for his success. Aided by relationships and family ties with Videla and Galtieri, his political career took off and he became an important figure in public life. Others who benefited included those involved in the construction industry, tourism, the mass media and communications. The state helped to finance those expenses which could be of national interest. Lacoste was a clear exponent of the links between football and politics, business and repression.

Once the dictatorship ended and Argentina became a democracy in 1983, opinions previously unvoiced because of censorship were then made known. This entailed a minute re-analysis of Argentina's recent history. Those who had suffered under the dictatorship sought to examine the wheeling and dealings that took place by the EAM'78 and revealed severe financial irregularities. Lacoste's responsibilities were removed and he was investigated for fraud relating to the World Cup. He has since been labelled by journalists as being the protagonist in running football's 'dirty war' during the World Cup and accused of having abused his power to achieve personal gain. He was by no means the only administrator to be guilty of financial irregularities during this period.

Another example of football being exploited to cover up deeper social unrest in Argentina was in 1979 when Argentina, captained by Diego Maradona, won the Youth World Cup. This coincided with an investigation into the allegations of state breaches of human rights which involved the presence of a number of foreign political figures of high status in Buenos Aires. The families of those who had disappeared while in state hands gathered in the Plaza de Mayo in Central Buenos Aires to demonstrate and demand an explanation of what had happened to their loved ones (as they still do every Thursday morning).

Rather than allow the demonstration to take place and provoke an embarrassing situation for the government and to avoid disbanding the group forcibly, which would probably have incited violence, the government led a campaign, spear-headed by the media, for people to go to the Plaza de Mayo to fete the victory of the youth team. Thus the real protest was hidden conveniently by a celebration of national pride. This media collaboration constitutes a key source of the state's power. For long periods in the twentieth century, the media have been state controlled. At the same time as the fiesta in the Plaza de Mayo, interviews with national team manager, Menotti, and captain Maradona were transmitted on the radio.

Football today is as large a business as it has ever been, and the mechanisms that link it with politics are still as strong as ever. Interestingly, the new laws mentioned earlier which were reluctantly introduced with the aim of reducing violence in football took into consideration the role of football as an industry. If any crime leads to a match being cancelled or suspended, the sentence is increased by one-third. Politics is protecting football as an industry.

Today, there is too much money involved in the football industry for politicians and businesses to ignore it. The media form part of the football business. Not only football matches themselves but also gossip surrounding the lives of footballers sells newspapers and attracts audiences on television and radio. Violence in football is part of the business too as it attracts media attention. Significantly, perhaps, it has been the media coverage via the installation of moral panic that has led to greater state control of football.

The media have to strike a balance, however, between sensationalism that sells newspapers and that which frightens the crowds away from football. In order to maintain a long-term, healthy market for the industry, the passion for football needs to be nurtured. Some of the media prefer to ignore football violence completely, unless a fatality is involved, and even then attempts are sometimes made to try and dismiss it as something else, not football-related. The business is protected while the media still manipulate football to suit political ends.

These two features of the sport, that is, its continued role in politics and as an industry, mean that those involved in football, whether as politicians, chairmen, directors or fans, will continue to enjoy a certain protection. Football clubs are still protected by their *padrinos*. Fans continue to enjoy protection, leading to articles in the press that criticize the way politicians, club directors and the judicial system protects *barras bravas*, pointing out that only 8 per cent of football-related deaths lead to a conviction and many prosecutions are dropped after intervention by a football club (*La Prensa* 8 May 1994; *La Prensa* 7 May 1992). No one accepts the responsibility for violence in football. Clubs say it is the responsibility of the police; the police complain they can do nothing without the backing of the clubs. The state has reluctantly become involved by establishing new laws, but is inconsistent in the application of the laws. As long as the links between football and politics continue, the system will be maintained. At present, there is no attempt to keep football and politics apart. The desire for power and money provides motivation for the continuation of relationships between the key players who control Argentine football. While the structures stay the same in football, the relationship between football and politics will also remain unchanged.

CHAPTER 8

Ultra-political: football culture in Italy*

This chapter explores the phenomenon of the politicization of football in Italy, paying particular attention to the culture of the *tifo estremo* (extreme football fanaticism). There is also evidence to suggest that the reverse process, the influence of football on politics (a sort of 'footballization' of politics), is taking place and hypotheses concerning the use of sporting metaphors in political language will be formulated.

The focus of the case study is not so much on the political dimension of the phenomena described but rather on the culture of football in Italy, its autonomy as an event and its possible political vulnerability. The aim of this chapter is to analyse the patterns of communication used by football fans (*tifo*) and illustrate how the styles of communication and patterns of language use are being transferred into the political context (some sociologists refer to this as the 'transcontextual' nature of communication).

In Italy the participation of fans in football has assumed various forms of organization. In line with its strong tradition of forming political, trade union and religious associations (known as 'associationism'), in football support also has an important, highly organized component. Therefore, in order to understand spectator culture in Italian football, it is necessary to outline its two main forms of association: the official supporters' clubs and the *ultras*. (For data on football fan associations see Dal Lago and Moscati 1992.)

A peculiarity of the official supporters' club is that they are recognized by the football authorities. Clubs linked to the same football team are usually all members of a *Centro di coordinamento* (Coordinating Centre) which, in turn, forms part of the Italian Federation of Football Supporters (FISSC). A similar association exists in England, the National Federation of Supporters' Clubs, to which some 140 'official' supporters' clubs are affiliated. In Italy, however, there exists no equivalent of the Football Supporters' Association, a national association of fans that is not club-based.

In the case of *Serie A* (Italy's first division) in particular, supporters' clubs are often based away from the city in which the football club is located. In these cases, a national federation or association often coordinates the various clubs which are scattered all over the country

*This chapter was written by Rocco de Biasi and translated and edited by Liz Crolley

and/or abroad: for example, *l'Associazione Italiana Milan Clubs*, founded in 1967, comprises 1,340 clubs, 11 of which are based outside Italy, and has around 200,000 members. The role of these supporters' clubs is crucial, for example, in the organization of transport to away matches, especially those played abroad. The most impressive example was the organization of the mass exodus of AC Milan fans to Barcelona in 1989 for the Champions' Cup Final against Steaua Bucharest. *L'Associazione Italiana Milan Clubs* ran no fewer than 450 coaches, a ferry and 25 aeroplanes to transport 25,000 *rossoneri* (Milan fans, known as such because of the Milan club colours of red and black). The image and prestige of AC Milan president, Silvio Berlusconi, was heightened noticeably and this event pre-empted his appearance in the electoral arena.

Still in Milan, Internazionale (known as Inter) supporters' clubs also play a key role in the organization of Inter fans. Inter was responsible for introducing the most passionate, visually impressive styles of football support into Italy, based on the Spanish model. The club supported the foundation of a group known as the *I Moschettiere* (The Musketeers) who initiated this style of support. It was no coincidence that the establishment of *I Moschettieri* was sought by, among others, Inter's manager Helenio Herrera. Today, Inter's Coordinating Centre comprises 800 supporters' clubs throughout Italy and has a total of around 90,000 members.

The activities of a supporters' club do not centre solely around the organization of fans in the football stadium. Clubs have a headquarters (often, though not always, a bar) in which various recreational activities take place, some involving figures from the football club, such as players or directors. The supporters' club can also represent for its members a place to socialize, to relax after work, an opportunity to do something different, apart from football-related activities, among a group of friends. Even for those who do not attend the club headquarters regularly, being a member brings advantages: the possibility of obtaining match tickets, often at reduced prices, especially beneficial when it might be difficult to obtain one via normal channels. This perk is also a feature of *ultra* groups.

While supporters' clubs have members of all ages and from very diverse social backgrounds (this varies mostly in relation to the region, city or neighbourhood in which the club is based), *ultra* groups consist mainly of young people. One aspect that distinguishes the *ultra* groups from the supporters' club is the spectacular nature of their support. Italians refer to the staging of a match as a *spettacolo*. No English word adequately conveys the *spettacolo*, but it involves the creation of a special atmosphere characterized by a combination of colour, vibrance and noise. They provide a vivacious and vociferous form of support along with impressive, hi-tech choreography typical of the *curva* (the part of the ground located behind the goal where traditionally the most vociferous supporters gather). The editor of this chapter was amazed on experiencing first hand the organization of a choreographic display at one match, Genoa vs Liverpool in May 1992, by the *ultra* group the *Fossa del Grifoni*. Even more astounding were the financial resources, estimated at some £20,000, that went into the event.

Although *ultras* have created their own specific form of support which changed the image and style of *tifo* in Italy, some of their attitudes and behaviour are often compared to those of old English football hooligans. *Ultras* in Italy, therefore, represent an extreme form of support and also represent (to a lesser extent) football hooliganism.

In the 1990s, a new era has begun in which the culture of the *curva* has become vulnerable and consequently runs the risk of losing its self-reference or autonomy. In particular, attempts to infiltrate *ultra* groups by elements of the extreme right (operations which largely failed in the 1970s) today find less resistance than in the past. This is partly owing to the period of crisis that some *curva* organizations are suffering, in which the generational changes within the leadership structures are accompanied by indications of a lack of governability along with the breaking up or fragmentation of *ultra* organizations. The subculture of the ritual or gratuitous chanting of insults is infiltrated by chants that encourage intolerance. These are inspired, to a greater or lesser extent, by the extreme political right (and at least partly by simplified, secessionist versions of political slogans of the political party the *Lega Nord*).

Changes are taking place in *ultra* culture. It is not necessarily the case that the *curva* in Italian stadiums are politically neutral. The football ground cannot be considered a place of politics, but to continue to treat football as simply a leisure activity would equally be a serious error.

Militant fans and political allegiances

The murder of Vicente Spagnolo, the young Genoa fan stabbed to death by a Milan *ultra* on 29 January 1995, can be seen as a tragedy waiting to happen. Yet until then, violence in football had not aroused the political interest of the militants of a well-known self-governed social and political club in Milan; two weeks after the events in Genoa, this club, *Leoncavallo*, organized its first meeting on the topic (*Leoncavallo* is the most important social club of extreme left-wing youth of this type in Italy). In the opening speech at the meeting, one militant from the social club explained: 'This assembly has been called today because two weeks ago in Genoa one of our comrades was stabbed to death'. (The term 'comrade' implies a communist militant.)

The situation had been defined in a different way from that which an observer from the outside world might have expected without previous knowledge of the context. The manner in which the event had been covered by the media and understood by the public was a different one to that evoked by the *Leoncavallo* meeting; it dealt with the murder of a 26-year-old Genoa fan, an *ultra*. Both of the interpretations of the tragedy in Genoa (the first being that provided by the media, the second that which was discussed in the meeting of the *Leoncavallo* politico-social club) can be considered as accurate. It is true that Vicente Spagnolo was killed because, to his attackers, he was a Genoa *ultra*, and not because he was a member of the left-wing political social club *Zapata* in Genoa, but it is important to emphasize the fact that the event could have been legitimately reframed in political terms in the context of the meeting referred to above.

The aim here is not to find out which was more significant to Vicente Spagnolo's personal hierarchy of values, that of the militant fan or that of a political militant. It is important to point out, however, that the two allegiances or identities coexisted, and that one cannot be considered to the exclusion of the other.

The mutual influences (or 'interference') between fans in the *curva* and political extremism has several dimensions. The one which has been commented upon most, in great detail, involves the links between football hooliganism and the radical right. However, it would be inaccurate to claim that *ultra* culture is right wing. The vulnerability of the *ultra* culture when faced with attempts by political groups to infiltrate or exploit it is one issue, another issue is determining the precise roots of a phenomenon which since the early 1970s has involved both young and not so young people. Not everyone who goes in the *curva* behind the goal is an adolescent. Although *ultra* members are usually between the ages of 14 and 25, it must be stressed that there exists, especially among the leaders, a generation in their mid-thirties.

Apart from the gravity of some violent incidents, the ritualistic and aggressive nature of fans on the *curva* constitutes a phenomenon that is largely apolitical. Thus it can be said that the *ultra* culture has its own particular autonomy, which has strict rules, its own code and specific rituals, which are more important than the ideological orientation of a limited number of supporters or genuinely politicized militants. The *ultra* world is one in which contrasting political views can circulate from time to time and are most certainly linked to radical extremism. The unifying element remains the *tifo*, the football fan, or more precisely, a certain way of understanding football support. All those who frequent the *curva* in the ground can be recognized as having a role to play; they unite as football fans regardless of their possible political allegiances. Any militant *ultra*, who is not usually very highly politicized, is aware of the repertoire of rules that govern the behaviour of fans of the *curva*. They are socialized into holding certain values – including the acceptance of violence or physical clashes with their opponents – and learn certain patterns of behaviour and observable forms of expression in the stadium during the football match. Their behaviour depends on the situation, on circumstance. There is a way in which they are expected to behave, a predetermined code, and circumstance is the catalyst to this code. These characteristics of the *ultras* come before any political beliefs they might hold. In the 1970s when they were established, *ultra* groups were not really extremist groups, either left or right wing, but rather the names or symbols adopted by *ultra* groups often alluded to political extremism (for example, the name *Brigate* (Brigades), now widespread, or the images of Che Guevara or Celtic crosses on their flags). Triani (1994) points out that *ultras* did not have or want to have political leanings.

Symbols of political extremism and parapolitical slogans have filtered into the culture of the *curva* fans, and been adapted (or 'recodified'). This process has been discussed elsewhere (see De Biasi 1993; Dal Lago and De Biasi 1994) and is known as 'reframing' or 'keying' (Goffmann 1974). It is true that several radical or extreme groups of young people have tried to transform the stadium into a political arena, but in most cases the attempts have failed. The unity of the *curva* has managed to prevail despite attempts to confer a unanimous political connotation onto the *ultra* fans which led to cracks appearing in the unity of *ultra* organizations. *Ultra* groups have not, however, remained entirely neutral or uncontaminated by these attempts. It is no coincidence that, for example, in Milan's Divisional Police Station, the political bureau that deals with the extreme left carries out investigative and preventive activities on the AC Milan *ultras* and similar activities on the Inter radical right. This does not, however, imply that political extremism is of greater priority to the fans of the *curva* than football support. It was simply easier for neo-fascist organizations (subsequently *naziskins*) to operate among Inter fans, just like the former exponents of the extreme left of the late 1970s became football militants after the crisis of the extreme left. On the one hand, around the end of the 1980s Lazio *ultras* provided a historical example of a *curva in nero* ('the black *curva*', black being the colour of fascism). On the other hand, the attitude that 'the *curva* is not political' or that 'politics divides while football fans unite' has remained unquestioned for numerous *ultra* associations, despite the contradictions outlined above.

The serious political vulnerability of the fans on the *curva* is without doubt a recent phenomenon; in fact, it is not an exclusively political vulnerability. *Ultra* organizations are now suffering a process of fragmentation; established in the 1970s, consolidated as highly struc-tured organizations in the 1980s, they are now showing visible signs of crisis. There are several symptoms: the absence of a generational change-over from the old leadership to a new one, their fragmentation or splitting into different groups, the emergence of violent, unofficial groups who escape the control of the recognized leaderships. As far as the other dimension to *ultra* culture is concerned – their style of support (choreography, passion for the game, and other aspects of football ritual) – the predominance of physical clashes with opposing fans involves less and less ritual, more and more 'aggro'. *Ultra* organizations risk becoming weakened and unstable, and consequently, perhaps, more dangerous. In the opinion of a senior police officer in Milan:

If these groups of fans come together under a certain flag, or label, under a symbol of some significance, and if there are people at the head of this group who are recognized as leaders, let's just say it all makes our life much easier. If on the other hand, it can be seen, as is the case in recent times – at least this seems to be the tendency – that there is a splintering of groups and gangs, then our police work becomes more difficult. This is because these groups and gangs can move around and hide themselves during the course of a season, and you then have difficulties in your police operations to stay on top of these continual developments. Whereas when the phenomenon was more clear-cut and more stable, it was much easier for us. When you talk to the people, and intervene when it is necessary to intervene, you can keep things stable, within the limits of certain possibilities. Then you have a situation that evolves in a positive manner. You try to speak to these people, to make them aware of the situation, and do it in a way that makes them understand that Sunday is a day for entertainment not for fighting. But when you start to see groups and gangs of all kinds forming, which are difficult to suss out because they keep moving around and hiding themselves throughout the season, and in addition there is splintering of the groups, then your work becomes more difficult. And that's true whether you are talking about mediation, confrontations, investigations or interventions.

The SIULP, the main union of police officers, also maintained, during recent discussions on anti-violence laws sparked by the events in Genoa, that it would be a dangerous mistake to impose the dissolving of *ultra* groups themselves because it would lead to the loss of even the slightest degree of endogenous control over the more violent fringes, or 'stray dogs', which still exist with these associations.

Are *ultras* right wing?

The stereotypical image of the *naziskins* has led to an assumption about *ultras*: the identification between the *tifoso di curva* and the militancy of the extreme right. The *skinhead* – one style among many, but not the only model for the *tifoso di curva* – has been reduced to a variety of *naziskins*. As Valerio Marchi has explained in attempts to correct this distorted view of the *skinhead*, 'Given that a style is not a club nor a party, where it is possible to join or to be expelled, and that there are no superior beings in a position to state who is or is not a *skinhead*, the question remains of why *skin* and *naziskin* became synonyms in the multimedia bombardment' (Marchi 1994: 63). Marchi, along the lines of Eric Dunning's (1986) analysis of the masculine style of violence of British hooligans, confirms that subcultures are extremely complex and that the subtle political differences between youth groups are important.

On the one hand, the term *skinhead* is too general and oversimplifies the wide variety of subcategories that exist and are subsumed within the single term. There are many groups, most of which hold widely differing political views, yet they are frequently all labelled together as *skinheads*. Thus there arises the need to develop more categories regarding the simple classification of the *ultras* in strictly politico-ideological terms, the need to develop subcategories of the term *skinhead*, which is just one of the numerous possible components of the *ultra* world. On the other hand, in more superficial sociological analyses the temptation arises to rely on common belief or stereotype attributing a specific, single ideological connotation to all extreme football fans, despite recognizing a lack of relevant supporting empirical evidence. For example, according to Sandro Segre,

Even when *skinheads* and football hooligans do not physically seem similar, they share the same subculture, leaning politically towards the extreme right. They are very aggressive and characterized by a sense of authoritarianism, masculinity and racism.

(Segre 1993: 197)

This perspective is more simplistic and does not analyse the political and ideological differences between groups.

It is one thing to recognize that for years the *curva* in Italian football grounds has been, among other things, a place where people are socialized into intolerance and aggression (De Biasi 1993), but another one to jump to the conclusion that any single political view will be held within a widely varied culture – youth or not. This is in fact unlikely to be the case. What has given the *ultra* culture strength since the mid-1970s has been their apolitical nature, and what is making them vulnerable today is the decline of their organizations and of the power of unity they embodied. There has been an abrupt change in the type of violence carried out (a movement from organized, small-scale fights to stabbings and forms of hooliganism that take place spontaneously in small groups, more akin to the old English style of hooliganism – see Dunning *et al.* 1988). Alongside this type of violence of the extreme *tifo*, which is related to the culture of the *curva*, episodes of instrumental violence with strongly defined political characteristics of the extreme right have recently broken out. An appropriate illustration of this type of violence took place in Brescia, during a match between Brescia and Roma, on 13 November 1994, when the Deputy Head of the Divisional Police was stabbed and a Chief Inspector of the National Police seriously wounded. During the hearing of the case in court it emerged that the attack on the police, and not on opposing fans as is usually the case, had been premeditated. Among those charged are an ex-member of the neo-fascist MSI party in Rome and the leader of the *Movimento Politico* (Political Movement), the leading so-called *naziskin* organization.

Another factor leads us to look for political connotations in what appears at the moment to be genuine attempted murder: the fact that some of those who took part in the Brescia incident were not regular attenders at football matches, but belonged to ultra-right groups associated with Mauricio Boccacci's Political Movement in Rome. 50–60 militants took part in the trouble in Brescia and they have all now been identified as extreme right-wing activists.

(*La Reppublica* 28 November 1994)

An analogous episode took place two weeks after the Brescia incident in the *Curva Nord* in the Olympic Stadium in Rome, during the Lazio–Roma derby. Again in this case the focal point was not violence between rival sets of fans, but a deliberate attack on the forces of law and order. The newspaper headlines read: 'Fifteen minutes of madness in the derby: eight police officers wounded. United against the police, Lazio and

Roma *ultras* joined forces and united under the same black flag'
(*Corriere della Sera* 28 November 1994).

Even bearing in mind the limited sources upon which we are basing
this line of thought (newspaper articles) it is obvious, nevertheless, that
these incidents involved more than the simple hostility between
traditionally rival fans. For a long time the vague parapolitical leanings
of some groups of fans were nearly always secondary to their
relationships of friendship or allegiances (*gemellagi*, literally twinning)
with other sets of fans. Otherwise, we would have quite a simple map
of rivalries between *ultra* groups, determined by their political tendencies. (As outlined by Eurispes (1994) the matter is considerably more
complex.)

The 'antagonistic left' and the fans of the *curva*

The relative autonomy of the *curva* culture is clearly situated within the
world of youth and is linked to the self-governed political social clubs
or to other elements of the antagonistic left. A militant from Milan's
(political) social club *Leoncavallo di Milano* explained how there are
clashes among left-wing fans, such as *Livorno–Pisa, Perugia–Terni* and
other fans who claim to be on the left, but then football factors become
more important than the political factors.

Returning to the original issue, after the death of Vicente Spagnolo, the
Genovese supporter stabbed to death by a Milanese *ultra*, the *Leoncavallo*
Social Club organized a meeting because a comrade had died. Vicente
Spagnolo's funeral was covered on television news bulletins all over Italy:
hundreds of young Italians with their left fist raised in salute, and at the
same time, wearing scarves of the *Fossa dei Griffoni* (the Genoa *ultra*
group of which Vicente Spagnolo was a member). Are the two symbolic
actions of equal significance? Can the football militancy of the Genoa fans
coexist alongside a political allegiance?

According to Eurispes' map of the *ultra* movement (1994: 296) 'left
wing ideology dominates' Genovese football support. However, during
conversations with the leader of the dissolved *Fossa dei Grifoni*, a group
that has already been the object of a detailed ethnographic study by the
author of this chapter (De Biasi 1993), it was confirmed that the
zapatisti, that is, those who attend the left-wing social club *Zapata*, are
one element (probably not the most important) of Genoa's *Gradinata
Nord* end in the Luigi Ferraris stadium. The same opinion was voiced by
a Genoa fan during the meeting of the *Leoncavallo* Social Club on 12
February 1995. As a young member of *Zapata* said,

The *ultras* have been defined as being right wing. I personally have nothing to
do with *ultras*. I go to the match and find it absurd to call it right wing. Of course
there will be right-wing people in the ground as in the rest of society. I see a
mixture in the stadium. Everyone together.

This reflects an opinion that is widespread among football fans in Italy and has been detailed in several sociological studies. But the most interesting thing is that this was said in a *political* meeting. As one Cosenza fan said in the same meeting, 'In my opinion, in antagonistic situations in Italy football fans in the *curva* have been treated diffidently, the *curva* and the *ultras* are bureaucrats who work for the state . . . it's an area of no interest to us.'

In effect, in the opinion of the radical right, youth groups and organizations of the antagonistic left, with a few exceptions, have shown little interest in confronting or exploiting an event which brings together a considerable number of young Italians across the country every Sunday. For example, the *leoncavalli,* the most politicized militants, have also looked in the past at the *ultra* world with distrust and even a certain scorn for their political apathy.

The discussions in the Milanese social club initiated by the death of Vicente Spagnolo is evidence of a renewed political interest and of an effort to understand an element of youth subculture.

There are comrades, people with a similar political conscience to ours who go to football. Parallels can be drawn between life in the social club and that of the football ground. Social clubs are places that give a sense of belonging, of community, of solidarity among people, and those who voluntarily frequent football grounds feel the same thing there.

(Introductory speech in the meeting of the *Leoncavallo,* 12 May 1995)

This explains the issue of double allegiance, of feeling a sense of identity, belonging or allegiance to both a football team and a political ideology, perhaps even a double militancy. It is not, however, resolved as an issue. The contradictions remain.

The 'footballization' of politics?

According to Milan manager, Fabio Capello, the answer is becoming more and more obvious. In October 1994, after some trouble in the Milan *curva* (more specifically after missiles had been thrown and several players injured) Capello declared, 'Is the *curva* infiltrated by people who want to harm Berlusconi? I'm certain of it, perhaps they were *leoncavallinos* [militant extreme left]' (*Corriere della Sera,* 28 October 1994). Here the Milan manager redefined in political terms an ordinary violent incident between football *ultras.* Moreover, the Milanese police discounted the possibility of any link between the above incident and an anti-Berlusconi sabotage of AC Milan by the *Leoncavallo.* It is pertinent here to point out that Capello had looked to political interpretations on another occasion a few weeks earlier, when he said to the press, 'Before Berlusconi entered politics, we had traditional, institutional and football rivalries. It's undeniable that now we have political rivalries too. It's perhaps the *progressitas* [left-wing electors] who dislike us most' (*Corriere della Sera* 3 September 1994).

The fact that football and politics influence each other (that 'interference' takes place between football and politics) assumes greater proportions here: it was not just the fans but AC Milan's manager who conferred a political dimension on football. This 'interference' between football and politics is evident in language and styles of communication too. This is a consequence of Berlusconi's involvement in football, or rather, of his entrance into politics. It involves not only the politicization of football, but also the reverse process, the influence of football on politics (or a kind of 'footballization' of politics). So, in recent years not only have football rituals become more vulnerable to the influence of politics, as the earlier examples illustrated, but also there are opposing tendencies: in some social contexts, and in particular on the political stage, certain types of ritual participation of the crowd are adopted, participation in expressive codes of football culture sometimes with strong analogies and very formal patterns.

Some communicative styles and metaphors are typical of a limited sphere of sport (of football as a spectacle). They seem today to characterize other social situations which are based on ritual conflict and collective exuberance. Mass demonstrations, electoral campaigns and the televised transmission of the political spectacle in Italy have all adopted a discursive style which originated in programmes dedicated to football. It is important to note that they involve contests in which there is always a public, an audience, which actively participates in social situations whose prime objective is not to entertain. As in the football ground, the public is excitable, emotional, can clap or boo, and the protagonists of the social performance no longer seem to follow the rules of fair play. Instead they offer those present (or the television viewer) a highly ritualistic performance which, unlike in the past, allows some relaxing of emotional control.

It is significant that some of these rituals on certain rather heated, animated programmes of political debate or political 'spectacle' on Italian television were initially characteristics of armchair football supporting. As Triani observes, in the Italian case, 'It is evident that behaviour and language from the football ground is spreading beyond its traditional confines and sporting metaphor is becoming a metaphor for life' (Triani 1994: 62).

While originally football chants on the *curva* had evolved, para-doxically, from the political slogans of the mass demonstrations of the 1970s, towards the end of the 1980s the opposite occurred: the reappearance of the mobilization of the people into the political conflict brought the football-style chanting with it. In 1993 during the second ballot of the local elections, in some large Italian cities the atmosphere where supporters of the two candidates met was just like the atmosphere at a football match.

The Berlusconi case is the most obvious example of this tendency. How useful has it been to AC Milan to construct an image of Berlusconi as a winner? As Berlusconi owns the largest private television station in Italy, he is in a position to manipulate his own media coverage. Some commentators are convinced that AC Milan's victories since 1988 have been identified almost automatically with Berlusconi and his company Fininvest and, consequently, have been associated with the rise of a political party. It is not our task here to establish the accuracy of this suggestion. It is, however, relevant to point out that the influence of football on politics, like the politicization of football, has surfaced recently in various contexts, not only in the Berlusconi case but also among his opponents as well as in the press in general.

At first Berlusconi's choice of the football slogan *Forza Italia* seemed a strange one to give to a political party. Yet it seemed to be largely approved of and extremely effective. (Similar successful adoptions of football slogans occurred during South American dicatorships in countries such as Brazil and Argentina.) Of course, we are not trying to attribute Berlusconi's success in the 1994 general elections to the choice of a sporting metaphor. Our aim is to gain a deeper insight into some formal aspects of football culture in Italy and into styles of communication and contexts (or 'frames') in which they function. It is from this perspective that we view the Berlusconi case.

Although in Italy Berlusconi's use of football terminology and metaphor is now well known to everyone, at first several opinion-makers derided it. It scandalized cultural purists but passion for football is one of the most important aspects of Italian culture and the language of football is one of the most expressive codes shared by a large section of the male population (see chapter 9 on male and female roles in football). Sections within the party were renamed clubs; the list of candidates for the elections became a 'purchasing campaign' as in football. Almost immediately after the World Cup the *Forza Italia* candidates were renamed the *azzurri* (the Blues, after the Italian national team). At this time, Candido Cannavò, director of the national newspaper *Gazzetta dello Sport* which ran a campaign against this labelling of *Forza Italia* candidates as *azzurri*, printed dozens of letters from fans who were protesting against it. But it was in vain and the *forzisti*, the exponents of *Forza Italia*, became known as *azzurri*. During the USA 1994 World Cup finals, commentators in Italy tried desperately to avoid using this term which has now become politically contaminated. The daily newspapers, who are either for or against Berlusconi, assimilate the football vocabulary into politics. So when Berlusconi's AC Milan won the league a few weeks after his electoral victory it was said that 'Even Milan's championship celebrations have turned into an anthem for *Forza Italia*' (*La Reppublica* 19 April 1994). Another example of mixing sporting and political metaphors appeared in the press when Berlusconi, on 18 May 1994, obtained a vote of confidence by the senate by just two votes on the same evening as AC Milan won the Champions' Cup final, beating Barcelona 4–0 in Athens: 'Berlusconi's figures: 159 in favour, 4 goals' (*L'Indipendiente* 19 May 1994).

It is not the political repercussions of those episodes that is important here but the fact that the communicative style was originally linked specifically to football culture and was then contaminated by political

connotations or overtones. This terminology forms a style of communication which has been transferred from the context of football into
politics. In sociological terms, it can be said that it is now 'transcontextual' terminology.

Although football is a form of entertainment, at the same time it
intertwines elements of culture that go beyond sport (symbolic, economic, ethnic, illegal, etc.) and which make it extremely complex.
Football fans are well aware that modern-day football is far from being
an ideal, pure game, yet for the football fan the football event has a
special autonomy: it is set apart from other events.

Yet this autonomy is purely perceptual and does not concern the
social or structural organization of football in Italy. This is not
autonomous. It would be difficult for it to have neutral or politically
innocent connotations because football is primarily an industry, and as
such is dependent on political and economic policies for its success (see
Hoberman 1988), but this aspect of football being a business takes a
backstage role (see Goffman 1969). It cannot be perceived to be all-
important and cannot be too visible as this would shatter the illusion of
what should primarily be a sporting event involving a football match and
the participation of the *tifosi*. As Rusconi outlines, 'Sport is a political
fact. But if we ask any sporting figure, any fan, any citizen of this
country, they will deny that politics enters (or should enter) into sport'
(Rusconi 1988: 9). This is despite recent indications of discontent
concerning the way football is being run. The illusion of football being
a sport not a business is a fragile one and economic factors take priority
in decision-making within the football structures. Economic factors
forced Juventus during the season 1994–95 to abandon playing at its
home ground, the Estadio delli Alpi (see Figure 8.1) owned by the local
authorities, in protest at the exorbitant rent charged (Juventus played its
'home' games in Milan's impressive San Siro). It was economic and
political factors that influenced this decision.

The *ultra* world, however, does enjoy a high degree of autonomy but
at the same time its vulnerability has been indicated. It is possible that
eventually the political element of some extreme groups might find a
niche in Italian football replacing some of the apolitical *ultra* groups.
Every act of communication is linked to a context and it is that context
which defines how any utterance will be interpreted. Expressions once
associated with the football context have now taken on political
connotations as the two communicative styles merge.

Football cannot be reduced to a single dimension. Within one stadium
there exists mutual influencing of different worlds ('interference'
between different worlds). The central event, the football match itself, is
menaced by events that can, using an expression of Goffman's, 'poke
through the thin sleeve of immediate reality' (Goffman 1961: 81). In
other words, the match does not take place in isolation. There are no
barriers between football events and the rest of reality. The participants
(the fans) do not cut themselves off from external matters. In a sense,
football does not cut out external factors but it acts more like a sieve than

Figure 8.1   The Estadio delli Alpi, home to both Juventus and Torino, was temporarily abandoned by Juve in protest at the high charges demanded by its owners, the local authority

a solid wall, and the sieve is not only selecting, but also modifying what it filters. This is true also in the case of the political symbols, that can assume another meaning in the football context and lose their original (political) sense.

It has been argued, therefore, that the mutual influences between football and politics are strong in Italy. It has been pointed out that the *ultras* of the *curva* are vulnerable to political infiltration but it is necessary to be aware of the dangers of assigning too much power to political extremism over the *ultras* of the *curva*. The double allegiances of some fans is demonstrated via the existence of politicized *curvas* such as those of the antagonistic left. Apart from that, and except for the infiltration of elements of the radical right, which have a specific political aim, the *ultra* world appears to have a rather ambivalent and contradictory relationship with politics. It continues to enter voluntarily into an apolitical conflict which involves the symbolic opposition of rival sets of fans in the football stadium.

There has been a sort of double movement: not only that of politics into football but also of football into politics. In Italy metaphor, codes, rituals, language and expressions typical of the football culture seem to have taken root in some areas of politics. It is undeniably a period of instability and change in the relationship between football and politics in Italy and many of the rituals and communicative styles linked to the football culture are no longer football-specific but have been adopted by the political world.

CHAPTER 9

Women can't play, it's a male ball: her story in football

In many countries, football is seen as the 'national' sport (see chapter 1). It is sometimes difficult to perceive the position of women within definitions of 'nation'; indeed women have been largely excluded from the main text of the book thus far. This is not owing to any bias on the part of the authors, far from it, but is a result of the fact that not only has football traditionally been regarded as a male sport in the countries in which the case studies have been carried out, but also the notion of state and the pioneering of nationalism have been largely male preserves (Dunning 1986).

It has become evident throughout the case studies that a state does not automatically equal a nation, in fact, it appears that it rarely does, and women can in many ways be seen as a submerged nation with a state. Although women as a nation do not have a defined territorial area, they can share other features which constitute the definition of nation – the sharing of common identity and sentiments, the myth of common descent (see chapter 1). Women are not represented in what is supposed to be the 'national' sport.

Historically, women have been politically unrecognized and marginalized. Over half the population has been ignored and has lacked representation in decision-making processes. Football is an extension of the state which continues, despite the huge advances made by women from the 1960s onwards, to be male-dominated. The political structures of the state are reflected in football, a sport created by men, for men.

Recent academic interest in sport has been reflected in the ever-increasing popularity of a relatively new discipline, the sociology of sport, in which the interest in women's sport has produced many publications. Relatively little research, however, has been carried out into women's role in football. Many of the studies into women and sport, along with much feminist interest in sport, have originated in the USA where football (or soccer) does not enjoy the popularity it commands in other countries. Moreover, football is distinctive in the USA as being a female rather than a male sport.

This chapter will focus on women's role in football in England, but conclusions can be drawn from the situation outlined in England for most states in which football is the national sport. Some of the reasons why women have been traditionally excluded from football in most countries will be described, and women's involvement in football at different levels will be documented: as players, as fans and in the media.

It will be demonstrated how women's involvement in football was discouraged and marginalized for a long time and that it is only recently that women's interest in football is being tolerated, even promoted, particularly as fans. The developments of the early 1990s and changes in women's relationship with football are discussed in some detail.

Separate, but related, issues concerning women's role in football are investigated in each of the three areas mentioned above: distributional issues (in which there is a relative absence of women in football at all levels, in all areas) and relational issues (which examine how women's involvement in football is seen in relation to men's involvement).

Reasons for women's exclusion from football

Before exploring the reasons why women have traditionally been excluded from the world of football, it is useful to emphasize that it is not unusual for women to be unrepresented in areas of public life. Sport, and football as a sport, is one expression of culture, and as with many other public aspects of society, such as political and economic activity and literary writing, it is the dominant social groups (often white males) who have access to that field. Feminist theories have accused men of deliberately seeking to legitimize their power through sport by reinforcing the concept of patriarchy. It is not the aim here to allocate blame for women's under-representation in football, indeed it is not our aim to decide whether or not blame is warranted, but it is enlightening to explore possible reasons for the absence of women from football.

It is necessary to explain the historical perspective. The first half of the nineteenth century in Britain was one in which men's dominance over women was challenged and began to erode following drastic transformations in the roles of men and women. In the latter part of the century, there was an opposite movement to emphasize distinct gender roles. Victorian social institutions promoted gender distinctions and sport served to reinforce the ideological conception of males' superiority over females. This superiority was both moral (to do with values) and physical. Men were in positions of power to reinforce such concepts.

Another historical factor is women's general and traditional lack of participation in leisure activities, of which sport (and therefore football) was just one aspect. Responsibilities for women lay in the home and in a duty to rear children and feed a hungry 'working' husband. There was little time to spend free from family commitments.

The principal reason, however, why women are excluded from the football culture involved the reinforcement of gender roles via football. The concept of patriarchy is key. A patriarchal society is one which is based on the belief that the male is the superior sex and many of the social institutions and social practices are then organized to reflect this belief. In a sense, a patriarchal society is one which is organized so that the belief in male supremacy 'comes true' (Spender 1985). The institution of football in many countries serves to perpetuate the existence of a patriarchal society. It does this via the reinforcement of gender roles on two levels – physical and moral – and this plays a part in contributing to the historical patterns of male empowerment and female disadvantage (Whitson 1990).

Moral gender roles

In football, as in most sports, the qualities admired most frequently are those of competitiveness, stamina, aggression, meritocratic (and patriarchal) values typical of male-dominated institutions and structures of dominance that exist outside football (in politics, for example). These are qualities that are considered desirable in men, but less so in women who have traditionally been socialized into passive roles where skills of persuasion, tact and subtlety are more admirable means to an end than direct and aggressive competition. Sex differences in patterns of sport socialization, 'have demonstrated how the dominant institutional forms of sport have naturalised men's power and privilege over women' (Messner and Sabo 1990: 2). Moreover, it was historically seen as 'unwomanly' or 'unfeminine' for a woman to possess those characteristics valued so highly in men which form part of the construction of male solidarity. Women's ability to possess these qualities is frequently questioned and many commentators are still genuinely surprised when a women is prepared to dedicate the same level of commitment, for example, to football as a man, be it as a player or as a supporter.

A man who travels weekly from Leeds to Liverpool for training sessions would be surprised at the level of commitment of a woman who travels from Liverpool to Doncaster for the same reason. Nick Hornby displays a similar level of distrust in the level of commitment of women as fans when he claims, 'I have met women who have loved football and go to watch a number of games a season, but I have not yet met one who would make that Wednesday night trip to Plymouth' (Hornby 1992).

Certain moral values, therefore, are perceived as being exclusive to men and they can be acquired through the football culture. Football forms part of the masculinizing process in which masculine values such as those mentioned above are ritualized. The superiority of masculine values are, therefore, underlined, the belief in male supremacy comes true.

The strong relationship between football and masculinity has been well documented (see Dunning *et al.* 1988) but for the purpose of this discussion it is important to note that in a society in which playing football, or even displaying an interest in football, is a firm stepping-stone for a boy to achieve the status of masculinity, it should be no surprise that girls do not follow the same process.

Physical gender roles

As with moral gender roles, patriarchal values reinforce physical gender roles. Football forms an important part of the social process of masculinization which turns boys into men. It is a well-worn cliché that football is supposedly 'a man's game'. Notions of physical strength, speed and power are appreciated as part of masculinity and while desirable attributes in men are not valued in women. Athletic women are acceptable providing they do not lose their 'femininity' (e.g. tennis player Chris Evert-Lloyd charmed her way into the public's hearts). If, however, women are muscular or appear physically strong they can be accused of being 'tomboys', 'unwomanly' or 'butch'.

Ironically, within (men's) football, strength and bully tactics alone are not respected. The Wimbledon team of the 1980s was loathed by football fans all over Britain for the players' use of physical force as intimidation and were accused of playing 'ale-house' football. Passing skills and dribbling abilities are valued too, although not to the exclusion of 'getting stuck in'. A player can be incredibly skilful, but if he does not go in for a 50–50 ball risking a broken leg, he is disparagingly labelled a coward (or worse still a 'woman' or a 'tart') and will never command the same respect from fans as a 'whole-hearted' less skilful but more overtly 'committed' player might do.

Women, it has been argued, are not as strong as men. Their participation in sport was resisted at the end of the nineteenth century and well into the twentieth. Some doctors even claimed that women needed to conserve all their energy for their reproductive organs (Kidd 1990). Even into the 1960s it was not uncommon to hear commentators express their opinions on the inappropriateness of women playing football. Former FA chief executive Ted Croker objected to women's participation in football, preferring women to be 'feminine'.

People who hold such opinions are trying to keep faith in the Victorian myth that women should be intellectually and physically frail. This myth persisted throughout the twentieth century and its legacy remains despite movements to dispel it, especially since the 1960s. The following sections explore these movements by looking at women's involvement in football as players, fans and in the media.

Women as players

Women's role in playing football will be outlined via the analysis of distributional issues and relational issues. As far as distributional issues are concerned women's role in football as players is relatively small. Indeed, compared to men, women's role in sport until the 1960s was minimal. The first Olympic marathon for men was in 1896, the first for women in 1988. The founder of the modern Olympics, Pierre de Coubertin, was not in favour of female participation in the Games, claiming that women playing sport went against the laws of nature and complaining that it was aesthetically displeasing. These attitudes survived for many years and, although heavily diluted in some cases, traces still remain. Those in control of sport are men. Women have no leadership models to follow. Of the 167 National Olympic Committee members worldwide in 1992, only 6 were women, and of the 94 International Olympic Committee members, 7 were women (and this is following a period of enlightened policy-making by the International Olympic Committee president Juan Antonio Samaranch – there were none before 1981).

Given the bleak prospects and lack of opportunities for women in sport in general, it is perhaps surprising that women's football did enjoy a boom period as early as the First World War; there are indications that women's eagerness to play football was present at the end of the nineteenth century (see Williams and Woodhouse 1991: 90) when the secretary of the British Ladies team, Nettie Honeyball, was instrumental in engendering interest. Women's enthusiasm was significant enough to spark action by the Council of the Football Association who in 1902 ordered that men and women should not play football together. Thus sex segregation in football was established.

This policy continues today, creating sporadic controversy among schoolchildren who believe that girls and boys should play together, especially before they reach puberty when there are no biological grounds upon which to justify segregation and the chances for girls to play in current all-boys teams would increase their opportunities of playing competitive football.

Football is part of the socialization process of a child and it is argued that segregation as early as in primary schools serves only to strengthen the gender roles. Segregation of the sexes in football took the form of a warning to male teams not to play with or against women and thus served to marginalize women in football. This marginalization has continued to the present day.

During the First World War men's football was suspended and women's football became increasingly popular. There is evidence, however, of women's football matches taking place much earlier. According to Newsham (1994: 14) the first recorded women's football match took place on 23 March 1895 when the British Ladies FC, whose president was Lady Florence Dixie (one of the early advocates of women's football), organized a game between the north and south of England (the north won 7–1). The best known women's team from the early twentieth century, when women's football hit its peak of popularity, was Dick Kerr's Ladies, formed in 1917 by female munition workers from Dick, Kerr & Company's factory in Preston. It was established to raise funds for charity. In December 1917 the team attracted a crowd of 10,000 against Arundel Coulthard Foundry (and won 4–0). Dick Kerr Ladies enjoyed tremendous success, acquired celebrity status and were in constant demand to play charity matches. Their function as fundraisers was crucial to their success. They made money and kept their sponsors happy: the name of the team became famous so they received positive publicity. In a sense Dick Kerr Ladies became the 'national' football team so that it was the women's team, arguably for the first (and only?) time in the history of sport in Britain, who were the prime source of national pride and the principal focus of attention in football.

Even during this boom period, however, there were many who were totally opposed to the idea of women playing football. The old 'relational' arguments involving the relationship between men and women in football emerged – that the woman's body was not built for football and could not cope with the physical strain involved. One of the Dick Kerr Ladies players, Molly Walker, was ostracized from her boyfriend's family because they did not approve of her participation in football (Newsham 1994).

However, it is important to point out that during the First World War women's football was not discouraged. Indeed in 1918 Dick Kerr Ladies were granted permission to play in (men's) league grounds, and played at Deepdale for a period. For a while at least then, both distributional and relational issues in women's football appeared to be more positive: women increased their participation and stigma attached to playing was (slightly) eroded, even though an undercurrent persisted.

Shortly after the First World War, however, following the return of the male footballers, the women were pushed aside. The relational issues concerning the appropriateness of women's involvement in football and their suitability to play, which were simmering during the war, came to the boil. Suddenly, the general (male?) opinion was that football was a dangerous sport and not one for women. Interestingly no one questioned the appropriateness of women playing hockey, arguably a more potentially dangerous sport, but one that was perceived as being acceptable for women to play. Such was the force of these opinions in football that in 1921 eventually women were outlawed from playing football in any league ground. This ban was to last until 1969, the year in which the Women's Football Association was launched.

So why were women accepted playing football during the First World War but not a few years later? This reversal of social standards was reflected in other spheres of life too. Women were forced to undertake traditionally considered male roles and occupations during the war in the absence of men, and were expected to revert back to their 'female' roles on the men's return. The relational issue of how women's football was perceived had appeared on the hidden agenda of the Football Association making their decision. The fact that more women participated in football and that women's football had been a success during the absence of male footballers meant that now men and women both wanted to play, the women constituted competition for the men thus threatening men's control of football. It was therefore in the interest of men's football that women should be discouraged. This is what happened. Women's football never again achieved the popularity, prestige and attention it did during the First World War.

Further attempts were made to discredit women's football by suggestions that funds raised by charity matches were not being channelled into the appropriate coffers and allegations of corruption in women's football spread. This contributed to the ever-increasing stigmatization of women's football. Although it is difficult to ascertain the veracity of the allegations, it is unlikely that the women themselves would have been responsible even if they were true given that they were rarely involved in the financial side of running clubs. Nevertheless, events conspired against the reputation of women's football and these factors contributed to justify the FA's decision to ban women from playing on league grounds. The chauvinists, the traditionalists, the medical 'experts' and the anti-women's football lobby had won and the threatened supremacy of male football was guaranteed. Women's football had been deliberately quashed.

Nevertheless, the women continued playing. There were many fewer teams, but those who played in the 1920s were in demand. Women's football continued to consist of charity matches and regularly attracted crowds of over 10,000. The largest ever recorded crowd at a women's match was on Boxing Day 1920 at Goodison Park when 53,000 witnessed Dick Kerr Ladies play St Helens (an estimated 10,000 to 14,000 were locked out).

At this time, enlightening ideologies were imported from France concerning the nature of women's football. It was during the 1920s that women's football in France began to form. Mme Milliat, founder of the Federation that governed women's football in France, was an influential figure and responsible for encouraging female participation in the sport. Unlike what happened in Britain, Milliat recognized that men's and women's football were different and that women should not try to beat the men at their own game but rather develop a particular 'women's' game. Women's football, she believed, was different from (not inferior to) the men's and should be judged by its own standards and own criteria, not by men's. These ideas were introduced into England via contact made during friendly matches played in England, which attracted considerable media coverage and an attendance of 25,000 for the first match, against Dick Kerr Ladies.

So women's football continued after the war. A Ladies FA was established in 1921 as leagues formed in different regions of England (e.g. Doncaster, Coventry, East Riding). It continued to be played in Scotland where Edinburgh Ladies dominated. Without the backing of the (men's) FA in England, however, women's football struggled financially and many teams gave up.

Opposition to women's football was to emerge sporadically from then to the present day. In 1938 Ted Robbins, a secretary of the Welsh FA, banned a women's charity match from taking place in Wales on the grounds that football was a man's game and it was not flattering for women to play. This was the same Ted Robbins who praised women's football in 1919 and approved of it providing women played against women (Newsham 1994). What made him change his mind? The reasons have already been outlined: a campaign against women playing football, their threat to men, increasing stigma associated with women playing in 1938 that was not so strong (or fashionable) in 1919. There are many such anecdotes illustrating the pejorative views and negative connotations of women's football.

By the early 1950s, there were around twenty-six women's football teams in England who played friendlies, charity matches and even trips abroad (e.g. Manchester Corinthians played in Jamaica, Italy and Latin America). Few changes of significance occurred in the history of women's football in the 1950s and early 1960s. It was in the late 1960s, possibly in part inspired by the victory of the men's England team in the 1966 World Cup final staged in England, that interest in women's football again intensified. Women were not ignored in the media coverage of the World Cup finals and there were special slots on television to explain the rules of the game to women.

Encouraged by signs of recognition from within the world of football, women's football once again increased in popularity. This eventually led to the launch of the Women's Football Association (WFA) in 1969. Its secretary was a man, Arthur Hobbs, thus women's football remained ultimately controlled by men. This era has been termed the 'new age' of women's football (Williams and Woodhouse 1991). The WFA had 44 founder member clubs; by 1972 this figure had increased to 182 and in the 1990s female participation in playing football is rising again.

Since the mid-1960s, there has been a gradual erosion of relational issues surrounding the appropriateness of women playing football, but the process is slow and (as is also the case with female fans) women are still not accepted in the 'man's game'. It is significant too that from the late 1960s onwards the women's movement really began to have an effect on British society. Women were encouraged to participate in what had traditionally been considered as male sports – contact sports such as football.

Feminism highlighted the inequalities and problems in both relational and distributional issues of women's participation in football. Concerning relational issues, feminism attempted to break down prejudices that women were incapable of physical activity or practising contact sports and to lessen the stigma associated with women who wanted to play sports such as football. Distributional issues centred around increasing the opportunities for girls and women to play football. One problem that the feminist movement has suffered in sport in general, but particularly pertinent to the discussion of women's football, is that different sections of the movement adopted different approaches and had different aims.

Simplifying extremely complex, sometimes subtle, divisions between sections of the movement, broadly speaking, liberal feminists demanded equal rights for women and men as individuals. Radical feminists claimed that equal opportunities are impossible within the present patriarchal structures and advocate a change in the system to allow women's football to develop within alternative structures. Socialist feminists believed equal opportunities, between men and women as between people of different social classes, are impossible in a capitalist society and they claim the first step towards equal opportunities must be socialism (Messner and Sabo 1990).

Despite the lack of unity of the feminist movement, considerable progress in the distributional issues surrounding female participation in football has been achieved (see pp. 137–8). As women have penetrated other male bastions in society, it is no surprise that they have also infiltrated football. However, as they have not succeeded in gaining control, power or equality (in terms of either relational or distributional issues) in other spheres of society, neither is it surprising that they are far from achieving this in the football world.

In recent years (especially since the mid-1980s in England and other Western European countries such as France, Spain and Italy – although slightly longer in Scandinavian countries), there has been an enormous escalation in interest and participation in football by women and girls. There are now some 15,000 registered players in England and 500 clubs affiliated to the FA (a 200 per cent increase since 1990). A national league was established in 1991. In 1994 some 2,159 females took FA Preliminary Awards, Football Leaders and teaching Certificate Awards (out of a total of 12,940) according to the FA Report for 1994. Women's football has strengthened at its grassroots, playing level. In the mean time, it has surrendered control of its institution. In 1984 the WFA affiliated to the (men's) FA and it was taken over as the Women's Football Alliance in 1993. The FA appointed a full-time coordinator of women's football, Helen Jevens. This loss of autonomy and control is the opposite to what the radical feminists wanted to see happen. Instead of developing independently as a sport, women's football is subsumed into a small, relatively insignificant, sub-element of men's sport.

Nevertheless, the FA tries to present an image that it is working hard to promote women's football; it does subsidize travel costs for women's teams in the national league and contribute towards officials' fees. The FA runs coaching sessions and organizes some training sessions. Indications are that much more needs to be done if women's football is to carve a niche for itself. Enthusiasm and commitment are present among girls of school age, just as it is among many boys, but there are still few outlets for such keen interest.

The FA claims to be making plans to develop the women's game at grassroots level and to encourage youngsters' participation, yet in its first full year in control of women's football (1994–95), the FA spent less on women's international matches than on (male) youth international matches; on operating expenses (administrative duties) it spent over 130 times more on men's football than on women's.

Not only is financial backing required if women's football is to continue to develop, but also attitudes need to change, via the education system and/or the media. In England, girls' football is rarely part of the school curriculum and teachers themselves provide some of the opposition. Those schools in which girls can play football rely on the dedication of teachers who give up their own time to run training sessions after school. Derek Marsden, one such teacher at Maghull High School, Merseyside, claims that girls' enthusiasm can be dampened by frustrated attempts to book pitches already in high demand by boys' teams.

In March 1996 Liverpool FC advertised a series of half-day coaching sessions for girls in the Merseyside area as part of a 'Kick Inequality Out of Football' campaign. The club was astounded by the response it received and had to alter initial plans to hold all sessions in one week to expand the scheme over several months. The lack of opportunities for girls in schools is still the source of many irate letters to schools or newspapers.

There is also concern over the limited opportunities for girls once they leave school. The FA is making some positive advances in this area. Over 1,000 women now hold football teaching certificates and 400 hold FA preliminary coaching badges. Middlesbrough Ladies have their own female coach who also teaches part-time in the 'Football in the Community' programme.

The football clubs themselves are trying to include female football in their programmes (although some with greater gusto than others). Some run five-a-side tournaments or training sessions (as in the example of Liverpool). Over three-quarters of FA Premier and Football League clubs now have a women's team affiliated.

It seems, therefore, that distributional issues are beginning to be addressed and although far more support (particularly financial) is needed to progress female football further, some indicators are encouraging. Yet despite the increased popularity, or arguably increased opportunities for females to play football, female footballers continue to be marginalized, even trivialized. Women's football does not receive anywhere near the recognition and prestige as men's and this is reflected not only in the meagre proportion of media space allocated to it (see pp. 141–3), but also in pay (or lack of pay), prize monies, sponsorship, etc. Doncaster Belles is the most successful women's team in the recent history of women's football, winning the (Women's) FA Cup twice and the Premier League twice in the period between 1991 and 1995 (see Figure 9.1), yet it cannot attract sponsorship to keep the club solvent and needs to hold fundraising events. Its case is typical in women's football. The women's league survived on a £25,000 grant from the Football Trust and £40,000 from the Sports Council and attracts no sponsorship.

Women's achievements in football remain a 'deviation from the norm' as evidenced in its title 'women's football' (as opposed to football). It is considered subordinate and inferior not only to men's football but also to boys' football. Commentator Archie Macpherson made a revealing statement on television about the status of women's football in 1994 when he criticized the overuse of Wembley Stadium to host competitions. He said that it was losing its special aura because of such overuse and that even women could play there.

The notion that women's football is substandard is even inherent in compliments. One of the authors, while attending the Women's Cup Final at Prenton Park, Tranmere, in 1995, overheard one (male) fan

Figure 9.1   Arsenal Ladies about to kick off against Doncaster Belles in the match which decided the women's national division championship in April 1995. The Stainforth Miners' welfare ground has no cover, seating or terracing

impressed by the high standard of play in the game enthusing, 'This isn't just women's football, this is football'.

Only by people watching, learning and appreciating women's football will attitudes change. Doncaster chairman Robert Kantecki claimed, 'Most of our supporters are men. They used to come to joke about watching the players swap shirts, but now they appreciate the football' (quoted in *The Times* 22 February 1993). Women's football is beginning to forge its own identity. Judith Draycott, chairperson of Aldwick Town, echoes the voice of Mme Malliat in the 1920s when she states, 'Women don't have to do things in the same way as men. We think differently and we've got different skills. It's men who have a problem if they think the only way to approach things is their way' (quoted in *Football Monthly* August 1991).

Finally, it is not automatic that football should be considered a male sport, or that it should form part of the masculinizing process. Thus, there is potential for change. The notion of football being too rough for females is merely a construction of our society. The evidence lies in the USA where the situation regarding football (or soccer) is very different from the one described thus far which is widespread in Western Europe.

Football in the USA is not a male preserve, but a woman's sport. The notion of football being 'a man's game' does not exist. On the contrary, 'soccer' is perceived as being a non-contact sport (the comparison being made with American football) and thus a sport for those who are not strong enough to play 'football'. Women's football is further developed in the USA than men's football. The USA won the 1991 Women's World Cup while the men would have been unlikely qualifiers for the finals had the country not been hosts in 1994.

In Sweden too, although football is still perceived as a male sport, the women's game is much stronger than in Britain. Sweden has acquired a reputation for egalitarianism in social differentiation and gender, and football responded to social changes and policies adopted by a series of Social Democratic governments. English football is toying with the idea of change at present, but resistance is strong involving not only women's participation in playing football, but also their role as fans.

Women's involvement as fans

Women's involvement in football as fans will be examined from both distributional and relational perspectives. A detailed analysis of the proportion of football support is not necessary for one to realize that women are not equally represented alongside men on the terraces (or in the stands). An investigation into women's experiences at football and the views of both female and male football fans might help highlight some of the relational issues which surround women as football fans and serve to explain the unequal distribution of fans. Finally, the recent rise in female support will be outlined and reasons for such an escalation in interest postulated.

It is relatively recently (from the mid-1980s onwards) that interest in football has augmented significantly among females. Today, according to most estimates in England as well as in Spain and Germany, on average women constitute between 10 and 15 per cent of football crowds at most clubs. It is possible that the number of female fans today at least in part reflects the successful policy of the 'feminization of football' which emerged as a response to football's hooligan problem of the early 1980s which seemed to be destroying football. The aim of Thatcher's policy was to adjust the distribution of female and male fans, increase the proportion of female fans and thus reduce the violence at football grounds: it was hoped that women would have a calming influence and would pacify the hooligans. Family stands were built as special areas where women and children would feel safe. It is possible that the feminization theory was a cover-up for the *embourgeoisement* of football, which was supposed to have the effect of pricing out the violent element, the working-class males who were considered responsible for most violent incidents in football. Thatcher's policies, continued by Major, can therefore be interpreted as an attempt to remove the working class from football culture and make more money from it in the process rather than to increase the presence of women.

Research carried out by Woodhouse (1991) into attitudes of female football fans suggested that they suffer a conflict of identities – between that of being a woman and that of being a football fan. The two identities clash as that of being a football fan is male gender based. Certainly research undertaken by one of the authors confirms the existence of such conflicts. While wishing away the sexism that is rife in the football context, many female fans are unwilling to promote any changes in football that might disturb the present gender balance. They are as reluctant to support attempts to attract female fans to football as men are. Just as any other 'true' football fan, female fans regard newly converted fans, male or female, with some suspicion, even scorn, and question their motivation and label them as 'glory-hunters' or 'part-timers'. Equally, female football fans consider promotions offered by some clubs for 'women and children to attend half-price' or to 'bring your girlfriend free' as degrading and patronizing.

Many female football fans do not want changes in football grounds any more than their male counterparts. Those that stand (or used to) do not want to sit any more than men do. They do not require any greater degree of comfort than men do. They do not even object to swearing, and they positively enjoy the hustle and bustle of packed terraces even though it might be filled with sweaty male bodies! Yet we are constantly told that changes in football grounds are taking place to attract more women. Little research has gone into what female fans like or dislike about football, and when women do voice their opinions, they are largely ignored. One of the authors complained to the West Midlands Police during a match between Wallsall and Liverpool in October 1988 in which most of the people who had stood around her at the start of the match had been ejected for swearing. It was explained that women found their language offensive. When it was pointed out that none of the women present objected to the use of such language, the response was, 'Well most women do!' As usual female voices are ignored.

In order to address the distributional imbalance in football support between males and females, it is necessary to look carefully at the relational issues including how women are treated at football and sexism in football in general. At present, women are frequently marginalized and their presence as fans trivialized. Women who attend (men's) football are often perceived as being 'oddities', a sort of 'tomboy'. The assumption is that she is there to please her boyfriend. It is not uncommon for a woman who attends football to be labelled 'a slag' just because of her passion for the sport. Even when it is accepted that she actually likes football (and has not gone along to admire the players' legs) men rarely ask her opinion on the match afterwards. They might ask about the atmosphere or the attendance, but not about the football. Even subconsciously in this case it is assumed that football is not a woman's specialism.

Some people, mainly (though not exclusively) men, find it difficult to understand how a female football supporter can feel the same level of commitment as a male (see Hornby quote p. 130). Yet according to the FA Premier League Survey (1995), 67.3 per cent of female football fans attend all league home games – a higher percentage than the men in the same sample.

Not only is sexism latent in attitudes towards female football fans, but also football culture can be overtly sexist too. It is offensive to a woman to sit and hear footballers 'insulted' by being called a 'woman' or a 'tart' just as it is degrading for a black person to hear a black player called a 'black bastard'. Yet the latter is stigmatized, the former is not. The latter leads to the automatic ejection of the guilty party (if they are located), the former does not. On the contrary, few people mind.

The fact that there are probably more female fans who attend football now than in the 1970s or 1980s (although few data have been available on the proportion of female fans in the past) does not, therefore, mean that women are marginalized less or accepted any more than before. Women are submerged into a male culture and either make very little attempt to change its male-dominated structures or have little success in doing so. It can be difficult for a woman to argue a point during a match without a man (possibly threatened by a woman who has superior knowledge on a 'male' subject than himself) resorting to bully tactics or trivializing strategies such as, 'Anyway, you're not entitled to an opinion, you're only a woman!' or 'Get back to your kitchen sink where you belong!' Though the presence of women is usually tolerated, women continue to be silenced, often through intimidation, marginalization and trivialization. Women have failed to construct their own structures and (as detailed earlier) often do not wish to do so. The radical feminists would frown upon such submissive acceptance of male structures.

They would, however, applaud the Spanish example. In Spain, female football fans have begun to join together as 'women's supporters' clubs' and to adopt their own style of support. The pioneers were a group known as *La Luna de Valencia* who were formed in 1986 and they were soon followed by many more such as Real Madrid's first all-female supporters' club *La Tentación Blanca*. As yet this has not happened in the UK and it appears, given the attitudes of female fans outlined earlier, that it is unlikely the idea will catch on among British female supporters.

Women and the football media

The distributional issue of women and the football media involves, first, the amount of space allocated to women and football, and second, the proportion of females involved in the media compared to men. The relational issue surrounding women and the media involves the portrayal of women's involvement in football (as players, fans or administrators).

Time and space allocated to women's football in the media are minimal. Most national daily newspapers give results from non-professional regional men's leagues but fail even to give the results of the women's national Premier League matches. There are occasional match reports on the Women's (FA) Cup Final and the odd match report when England play. Sporadically, the nationals run feature articles, usually on the most successful women's team of recent years, Doncaster

Belles, or on female football fans. A similar representation of women's football is gleaned by perusing newspapers abroad, although those devoted entirely to sport do often give results of women's games, though little more.

Women's football therefore is unreported. A similarly bleak picture is present in television coverage of women's football. There is currently no coverage on terrestrial television. A series of matches shown by Channel 4 attracted unexpectedly large audiences of up to 2.8 million, but were never repeated despite such popularity. The Women's FA Cup has earned a contract with satellite channel UK Living which will provide some much-needed sponsorship for women's football. The radio offers an even less promising perspective. There are no match commentaries and only rare match summaries or results. Occasional feature programmes are the only source of information on national radio.

Women's football, therefore, goes unreported and is marginalized. This is disappointing for those involved in the sport. A glimpse at what a few weeks' positive media coverage can do for a sport was provided by Channel 4's broadcasts which gave a tremendous boost to women's football. Instead, girls remain with no role models and women's football is invisible.

A far more positive distributional issue concerns women's active involvement in the football media. Many women have very recently become household names and women are represented in all forms of national and local media, for example Eleanor Oldroyd and Charlotte Nicol work at BBC Radio Five Live, Cynthia Bateman writes for the *Guardian*, Hazel Irvine and Jane Hoffen work on television and Karen Buchanan is editor of the glossy *FourFourTwo* magazine. In the local media, for example, Rachel O'Connor, Yorkshire Sportswriter of the Year 1995, who writes for the *Wharfedale and Airedale Observer*, believes that women sportswriters do not experience serious problems working in a predominantly male environment but that it is harder for a woman to earn the respect of her male counterparts. In her case, she admits to being fortunate as she grew up in the environment she was later to work in, knew everyone and was respected for her commitment to and knowledge of football before entering journalism.

Other female sportswriters share O'Connor's view. Louise Aughty's research into attitudes towards female sportswriters confirms that women do not feel that they suffer prejudices on entering a male-dominated sports media, but believe they need to display a greater confidence and knowledge than their male counterparts. Most women interviewed agreed that providing they demonstrated knowledge, they rarely suffer prejudices today.

It was also felt that female sportswriters were accepted by men with the proviso that they 'weren't too feminist'. Women were resented in sports journalism when writing a feature on football only when it was clear they had little knowledge about their subject-matter and/or exhibited little enthusiasm. In those cases, it does appear that women were resented more than men in similar positions – perhaps because it is assumed that men are knowledgeable, unlike women; this forces women to prove their knowledge while men have to disprove knowledge, obviously less likely to happen when interviewing. Footballers interviewed expressed indifference as to whether they preferred to be interviewed by a man or a woman, although one expressed his caution and distrust of women as they could be 'more manipulative by making you relax!'.

Although the proportion of women in the media is low, their profile and presence have enhanced considerably since the late 1980s. Advances have been made in women's position in some of the distributional issues of football, but others lag behind. As far as the portrayal of women in football in the media is concerned, there are conflicting tendencies.

When covered at all, women's football is not generally portrayed in a negative light. Sometimes encouraging remarks are offered regarding the quality of the football, usually analysed from a comparative perspective – that women's football is less physical (than men's), etc. Women's football is deviant from the (male) norm. Magazines, however, display more complex characteristics. The early 1990s witnessed the rise of glossy, 'intellectual' football magazines such as *FourFourTwo* which have run in-depth features on women's football; general magazines have also run some balanced features (e.g. *Cosmopolitan* September 1995). Other magazines offer a less balanced view of women's football, for example *Total Football* ran a feature of women's football in which the titles 'Nice Legs' and 'Tomboys' sum up the contents. Perhaps this trend is symbolic of the return to the 'laddie' culture and of a rejection of modern 'feminized' culture. Women in the media generally remain silent on the issues surrounding women's football and rarely promote women's football or highlight problems that female football fans endure, such as verbal insults and physical harassment. The potential is present for successful integration of women into the football media but they have by and large assimilated into the male football media and make decisions (sometimes consciously) that do not 'rock the boat'.

Given the strength of the media in moulding public opinion, it is in a powerful position to shape the future of women's role in football. It has certainly played a key role in the development of football in the 1990s. Thus far, there has been little media interest, which translates as low levels of sponsorship and no financial support. The media also supply the key to why interest in women's football has augmented. It forms part of the general attempt to target female support – not through any desire to feminize football or any philanthropic desire to involve the female population in the 'national' sport, but rather in an era of ever-increasing commercialism, expansion of the market of a product by 100 per cent can be only beneficial to the industry. An increase in demand while supply of football remains constant (or even reduced within the football grounds that have been converted to all-seater) allows prices to rise and greater profit. Similarly, women are targeted in terms of football merchandise. It appears, therefore, that the media, via advertising, are encouraging women to play a part in the world of football, but the part is a passive one. They have no power to tamper with the structures of the football hierarchy.

As far as the distributional issues are concerned, women's role as players has increased, particulary since the mid-1980s, but female players receive little support. Equally, there has been a small but significant rise in the proportion of female fans who attend football. This time women's interest is encouraged. The most significant advance in terms of women's profile in football is in the media where female presence is conspicuous. Conversely, this is also the Achilles' heel of women's football. Its invisibility is almost total and is attributed similar status to (men's) minority sports such as rowing or fencing.

Regarding the relational issues, much less progress has been made since Dick Kerr Ladies raised the prestige of women's football and began to change attitudes at the start of the twentieth century.

The values of our patriarchal society are changing gradually, but the structures remain in place. It is women who are joining the men's game, on men's terms. The feminization of football promised in the 1980s has been superimposed by the smale-scale footballization of women. If football were to be a truly 'national' sport, it would not represent just half the population. It would not be male-dominated and male-controlled as both men's and women's football are at present. Not only would there be a need to readdress the distributional issues, but also the reasons which currently exclude women from football would need to be removed and women's involvement demarginalized so that women's football and women's involvement are as acceptable as men's. Thus the moral and physical gender roles would not be reinforced via football which would not be part of the masculinizing process but would become part of a more gender-neutral socialization process which included both males and females.

References

Anderson, B. (1983) *Imagined Communities: Reflections on the Origin and Spread of Nationalism*, London: Verso.

Archetti, E. (1994) 'The moralities of Argentine football', paper presented at the *Third European Association of Social Anthropologists Conference*, Oslo, June.

Bale, J. and Maguire, J. (eds) (1994) *The Global Sports Arena*, London: Frank Cass.

Bayer, O. (1990) *Fútbol argentino*, Buenos Aires: Editorial Sudamericana.

Boin, V. (1949) *Het Gulden Jubileumboek Van De K.B.V.B. 1895–1945*, Brussels: Leclercq and De Haas.

Boletín del Real Madrid, December 1959, Madrid.

Boletín del Real Madrid, January 1961, Madrid.

Bromberger, C. (1990) 'Ciucco e fuochi d'artificio. Indagine sul rapporto fra la squadra di calcio napoletana e la sua città', *Micromega* 4.

Broussard, P. (1990) *Génération supporteur*, Paris: Laffont.

Cazal, J. *et al.* (1993) *La Coupe de France de Football*, Fédération Française de Football.

Cazorla Prieto, L.M. (1979) *Deporte y Estado*, Barcelona: Labor.

Cerecedo, F. (1974) Sociología del fútbol español, in *Posible* 1 (Nov.).

Curran, F. (1986) *The Derry City Football Club Story 1928–86*, Derry: Wholesale Newspaper Services.

Dal Lago, A., and De Biasi, R. (1994) 'Italian football fans: culture and organisation', in R. Giulianotti and N. Bonney (eds) *Football, Violence and Social Identity*, London: Routledge.

Dal Lago, A. and Moscati, R. (1992) *Regalateci un sogno. Miti e realità del tifo calcistico in Italia*, Milan: Bompiani.

Dearlove, J. and Saunders, P. (1984) *Introduction to British Politics*, Cambridge: Polity Press.

De Biasi, R. (1993) 'Le culture del calcio. Un'analisi comparativa dei rituali e delle forme del tifo calcistico in Italia e in Inghilterra', PhD thesis in Sociology, University of Trento.

Depestel, R. (1960) *Jubelbrochure Kon.S.K.Roeselare: Kampioen Bevordering C 1959–60*, Roeselare: Roularta.

Duke, V. (1994) 'The flood from the east? Perestroika and the migration of sports talent from Eastern Europe', in J. Bale and J. Maguire (eds) *The Global Sports Arena*, London: Frank Cass.

Duke, V. and Crolley, L. (1996) 'Football spectator behaviour in Argentina: a case of separate evolution', *Sociological Review* 44 (May).

Dunning, E. (1986) 'Sport as a male preserve: notes on the social sources of masculine identity and its transformation', *Theory, Culture and Society* 3(1): 79–80.

Dunning, E., Murphy, P. and Williams, J. (1988) *The Roots of Football Hooliganism: An Historical and Sociological Study*, London: Routledge.

Essinague, J. (1971) 'Relaciones entre deporte y política', *Cuadernos para el diálogo*, Madrid.

Eurispes (1994) *Ultra: Le sottoculture giovanile negli stadi d'Europa*, Rome: Koiné.

Fernández Santander, C. (1990) *El fútbol durante la guerra civil y el franquismo*, Madrid: Editorial San Martín.

Fusi, J.P. and Carr, R. (1979) *España: de dictadura a la democracia*, Barcelona: Ediciones Planeta.

Goffmann, E. (1961) *Encounters: Two Studies in the Sociology of Interaction*, Indianapolis: Bobbs-Merrill.

Goffmann, E. (1969) *Behaviour in Public Places: Notes on the Social Organization of Gatherings*, New York: Free Press of Glencoe.

Goffmann, E. (1974) *Frame Analysis: An Essay on the Organization of Experience*, Harmondsworth: Penguin.

El Gráfico (1993) (special series) 'Historia del fútbol argentino'.

Govaerts, A. and Vankesbeek, D. (1929) *Racing Gedenkboek*, Mechelen: Gebroeders Laurent.

Hargreaves, J. (1995) 'The Catalanisation of the Barcelona Olympic Games: a case study of nationalism in contemporary Spain', paper presented at the *Conference on Nationality and National Identity in the Iberian Peninsula*, University of Southampton, March.

Harrison, P. (1974) 'Soccer tribal wars', *New Society* 29.

Hoberman, J. (1988) *Politica e sport. Il corpo nelle ideologie politiche dell'800 e del 900*, Bologna: Il Mulino.

Holt, R. (1989) *Sport and the British*, Oxford University Press.

Hornby, N. (1992) *Fever Pitch*, London: Victor Gollancz.

Hutchinson, J. and Smith, A. (eds) (1994) *Nationalism*, Oxford University Press.

Jacobs, J. *et al.* (1978) *Ons Land Op Voetbal Schoenen*, Tielt: Lannoo.

Janart, J. (1919) *La Histoire du Football Club Roulers 1910–1915*, Roulers.

Kennedy, J. (1989) *Belfast Celtic*, Belfast: Pretan.

Kidd, B. (1990) 'The man's cultural centre: sports and dynamics of women's oppression/men's repression', in M. Messner and D. Sabo (eds) *Sport, Men and the Gender Order*, Illinois: Human Kinetics Books.

King, R. (1946) *History and Reminiscences of Berwick Rangers Football Club*, Berwick-upon-Tweed: Berwick Advertiser.

Kuper, S. (1994) *Football against the Enemy*, London: Orion.

Langmack, T. (1981) *Berwick Rangers Football Club 1881–1981*, Berwick-upon-Tweed: Tweeddale Press Group.

McCrone, D. (1992) *Understanding Scotland: The Sociology of a Stateless Nation*, London: Routledge.

Marchi, V. (1994) *SMV. Stile Maschio Violento. I demoni di fine millennio*, Genoa: Costa & Nolan.

Marien, R. (1973) *100 Jaar Voetbal En Clubleven*, Antwerpn: Nederlandse Boekhandel.

Messner, M. and Sabo, D. (eds) (1990) *Sport, Men and the Gender Order*, Illinois: Human Kinetics Books.

Moorhouse, H. (1991) 'On the periphery: Scotland, Scottish football and the new Europe', in J. Williams and J. Wagg (eds) *British Football and Social Change*, Leicester University Press.

Newsham, G. (1994) *In a League of their Own!*, Chorley: Pride of Place Publishers.

Platt, W. (1986) *A History of Derry City Football and Athletic Club 1929–1972*, Coleraine: Platt.

Romero, A. (1986) *Muerte en la Cancha*, Buenos Aires: Nueva América.

Romero, A. (1994) *Las barras bravas y la contrasociedad deportiva*, Buenos Aires: Editorial Latino América.

Rous, S. (1978) *Football Worlds*, London: Faber & Faber.

Rusconi, G. (1988) 'Introduzione', in J. Hoberman, *Politica e sport. Il corpo nelle ideologie politiche dell'800 e del 900*, Bologna: Il Mulino.

Scher, A. and Palomino, H. (1988) *Fútbol: pasión de multitudes y de elites*, Buenos Aires: Nueva América.

Segre, D. (1979) *Ragazzi di stadio*, Milan: Mazzotta.

Segre, D. (1993) 'Teppisti del calcio e skinheads: una spiegazione commune ed ingratata dei loro comportamenti delinquinziali', *Marginalità e società* 23.

Shaw, D. (1987) *Fútbol y franquismo*, Madrid: Alianza Editorial.

Sobrequés, J. (1991) *Terra Nostre: F.C.Barcelona, un club ai servei de Catalunya*, Barcelona: Editorial Labor.

Spender, D. (1985) *Man Made Language* (2nd edn), London: Routledge & Kegan Paul.

Tolleneer, J. (1996) *Soccer and Cultural Separateness: The Flemish Football Association 1930–1944*, Catholic University of Leuven.

Tomlinson, A. (1994) 'FIFA and the World Cup', in J. Sugden and A. Tomlinson (eds) *Hosts and Champions*, Aldershot: Arena.

Triani, G. (1994) 'Curva sud e Lega Nord: dai calci alla politica', in G. Triani (ed.) *Tifo e Supertifo. La pasione, la malattia, la violenza*, Naples: Edizioni Scientifiche Italiane.

Ward, A. (1989) 'Some notes on the history of women's soccer' (unpublished paper).

Whitson, D. (1990) 'Sport in the construction of masculinity', in M. Messner and D. Sabo (eds) *Sport, Men and the Gender Order*, Illinois: Human Kinetics Books.

Williams, J. and Woodhouse, J. (1991) 'Can play, will play? Women and football in Britain', in J. Williams and S. Wagg (eds) *British Football and Social Change: Getting into Europe*, Leicester University Press.

Williams, J., Dunning, E. and Murphy, P. (1984) *Hooligans Abroad*, London: Routledge.

Wils, L. (1992) 'A brief history of the Flemish movement', *Historica Lovaniensa* 246, Leuven.

Woodhouse, J. (1991) *A National Survey of Female Football Fans*, Leicester: Sir Norman Chester Centre for Football Research.

INDEX

Abacus League 21
Aberdeen FC 15, 80
AEK 77
Afan Lido FC 20
Africa 1, 2, 14, 16
    members of FIFA 14, 19
    World Cup places 3
Akasztó 98
Akhna 77
    Ethnikos Akhna 77
Albania 88
    national team 91
    socialist organization of sport 85
Aldwick Town FC 138
Alnwick FC 68
Alumni FC 101
Amateur Football Association 13
amateurism 79
    amateur players and FIFA 13
American football 1
Andalusia 25, 40, 47
Anderson, B. 4
Andes Talleres 100
Anorthosis Famagusta
    phoenix symbol 80 see also
        Famagusta
Antwerp 51, 54, 59
    Antwerp Football and Cricket
        Club 59
    Antwerp Football Club 51, 54, 59
    Beerschot Athletic Club 59
    Koninklijke Beerschot Voetbal en
        Atletiek Vereniging 59
    Koninklijke Berchem Sport 59
    Royal Beerschot AC 59
    Royal Berchem Sport 59
Apoel Nicosia see Nicosia
Aragón 24, 40–41
Ararat Yerevan 94

Archetti, E. 101
Ards FC 71, 72
Argentina 7, 31, 48, 53, 56, 125
    and FIFA 2, 14
    anti-violence laws 111, 113, 114
    corruption in football 107,
        111–112, 113
    elections in football 103, 109
    English influence 100, 101
    establishment of football league
        100, 101, 103
    football as political propaganda
        103, 110, 111–113
    Football Association 7, 11, 100,
        102, 104–105, 107
    and the state 104, 106
    media 100, 103, 106, 108, 110,
        112, 113–114, 125
    national image 111–112
    national team 12, 106
    padrinos 105, 106, 107, 114
    police 108
    political structures 100, 102, 104
    presidentes 103, 104, 105, 107,
        109
    professionalization of football 103,
        104
    role of business in football 100,
        102, 103–104, 105, 106,
        113–114
    role of football clubs 100, 102,
        105, 106, 107, 110
    role of state/politicians in football
        102, 103, 104, 105, 106, 108,
        111–113, 114 see also padrinos
    role of supporters in football 7,
        100, 102, 103, 106–111, 114
        see also barras bravas
    sponsorship 102, 106

spread of football 100–101
violence in football 107, 114
see also Football Associations
(Argentina), *barras bravas*
Argentinos Juniors 101, 108, 109
Armenia 16, 94, 95
army involvement in clubs 30, 92–93,
97, 98
Arsenal FC 41, 89
Arundel Coulthard Foundry 132
Asturias 40
Ashton United FC 21
Asia
and FIFA 2, 14
globalization of football 65
World Cup places 3, 14
Asian Football Confederation 95
Asil 77
assimilated players 16
Association Athlétique La Gantoise
see Ghent
association football 1, 11, 18, 19
Association Sportive Ostendaise 52
Atheneum Voetbal Vereeniging 51
Athletic de Bilbao *see* Bilbao
Athletische Sportvereeniging
Oostende *see* Oostende
Atlético Aviación 30
Atlético Bilbao *see* Bilbao
Atlético de Madrid *see* Madrid
Atletiek Associatie Gent *see* Ghent
attendances 21, 22, 28, 64, 66, 72, 97,
103, 106
Austria 13, 87, 90, 97, 99
national team 12
Austrian teams playing in German
league 66
Australasia
globalization of football 65
Australia 65
Australian National League 65
Kangaroos play in Singapore 65
Autonomous Communities *see* Spain
Aviación Atlético *see* Madrid
Azerbaijan 16, 94, 95

Baf Ülkü Yurdu SK 77, 78
Bahía Blanca 100
Bale, J. 61
Ballymena United FC 72
Baltic Republics 5 *see also* Estonia,
Lithuania, Latvia

Banfield FC 110
Bangor City FC 20
Banik Ostrava 92
Barça *see* Barcelona
Barcelona 26, 29, 39, 41, 45, 116, 125
FC Barcelona 26–29, 30, 32, 33,
36, 37, 42–43, 44, 45, 46, 47,
48
FC Barcelona tour 31, 32, 38
and Catalan nationalism 17, 28,
30, 36, 42, 43
and democracy 33
knock Spain out of Europe 38
rivalry with Español 27, 28, 40
rivalry with Real Madrid 27, 28,
38–40, 44
political neutrality 45
persecution complex 27, 39
symbol of Catalonia 26, 27, 28, 38,
39, 43
barras bravas 107–111, 114
activities 108–110
and institutionalization of violence
107
militarization of support 107
payment for services 107–108
unite against police 108
Barry Town AFC 20, 21
Basque Country 6, 25, 26, 29, 30, 31,
36–38, 42, 46–47, 48
Basques 26, 29, 32, 41, 42, 48
Basque tour 31, 32, 38
ikurriña 36, 37, 46
language 37, 38
nationalism 25–26, 29, 37–38, 42,
46
Bayer, O. 100
Beerschot
Athletic Club 55, 59
Koninklijke Beerschot Voetbal en
Atletiek Vereniging 55, 59
Belarus 16, 95
Belfast Celtic FC 71
Belgium 6, 11, 12, 50–59, 87
choice of royal designation 52,
53–54
constitutional reform 56
derby matches 56, 57
English schools and football 58
Koninklijke 53–54, 57
language issue 6, 50–59
language boundary fixed 56

national league 53–54, 91
political parties split on linguistic
  basis 56
Royal clubs 53–54, 59
see also Football Associations
  (Belgium), *vervlaamsing*
Belgrade
  Red Star Belgrade 92, 93
Berchem
  Berchem Sport 54
  Koninklijke Berchem Sport 55,
  59
  Royal Berchem Sport 55, 59
Berlusconi, S. 7, 41, 109, 116,
  123–125
Bernabéu, S. 35
Berwick Rangers FC 6, 22, 62, 63, 64,
  67–70
  affiliation to (English) FA 69
  joins Scottish league 70
  pressure to leave English league
  69–70
Betis *see* Real Betis de Sevilla
Beyarmudu 77
Bilbao 38, 41, 47
  Athletic de Bilbao 27, 29, 30, 31,
  36–38, 46, 48
  and Basque nationalism 30, 36–38,
  46
  Basque-only policy 29, 37, 43, 46
  symbol of Basque Country 29, 30
Binatli Yilmaz 77
Blackburn Rovers FC 86
black market 107–108
Blancos 100
Blyth Spartans FC 68
Boca Juniors 101, 103, 108, 109
  and *fútbol espectáculo* 107
  new stadium 105
  relationship with River Plate 103
Bohemia *see* Czechoslovakia
Boin, V. 51
Boixos Nois 47, 48
Border League 68, 69
Bosman case 16
Bosnia-Hercegovina 85, 96
Brazil 13, 125
  national team 13, 19, 91
Brescia 121
Brigadas Blanquiazules 45–46, 47
British Ladies FC 132
Brittany 11

Brno
  Boby Brno 96, 98
  Zbrojovka Brno 96
Broussard, P. 48
Bruges 53, 54, 56, 58, 59
  Brugsche Football Club 58
  Cercle Sportif Brugeois 55, 58, 59
  Club Brugge Koninklijke
  Voetbalvereniging 55, 59
  Football Club Brugeois 55, 58, 59
  Koninklijke Sportvereniging
  Cercle Brugge 55, 59
  Rapid Football Club 58
  Vlaamsche Voetbal Club 58
Brussels 50, 51
  officially bilingual 55, 56
Bucharest 87, 90, 93
  Dinamo Bucharest 93
  Olimpia Bucharest 87
  Rapid Bucharest 94
  Steaua Bucharest 92, 93, 97, 116
  Victoria Bucharest 94
  Viitorul Bucharest 90
Budapest 86, 89, 90, 92, 93
  Honvéd 92, 93, 96
  AC Kispest 92, 96
  Kispest-Honvéd 96, 98
  MTK 86
  team changes names 93, 96
  secret police team 93
Buenos Aires 100, 101, 102, 103, 113
  Buenos Aires Cricket Club 100
  Buenos Aires Football Club 100
  Buenos Aires FC 100
Bulgaria 87, 91, 93
  football clubs change names 93, 96
  football clubs forced to merge 93
  match-fixing 95
  national league established 87
  national team 91, 99
  socialist organization of sport 85,
  91, 92–93
  business 87
  links with football 1, 7, 22, 126,
  139, 143 *see also* Argentina

cabezas rapadas 47
Caernarfon 22
Caernarfon Town FC 20–23
calcio 11
Canada 1, 12
Canary Isles 47

Capello, F. 123
capitalism 7, 85, 88, 92, 97
Cardiff City FC 19, 20, 64, 65, 89
Caribbean 2
Carr, R. 34
Catalans 26, 41, 42, 48
Catalonia 5, 6, 25, 26, 27, 28, 30, 31,
    36, 38, 42, 43–44, 45, 47, 48
  Catalanism 26, 36, 45
  language 37
  Lliga 26
  senyera 27, 36, 37, 43, 45
  and nationalism 5, 24–26, 28, 37,
    41, 42
Catholic 18, 50, 54, 57, 59, 67
  Catholic workers' movement 54
  conflict with Protestant population
    70–76
  and Flemish language 57
Cazal, J. 62
Cazorla Prieto, L. 36
Celta de Vigo 47
Celtarra 47
Central America 1, 2
Central Argentino 100
Central Norte 100
Centre for Historical and Statistical
    Research into Football in Spain
    30
Cercle Sportif Brugeois *see* Bruges
Cerecedo, F. 37
Cheb
  Ruda Hvezda Cheb 96
  Union Cheb 96
Chelsea FC 89
Chetin Kaya Turkish Sports Club 76,
    79
  on the frontline 79
Chile 91
  FA 11
  and FIFA 2
China 11
  and FIFA 3
Chorzow 90
Clemente, J. 42
Cliftonville FC 71, 72
Club Brugge Koninklijke
    Voetbalvereniging *see* Bruges
Club Sportif Anversois 51
Coldstream FC 68
Coleraine FC 71, 72, 73
collectivism 88

Colorados 100
Colwyn Bay FC 20, 21, 22, 23, 64
communism 2, 7, 14, 80, 85, 88, 90,
    92–94
  construction of stadiums 90
  postcommunism 7, 95–99
  see also socialism
Cook Islands 2
corruption 97
  blackmail 109
  match-fixing 95, 97
Cosenza 123
Coubertin, P. 131
Courtrai Sports 55
Coventry 134
creolization 101
cricket 1–2, 18, 58
Croatia 5, 16, 85, 88, 96, 99
  national team 99
Croker, T. 131
Crolley, L. 107
Crusaders FC 72
Cruyff, J. 27, 44
Curran, F. 37
curva culture *see* Italy
Curzon Ashton FC 20, 22
Cymbran Town FC 20, 21
Cymru Alliance 20
Cyprus 6, 62, 67, 76–81
  conflict between Greek and
    Turkish 76
  Greek Cypriot champions join
    Greek league 76
  Greek Cypriot league 76, 77
  ownership of stadiums 78–79, 80,
    81
  partition 76
  political orientations of clubs 80
  refugee football clubs 6, 67, 76–81
  support for refugee clubs 78, 79,
    80
  Turkish clubs form own league 76,
    79
  Turkish Cypriot clubs withdraw
    from Cypriot league 76
  Turkish Cypriot league 76, 78
  see also Famagusta
Czechoslovakia 2, 5, 14, 16, 61, 66,
    86–87, 93, 95
  attendances at football 97
  Bohemia 86–87
  Czechoslovakian teams playing in

German league 66
Czechoslovak League 86, 98
and FIFA 86
and hooliganism 95
national team 90, 91, 98
payment of illegal bonuses 95
professional football 87
socialist organization of sport 85,
    92–93
status of players 92
transfer of footballers 98–99
unofficial defections 94
Czech Republic 16, 85, 95
attendances at football 97
clubs change names 96
national team 99

Dal Lago, A. 115–119
Darwin Cubs FC 65
playing in Singapore League 65
De Biasi, R. 119, 121, 122
Dearlove, J. 4
Delegación Nacional de Deportes 32,
    33
democracia orgánica 33
democracy in football 32, 33, 40, 48,
    52 *see also* elections in
    football
Dendermonde
    Association Athléticque
        Termondoise 55
    K Athletische Vereeniging
        Dendermonde 55
Denmark 11
    and FIFA 12
Deportivo La Coruña 47
Depestel, R. 57
Derby County FC 94
derby matches 56, 57
Derry City FC 6, 18, 22, 62, 66–67,
    70–76
    conflict with Irish League 70, 72,
        73
    fans 75
    financial pressures 72
    joins League of Ireland 74–75
    matches suspended at Brandywell
        71–72, 73
    withdrawal from Northern Irish
        football 70–71, 73
    without professional football 73
Derry FC 73, 74

Dick Kerr Ladies FC 132–133, 134,
    144
dictatorship 7, 32–40, 104, 111–113
Dighenis Akritas 77, 78
Distillery FC 72–73
    forced to abandon Grosvenor Park
        72
distributional issues 8, 129, 131–137,
    139, 140, 141–143, 144
Dixie, F. 132
Dogan Türk Birligi SK 77, 78
Doncaster 134
    Doncaster Belles FC 137, 138,
        141–142
    women spectators uncovered 138
Donegal Celtic FC 74
Doxa 77
Dresden
    Dynamo Dresden 93
Duke, V. 61, 107
Dunning, E. 4, 120, 121, 128, 130
Duns FC 68
Dynamo/Dinamo clubs sponsored by
    ministry/secret police 93
Dynamo Kiev *see* Kiev
Dynamo Moscow *see* Moscow

Eastern Europe 7, 16, 31, 85–99
economic pragmatism 6, 62, 63,
    63–65, 67, 69, 70
Egypt national team 3
elections in football *see* Argentina,
    Italy, Spain
Ellesmere Port 21, 22
embourgeoisement 139
England 65, 87, 90, 94, 99, 128
    English FA *see* Football
        Associations (England)
    and FIFA 5
    national team 11, 34, 87, 89, 135
    –Scotland border 62–63, 64 *see*
        also Berwick Rangers,
        Gretna FC
    supporters 4, 46
    World Cup 14, 15
enosis 76
Español 26, 27, 28, 40, 44–45, 47
    and Catalanism 44–45
    division between fans 45
    political neutrality 45
    relationship with Real Madrid
        46

rivalry with FC Barcelona 27, 28, 39
symbol of Francoism 28, 30, 40
Espanyol *see* Español
Essinague, J. 34
Estonia 5, 16, 95
Estudiantes 101
Ethnikos (Akhna) 77, 78
Ethnikos (Asha) 77
ethnies (ethnic communities) 5
eurocentrism 2
European Champions' Cup 12, 15, 16, 20, 38, 46, 62, 80, 92, 97, 116, 125
European Championship 15, 90, 91, 99
European Cup Winners' Cup 15, 19, 20, 41, 62, 80
European Union 16, 43
law 23
Euskadi 31, 32 *see also* Basque Country
Euskera 37
Everton FC 86
Evita Youth Championships 105
Eyemouth FC 68

FA *see* Football Association
FC Barcelona *see* Barcelona
Famagusta 80
Anorthosis Famagusta 77, 78, 80, 81
Nea Salamina 77–78, 79, 80, 81
membership of clubs 80–81
political orientations of clubs 80–81
relationship between clubs 80
fans *see* football spectators
fascism 48, 52, 119
Federación Española de Fútbol see Football Associations (Spain)
feminism 129, 135–136, 141
influence in football 135
feminization of football 139, 143, 144
Ferencváros 93, 94, 98
changes name to EDÖSZ 93
changes name to Kiniszi 93
and hooliganism 95
Fernández Santander, C. 30, 34, 35, 103
FIFA 2–3, 6, 14, 18, 19, 21, 23, 31, 52, 61, 86, 87, 99

and amateurism 13
dispute with FA of Wales 21–23
foundation 2, 12–13
and independent states 4, 5–6
membership 2, 6, 12–13, 14, 19, 86, 87
presidents 13
and UK associations 5, 12–17, 18
Finland 1
Finn Harps FC 73, 74
Fiorentina 94
Flamenpolitik 55
Flanders 6, 50, 52, 54
and Catholicism 55, 57
officially Flemish-speaking 55
upsurge in nationalism 5
see also Football Associations (Flanders)
Flemish 54
clubs withdraw from playing Belgian clubs 52
flemicizing *see vervlaamsing*
football league 6, 52–53
language 6, 50–59
nationalism 6, 54, 55–56
role of local authority 56
Football Associations
Argentina 7, 11, 100, 102, 104, 106
Belgium 6, 51, 52, 53 *see also* Flanders
Chile 11
Czechoslovakia 86, 95
Denmark 11
England 11, 12, 13, 63, 68, 69, 131, 133, 134, 136
Flanders 52, 53 *see also* Vlaamsche Voetbalbond
France 61
Hungary 18, 86, 95
Italy 11
Malaysia 64
Netherlands 11
New Zealand 11
Northern Ireland (IFA) 11, 12, 72, 73, 74, 75
Poland 87
Republic of Ireland (FAI)12, 18, 76
Romania 90, 97
Scotland 11, 68, 70, 74
Singapore 11

South Africa 11
Spain 30, 33, 39, 41, 44
Switzerland 11
Wales (FAW) 11, 16, 19–23, 134
Women's 133
Yugoslavia 88
Football Association rules 11
football chants 7, 46, 47, 109, 124
football fans *see* football supporters
football stadium *see* stadium
football supporters 4, 7, 15, 44, 45,
    46, 47, 53, 75, 97, 103, 125,
    128, 131, 139–141
commitment 130, 140
female fans 128, 130, 139–141
see also Argentina, *barras bravas*,
    socios, tifo, ultras, violence
Football Supporters' Association 115
footballers 30, 32, 34, 35, 37, 41, 44,
    53, 59, 68, 79, 94, 98, 108–109,
    131–139
foreign players 16, 27, 28, 61
nationalist gestures 31, 33, 36, 38
strike in Argentina 103
victims of blackmail 109
women 128, 131–139
see also Basque-only policy,
    Bosman case, transfers
footballization
of politics 123–127
of women 144
Forza Italia 125
France 31, 50, 61, 65–66, 99, 134
organization of FA Cup 61
and FIFA 12, 13
French language 50–59,
    domination in Flanders 50–51
French League 65–66, 87
French teams playing in German
    league 66
established World Cup and
    European Champions' Cup 61
women's football 134, 136
World Cup hosts (1936) 13, (1998)
    3
Franco 30, 32–34, 36, 37, 40, 42, 48,
    105 *see also* Spain
Francoism 38, 48
francophone referees sent off to
    Flemish villages 52
French Guiana 61
Frente Atlético 47

furia española 29, 34
Fusi, J. 34
fútbol-empresa 106
fútbol-espectáculo 106–107

Gaelic Athletic Association 18
gaelic football 18, 75
Galicia 25, 31, 40, 47, 48
Gand *see* Ghent
Gdansk 98
    Lechia Gdansk 98
Gencler Birligi 77
gender roles 129–131, 132, 133,
    144
moral gender roles 130, 144
physical gender roles 131, 144
Genoa 117, 118, 120, 122
Genoa 117
    Fossa dei Grifoni 117, 122
Gent *see* Ghent
geographical proximity 6, 62, 62–63,
    67
Georgia 16, 90, 94, 95
Germany 13, 47, 53, 55, 66, 85, 87,
    89, 99, 139
German Democratic Republic 85,
    94
national team 3, 89, 91
Ghana 3
Ghent 53, 54, 55, 59
Atletiek Associatie Gent 55, 59
Association Athlétique La
    Gantoise 55, 59
Racing Club de Gand 55, 59
Racing Club Gantois 59
Racing Club (of) Gent 54, 55,
    59
Glasgow Celtic FC 15, 18
Glasgow Rangers FC 15, 18, 80, 81,
    89
glasnost 94–95
Gloucester City FC 20, 22
Govaerts, A. 56
Goffmann, E. 119, 126
Goole Town FC 22
Greece 6, 11, 67, 76–81, 97
Gretna FC 22, 62, 63
affilition to (English) FA 63, 64,
    65
Grondona J. 104, 105
Guadaloupe 61
Guruceta 39

Hajduk Split 88
Halle
    K Cercle Sportif Halle 55
    R Cercle Sportif Hallois 55
Hampden Park 17
Hargreaves, J. 42
Havelange, J. 13, 14
Hasselt 52
    R Excelsior Football Club Hasselt
        55
    K Sporting Club Hasselt 55
Heracklis 77
Herri Norte 48
Heysel stadium 16
Highland Light Infantry 70
Hoberman, J. 126
Holt, R. 12
Home Farm FC 75
Honduras 4
hooliganism 95, 117, 118, 139 *see
    also* violence in football
    in Eastern Europe 95
    and radical right in Italy 118,
        120–122
Hornby, N. 130
Howden Rangers FC 68
Hungary 13, 61, 86–87, 90, 93, 94, 97,
    98
    and FIFA 86
    clubs change names 96
    corruption in football 95
    Hungarian League established
        86
    national team 12, 87, 89, 90, 91
    professional football 87
    socialist organization of sport 85,
        92–93
    status of players 92
    style of play 89
    transfer of footballers 99
    see also Football Association
        (Hungary)
Huracán 105
Hutchinson, J. 4

ice hockey 1
ikurriña see Basque Country
Independiente FC 101, 108
    Club Atlético Independiente 101
India 2
Indian Ocean 61
industrialization 29

International Football Association
    Board 14
Ireland 11, 12, 70–76
    All Ireland League 75–76
    and FIFA 13, 18
    Football Association of Ireland
        (FAI) *see* Football Associations
    Irish FA (IFA) *see* Football
        Associations
    League of 6, 18, 67, 71, 73, 74, 75
    (Northern) Irish League 70, 71, 72,
        73, 74, 75
Israel 2
Italy 1, 11, 13, 47, 66, 88, 91, 94, 98,
    99
    curva culture 116–117, 118–119,
        121, 122, 124, 127
    elections in football 116, 124–125
    football as a business 126
    linguistic metaphor 7, 115,
        124–127
    and national identity 4
    national team 3, 91
    official supporters' clubs 115, 116
    organization of football fans
        115–116, 119–120 *see also*
        ultras
    police 119–120, 121–122
    political vulnerability of fans 115,
        119
    style of football support 116, 117,
        118, 119
    and teams from San Marino 62–63
    women's football 136

Jacobs, J. 56
Janart, J. 57
Japan 11, 64
Juntas Españolas 47
Juventus 16, 46, 94
    abandons home ground 126

Kazakhstan 95
Kelso 68
Kennedy, J. 71
Kidd, B. 131
Kiev
    Dynamo Kiev 90, 94, 97
King, R. 67
Kirghizstan 95
Koeman 27
Kortrijk Sport 55

Kraków 87
    Cracovia 87, 93
    Hutnik Kraków 97
    Wisla Kraków 87
Kuper, S. 5, 44, 97, 108, 112
Kyrenia
    PAEEK Kyrenia 77, 79

La Plata 103
Langmack, T. 67
language 6, 25, 37, 38, 40, 43, 46, 56,
    115, 124, 127
    see also Belgium (language issue),
    Italy (linguistic metaphor)
Larnaca 78, 79, 80, 81
    Alki Larnaca 80
    EPA Larnaca 80
    political orientations of clubs 80
Las Palmas 47
Latvia 5, 16, 95
Lazio 119, 121
League of Ireland *see* Ireland
League of Wales *see* Wales
Lega Nord 117
Leoncavallo club 117–118, 122, 123
Levante 31
Liechtenstein 62
    no national league 62
Lier 52
    Liersche Sportkring 52
    Turn en Sport Vereeniging Lyra 52
Liga Mediterránea 3
Lille 61
Limassol 78, 80, 81
    AEL Limassol 79
    Türk Ogaci Limassol 77
Lineker 27
Linfield FC 71
    conflict with Derry City FC 71, 72
Lisbon 61
Lithuania 5, 16, 94, 95
    national team 44
Liverpool FC 15, 16, 117, 137
Llanelian Road 22
Lliga *see* Catalonia
Lódz 87
    LKS Lódz 87, 97
    Widzew Lódz 87
Luxembourg 66
    FV Stadt Dudelingen 66
    Luxembourg teams playing in
    German league 66

Macedonia 16, 85, 96
Madeira 61
Madrid 26, 43, 47, 61
    anti-madridismo 43
    Atlético de Madrid 30, 32, 36, 46,
    47, 109
    Aviación Atlético 30
    Real Madrid 6, 26, 27, 35, 44, 47,
    141
    Real Madrid as a national symbol
    35, 36, 38, 112
    relationship with Español 46
    rivalry with FC Barcelona 26, 28,
    38–40, 44
Maghull High School 137
Maguire, J. 61
Malaysia 64
    and Singapore 64–65
Malines *see* Mechelen
FC Malinois *see* Mechelen
Malta 42
Manchester Corinthians FC 135
Maradona, D. 113
Marchi, V. 120
Marien, R. 58
Marítimo 61
Marseille 66
masculinity 121, 130, 131
    masculinizing process 130, 131,
    144
match-fixing 64, 95, 97
McCrone, D. 17
Mechelen 54, 56–57
    Football Club Malinois 55, 56, 57
    and social class 56–57
    Koninklijke Racing Club
    Mechelen 55, 57
    Koninklijke Voetbalclub Mechelen
    55, 57
    Racing Club de Malines 55, 56,
    57
    and social class 56–57
    Racing Club Mechelen 54
media 15, 31, 36, 41, 46–47, 72, 88,
    103, 106, 108, 110, 121–122,
    128, 141–143
    and Berlusconi 124–125
    role in communist states 89–90
    role in dictatorship 34, 38,
    112–114
    coverage of women's football 134,
    137, 143

women in football media 128, 129,
   135, 141–143
Meenen
   K Sporting Club Meenen 55
   R Sporting Club Meneeois 55
Mendoza, R. 44
Mendoza 100
Menotti 113
Merthyr Tydfil FC 20–23
Messner, M. 130, 136
metaphor *see* Italy (linguistic
   metaphor)
Mexico 1, 31
Middlesbrough Ladies FC 137
migration of football talent 16, 61, 94,
   98–99
Milan 116, 117, 119, 123–125, 126
Associazione Italiana Milan Clubs
   116
   AC Milan 109, 116, 117, 119
   Internazionale 116, 119
militarization of football 30, 32
   of football support 107
Millonarios 39
Moldova 16, 95
Monaco 65–66
   Association Sportive de Monaco
      65–66
   attendances 66
   new stadium 66
   playing across border 66
   royal patronage 66
Moorhouse, H. 12, 17
Moravia 86
Morocco national team 3
Moscardó 30, 32
Moscati, R. 115
Moscow 61, 86, 90, 94
   Asmaral 61
   CSKA 61, 92
   Dynamo 61, 86, 88, 89, 93, 98
   Lokomotiv 61, 92
   Spartak 61
      the people's team 94
   Torpedo 61, 92
Mulhouse
   FC 1893 Mulhausen 66
Murphy, P. 4, 121, 130

Nacional (Madeira) 61
Nacional (Uruguay) 18
nation 1, 16, 35, 41, 42, 88

definition of 3–5, 128
latent 5, 6
relationship between nation and
   state 3–5, 128
see also submerged nation
national identity 4
   in Spain 24, 34, 43
national image 111
national sports 1, 17, 128, 144
nation-states 5, 13, 86
nationalism 4–5
   and loyalty to state 5, 88
   and national team 4, 41–42, 88–89
      see also Spain
   and social class 4
   in Spain 24–26, 28, 29, 31, 33–4,
      36–38, 40–49
   popular nationalism 88
nationality
   historic nationality 6, 25, 41, 42,
      48
Navarre 25
naziskins 119, 120, 121
Nea Salamina *see* Famagusta
Netfchi Baku 94
Netherlands 12, 50, 52, 87
   FA 11
   national team 112
Newport AFC 20, 21, 22, 64
Newtown FC 20
New York 31
New Zealand 11
Newsham, G. 132, 133, 134
Nicosia 78, 79, 81
   Apoel Nicosia 76, 79, 80
   Olympiakos Nicosia 76
   Omonia Nicosia 80
   political orientations of clubs 80
Northern Alliance 69
Northern Ireland 5, 6, 12, 15, 18,
   66–67, 70–76
Northern Premier League (English)
   62, 65
North Northumberland League 69
Northumberland League 68, 69
Northwich Victoria FC 20, 22
Nueva Chicago 110
Núñez 44

Oceania 2
FC Olt 94
Olympiakos Nicosia 76

Olympic Committee 131–132
Olympic Games 7, 42, 43, 88, 89, 90, 91
Oostende 54
  Association Sportive Ostendaise 55
  Athletische Sportvereeniging Oostende 54, 55
  Van Neste Genootschap Oostende 54
Orekhovo SK 86
Osasuna 30, 32
Oswestry Town FC 22
Oval, The 22, 23

Pacífico 100
Pacific Ocean 61
padrinos see Argentina
Palestine national team 3
Palomino, H. 101, 104, 108, 112
Panathinaikos 97
Parmalat 96, 98
Partido Justicialista 104
patriarchy 8, 129–130, 131, 144
Pele 91
peña 43, 46, 47
Peñarol 18
Percy Rovers FC 68
perestroika 94–95
Perón, Juan Domingo 104, 105
Peronism 105
  Peronist medals 105
Perth Kangaroos FC 65
  playing in Singapore League 65
Peru national team 111–112
Petra Drnovice 98
Pile 77
Plastika Nitra 92, 97–98
Platt, W. 71
Plaza de Mayo 113
Plovdiv
  Botev Plovdiv 87, 96
  Trakia Plovdiv 96
players *see* footballers
Poland 31, 66, 87, 91, 93, 97, 98
  FA 87
  match-fixing 95, 97
  national championship established 87
  national team 91
  Polish teams playing in German league 66

socialist organization of sport 85, 91, 93
  clubs change names 93
  political pressure 59, 66–67
  politics 6–8, 24, 26, 29, 31, 36, 44, 54, 75, 76–77, 79, 88
    in Argentina 100–114
    football as political propaganda *see* Argentina, Spain
    footballization of politics 115
    intervention in football 32, 34–35, 55, 59, 66–67, 70, 85, 90, 105
    structures converge with football 6–7, 128
    see also socialist organization of sport, Peronism
Popescu 27
Portadown FC 73
Portuguese league 61
Poznan 98
  Lech Poznan 97
  Olimpia Posnan 98
Prague 86, 89, 94, 98
  Bohemians Prague 93, 95
  financial scandal 95
  Dukla Prague FC 91, 92, 93, 98
  Dynamo Prague 93
  Nationalsozialistiche TG Prag 66
  Slavia Prague 86, 93, 94, 98, 99
  Sparta Prague 86, 93, 95, 97
  Spartak Sokolovo 93
  teams change names 93
presidente see Argentina, Spain
Primo de Rivera 28
professionalization 7, 87, 95, 103, 104
professionalism 92, 95
Protestant 18, 50, 67, 72
  conflict with Catholic population 70–76
Prussia 87

Quilmes 101, 110
  Argentinos de Quilmes 101

Raba Györ 92
Racing 101
  new stadium 105
Racing Club Tienen 54
Racing White Daring Molenbeek 52
racism 47, 121
Rapid Football Club *see* Bruges
Real Betis de Sevilla *see* Seville

Real Madrid *see* Madrid
Real Sociedad 29, 36, 37, 38, 46, 48
    and Basque nationalism 36–38
    Basque-only policy 29, 37, 43, 46
Red Star Roeselare *see* Roeselare
referees 15, 26, 27, 34, 35–36, 39, 89,
    108
    corruption 97
    francophone referees imposed in
        Belgium 52
    political refereeing 27, 44
refugee football clubs *see* Cyprus
region 1, 41
    definition of 4
    relationship between nation and
        state 4–5, 41, 42
regionalism 25, 36 *see also* Spain
relational issues 8, 129, 131, 133, 135,
    139, 140, 143, 144
religion 4, 70–76, 115
Renaix 55
    Association Sportive Renaisienne
        55
    Football Club Renaisien 55
    Sportkring Ronse 55
Renaixença 26
Republic of Ireland 6, 15, 22, 70–76
reyes católicos 24
Rhyl FC 20
Riazor Blues 47
River Plate 39, 101, 103, 108
    and *fútbol-espectáculo* 107
    new stadium 105
    relationship with Boca Juniors 103
Roeselare 54, 57
    Football Club Roeselare 54, 57
    Football Club Roulers 52, 54, 57
    Red Star Roeselare 57
    split into two clubs 57
    Sportkring Roeselare 57
    Sport Vereeniging Roeselare 57
    Union Sportive Roularienne 57
Romania 87, 90, 91–92, 93, 94, 97
    and corruption 97
    and FIFA 87
    national team 91–92, 98, 99
    socialist organization of sport 85,
        92–94
    transfer of footballers 98
Romans 11
Rome 121
    AS Roma 121

Romero, A. 100, 107, 108
Rosario 100
    Rosario Central 100
    Rosario el Central Argentine
        Railway Athletic Club 100
FC Roulers *see* Roeselare
Rous, Sir Stanley 13, 14
Royal Antwerp Football Club *see*
    Antwerp
Royal Beerschot AC *see* Antwerp
Royal Berchem Sport *see* Antwerp
Ruabon FC 19
rugby 11
rugby union 1, 18, 19, 75
Rusconi, G. 126
Russia 61, 86, 87, 95
    national team 34, 99
    Revolution 85, 86
    style of football 89
    tour of Britain 88–89

Sabo, D. 130, 136
St Helen's Ladies FC 134
St Patrick's Athletic FC 74
St Pauli 94
St Petersburg 86
El Salvador 4
Samaranch, J. 132
San Lorenzo 108, 109
San Marino 62
    and FIFA 2
    Calcio San Marino 62
    national league established 62
    teams playing in Italy 62–63
San Sebastián 29
Sanz, L. 44
Sarajevo
    Zeljeznicar Sarajevo 66
Saunders, P. 4
Scher, A. 101, 104, 108, 112
Scotland 5, 11, 12, 15, 17–18, 67–70,
    74, 134
    –England border 62–63, 64, 67 *see
        also* Berwick Rangers, Gretna
        FC, Border League
    and FIFA 5, 13
    national team 11, 17–18
    Scottish FA *see* Football
        Associations (Scotland)
    Scottish League 6, 18, 62, 67, 70,
        74
    Scottish National Party 18

Scottishness 17
women's football 134
and World Cup 18
Seaton Burn FC 69
Segre, D. 121
Selección see Spain (national team)
semi-professional football 99
in England 20, 21, 22, 65
in Hungary 86, 99
in Scotland 65
in Wales 19–23, 64
senyera see Catalonia
Seville 41
Real Betis de Sevilla 47
sexism 140, 141
Shakhtor Donetsk 97
Shamrock Rovers FC 74
Shaw, D. 34, 37, 39, 43
Singapore 11, 64-65
Slovakia 5, 16, 85, 86, 95
national league 86
national team 86
Slovenia 1, 16, 85, 96
Smith, A. 4
Sobrequés, J. 26
social class 4, 29, 52, 56–57, 86, 92,
98, 102, 139 *see also*
working-class organizations
social drug 34, 103, 106
socialism 7, 88, 96, 97
football reinforces values 88
socialist organization of sport 85,
86, 90, 92–94, 96
compulsory national service 93
socios 28, 33, 40, 41, 48, 103, 109 *see
also* football supporters
Sofia 87, 90
clubs forced to merge 93
CSKA Sofia 92, 93
Dinamo Sofia 93
Levski Sofia 87, 93
name changes 93
Slavia Sofia 87, 93
Sofia league 87
Strojtel Sofia 93
Udarnik Sofia 93
Sokol Pniewy 98
soule 11
South Africa 1, 11
South America 1, 2, 3, 14, 31
Soviet Union 2, 5, 7, 14, 16, 19, 61,
85, 86, 90, 92, 95, 97

establishment of national league
86
and international football 88
role of national team 88, 90
Spain 6, 12, 24–49, 61, 99
autonomous communities 25, 40,
41, 42–43, 49
elections in football 29–30, 32, 33,
40, 44
football as political propaganda
31–32, 33, 34–36, 41
football supporters *see also socios*,
peñas 44, 45, 46, 141
Franco regime 6, 24, 25, 28,
32–40, 42, 45, 48, 105
national identity 24, 34, 40, 48
national image 34–36
national team *(Selección)* 3, 32,
34, 35, 41–42, 46–47, 49
nationalism 24–26, 28, 29, 33–34,
36–38, 42, 47–49
presidentes 28, 30, 32, 33, 37, 40,
44, 47
regionalism 25–26, 37, 40–43, 47,
48
Spanish Civil War 6, 24, 28, 29,
30–32, 39
Spanish Constitution 25
transition to democracy 6, 24, 38,
40–49
women in football 136, 139, 141
see also Basque Country,
Catalonia, Galicia, Football
Associations (Spain)
spectators *see* football supporters
Spender, D. 129
sponsorship 92, 94, 96, 97–98, 99,
102, 106, 137, 143
Sporting Club Tirlemontois 52
Sporting Gijón 36, 47
Sportkring Roeselare 54
Stade Leuven 55
Stade Louvaniste 55
stadium 5, 14, 17, 40, 66, 76, 78–79,
80, 81, 90, 98, 105, 106, 116,
127, 140
FC Stadler 98
state 1, 5, 42, 50, 62, 65, 76, 86
control via football 34, 102–103
definition of 3–5, 128
status presence 6, 62, 64, 65–66
Di Stefano 39

Stoichkov 27
Strasbourg
    SS SG Strassburg 66
strike (players' in Argentina) 103
submerged nations 5, 12, 15, 16, 17,
    128
Swansea City FC 19, 20, 64, 65
Sweden 12, 139
Switzerland 11, 12, 62
    Swiss League 62
Székesfehérvar 98

Tadjikistan 95
taksim 76
Tatabánya 92
Tbilisi
    Dynamo Tbilisi 93, 94
Tenerife
    Club Deportivo Tenerife 61
Tienen
    Racing Club Tienen 54, 55
    Racing Club Tirlemont 55
tifo 115, 117, 118, 126 *see also ultras*
    tifo estremo 115, 121
Tirana
    Dinamo Tirana 93
Tolleneer, J. 52
Tomlinson, A. 4
Tongeren 54
    R Cercle Sportif Tongrois 55
    K Tongerse Sportvereeniging
        Cercle 55
    Patria Football Club Tongeren 55
Tongres 54
    Patria Football Club Tongres 55
totalitarianism 7
Tottenham Hotspur FC 89
Tow Law FC 68
trade unions 7, 92, 93, 110, 115
transfers 39, 94, 97, 98–99
Treaty of Rome 16
Triani, G. 119, 124
Tucumán 100
Tunisia national team 3
Turkey 6, 67, 76–81
Turkmenistan 95
Turn en Sport Vereeniging Lyra *see*
    Lier
Türk Ogaci Limassol 77
Tweedside Albion FC 68
GKS Tychy 98
Tynefield FC 68

UEFA 2, 20, 22, 74, 75, 77, 78
    and Bosman case 16
    and Eastern Europe 16
    and former Soviet Union members
        95
    membership 16, 19
    restrictions on number of
        non-nationals 16
    status of players 92
    UEFA Cup 15, 20
Ujpest TE 86
Ukraine 16, 90, 95
    and corruption 97
Ulster 18
Ultra Boix 47
ultras 7, 45, 46–48, 118, 120–122
    apolitical nature 118, 121,
        122–123, 126
    militant fans 117–120
    naziskins 119, 120, 121
    organization 115, 116, 117,
        119–120, 121, 126
    and political militants 117–120,
        122–123, 127
    skinheads 120–121
    violence 117, 118, 119, 120,
        121–122
Ultras Mujica 48
Ultrasur 47, 48
Uniao (Madeira) 61
*Union Belge des Sociétés de Sports
    Athlétiques* 51, 57, 58, 59
Unión Cívica Radical 104, 105
*Union (Royale) Belge des Sociétés de
    Football Association* 51, 52
Union Sportive Roularienne 51, 57
United Kingdom 5–6, 56
    associations 2, 11, 13–17
    and FIFA 5–6,
    founder of football 6
United Nations 2, 77, 79
United States of America 1, 2, 3, 12,
    13, 15, 85, 128
    women's football 128, 138–139
Uruguay 13, 14, 18, 87
    Uruguay national team 12
Uzbekistan 95

Valencia 25, 44, 48
Van Neste Genootschap Oostende *see*
    Oostende
Vankesbeek, D. 56

Varna 87
  Cherno More Varna 87
Vélez 108, 110
  new stadium 105
Venables, T. 27
Venezuela 1
vervlaamsing 6, 51, 52, 53–59
Videoton 96
  changes name 96
Vienna 86
  First Vienna FC 66
  Sport Klub Rapid Wien 66
  Wiener Sport Club Admira 66
Viktoria Zizkov 98
village teams play in first division 98
Vilvorde Football Club 55
violence in football 47–48, 75, 107
  barras bravas in Argentina
    108–110
  FC Barcelona and Español 28, 46
  FC Barcelona and Real Madrid
    38–39
  Derry City FC and Linfield FC 72
  neo-fascist groups in Spain 47–48
  right-wing groups in Italy 120–122
  see also hooliganism, *ultras*
    (violence)
Vizcaya 29
Vlaamsch National Verbond 52
Vlaamsche Voetbalbond 52, 53
  political militancy 52–53
Vlaamsche Voetbal Club *see* Bruges
Vladivostok 61
  Luch Vladivostok FC 61
Volksunie 56

Wales 1, 3, 11, 12, 15, 19–23
  and FIFA 5, 13, 21–23
  League of Wales 6, 11, 18–23, 64,
    65
  and semi-professional clubs
    19–20, 64
  upsurge in nationalism 5
  Welsh FA *see* Football
    Associations (Wales)
  Welsh clubs playing in England
    19–23, 64
  Welsh national team 15
  winners of Afro-Asian qualifying
    group 3
  women's football 134
Wallonia 50, 51, 55

officially French-speaking 55
war 66
  El Salvador versus Honduras 4
  First World War 2, 6, 13, 51, 52,
    57, 86, 87, 88, 91, 132, 133
  Franco-Prussian War 58
  Second World War 7, 50, 53, 55,
    66, 85, 92, 93
Warsaw 66
  Legia Warsaw 92, 97
  SG Ordnungspolizei Warschau 66
Wembley 17
West Calder Swifts FC 70
White Star Athletic Club 52
Whitley Bay 20
Whitson, D. 130
Williams, J. 4, 47, 121, 130, 132, 135
Wils, L. 55
Wimbledon FC 131
women 110
  football fans 8, 128, 139–141,
    142
  marginalization 8, 129–130, 132,
    137, 141, 142, 144
  players 8, 128, 131–139
  role in football media 8, 128, 137,
    141–143
  Women's Football Alliance 136
  Women's Football Association
    133, 135, 136
  see also feminism, distributional
    issues, relational issues
Woodhouse, J. 132, 135, 139
Worcester City FC 20, 21
working-class organizations 85, 92
World Cup 1, 4, 12, 15, 62, 90
  organization of finals 3
  1930 13, 87, 91
  1934 3, 13, 90, 91, 106
  1938 13, 91
  1950 13
  1954 89, 91
  1958 3, 15, 18, 19, 88, 106
  1962 3, 91
  1966 3, 14, 15, 90, 135
  1970 3
  1974 91
  1978 7, 110, 111–113
  1982 3, 18, 41, 46, 91
  1986 14, 18, 108
  1990 1, 3, 14, 98
  1991 (Women's) 139

1994 1, 3, 15, 42, 91, 92, 108, 125, 139
1998 3
Wrexham FC 19, 20, 64, 65

xenophobia 47

Y Bogazici 77
Youth World Cup 1979 113
Yugoslavia 2, 5, 14, 16, 19, 88, 93, 96

national team 91
socialist organization of sport 85, 92–93

Zaglebie Lubin 97
Zagreb
   Dinamo Zagreb 93, 96
   Croatia Zagreb 96
Zapata 118
Zaragoza 40–41
Zhalgiris Vilnius 94